BREAKING BOUNDARIES

BREAKING BOUNDARIES

Public
Policy vs.
American
Business
in the
World
Economy

Joseph E. Pattison

PETERSON'S/PACESETTER BOOKS
PRINCETON, NEW JERSEY

Dedicated to
Joseph Surtees Pattison

Visit Peterson's at http://www.petersons.com

Peterson's/Pacesetter Books is a registered trademark of Peterson's, A Division of Thomson Information Inc.

Library of Congress Cataloging-in-Publication Data

Pattison, Joseph E.
    Breaking boundaries : public policy vs. American business in the world economy / Joseph E. Pattison.
       p.   cm.
    Includes bibliographical references and index.
    ISBN 1-56079-611-1
    1. United States—Foreign economic relations. 2. United States—Commercial policy. 3. Business enterprises—United States. 4. Competition, International. I. Title.
HF1455.P332   1996
337.73—dc20

                        96-11301
                            CIP

Editorial direction by Andrea Pedolsky
Production supervision by Bernadette Boylan
Copyediting by Kathleen Salazar
Composition by Gary Rozmierski

Creative direction by Linda Huber
Interior design by Cynthia Boone
Jacket design by Kathy Kikkert
Jacket illustration by Christopher Zacharow

Printed in the United States of America

10 9 8 7 6 5 4 3 2 1

CONTENTS

Preface   vii

1. Falling Off the Flat Earth   1

2. The Death of Trade: Getting to the Global View   26

3. Protection from Productivity: America's Burden of Managed Trade   51

4. The New Protectionism: Washington's War on Global Innovation   76

5. Dinosaurs on the Prowl: Competition Policy in a Changed World   108

6. Losing Its Place: The New Global Capital   142

7. Putting the Chill on Investment: The Battle for Global Presence   172

8. Government from a Global Core: Building the Innovation Infrastructure   195

Notes   221

Index   237

PREFACE

nnovation devalues institutions. That phenomenon is as old as human society itself. In their time, bows, gunpowder, and aviation overturned conventional armies; navigational advances destroyed established patterns of trade; and new manufacturing techniques overwhelmed traditional guilds. Change is fundamental to enterprise; ultimately, by allowing the entrepreneur to create new value, it is the essence of economic progress.

But nothing in our past has prepared us for the speed and scope of the changes brought by the global economy. That new economy has become an irrefutable fact of life at the end of the twentieth century, inseparable from our way of life. We inexorably rely upon it for our jobs, our vehicles, our food, our entertainments, and a thousand and one other products and services that are intertwined with our standard of living—as well as the knowledge and ideas that define who we are. But our economic institutions in both the public and private sector have largely ignored that change. The primary laws regulating commerce in all its aspects have not significantly changed in concept in the last five decades; they've only expanded in their scope and scale of enforcement. Although frequently altered in appearance according to prevailing fashion, the frameworks relied upon in mapping strategy for many businesses have evolved little in their basic assumptions of cause and effect. Reactions to the global economy are dominated by rigid notions of a national economy that prevails by battling other economies, deep suspicions of international enterprise, and a preoccupation with manufacturing. As a result, policymakers are blinded to the fact that practices and institutions that were once a source of strength for American enterprise have instead become painful liabilities.

This book is about the effects of such intransigence, about the implications of the new global economy for public policy and management concepts that have remained static, rooted in a world that no longer exists. It focuses not on the global economic earthquake of the last decade but on the neglected fractures that earthquake has caused in the foundations of government and business. It is about the ways in which the new economy has overthrown traditional criteria for measuring the effectiveness of governments and enterprises and the high-stakes challenge involved in identifying new criteria. It is about the dangerous mentality that was encountered, for example, when a manager of a California electronics firm recently met with a senior member of the U.S. House of Representatives to discuss the need for open access to electronic memory components manufactured in Asia, components that the firm needed to remain competitive at home and abroad. "I don't believe in the global economy," the powerful lawmaker groused, "and I'll be damned if I'll let any American firm be held hostage to suppliers across the Pacific."

This book is also about managers like those at Gerber, who announced in 1994 that they could not find a strategy to compete in their newly global industry and "surrendered" to an acquirer from Switzerland, or those at Kodak, who, when pressured by a global competitor from Japan, decided to cut back employees in Japan, sell the firm's research facility in Japan, and petition Washington regulators to fashion a competitive remedy by decree. Ultimately this volume is about the little-understood reasons America's commercial and political institutions are not coping adequately with the emerging economy. When MIT's Commission on Industrial Productivity evaluated American firms by the criteria of that new economy, it concluded that only *one half of 1 percent* of American firms had transformed themselves into effective global competitors.

Policymakers are in a "competitiveness" quandary, uncertain where to go but compulsively inclined to apply worn-out solutions to new economic challenges. The result is a delusion with painful consequences for America: Pretending they are regulating and guiding the global economy and global enterprise, they instead restrict America's share of that economy. They have failed to grasp how new realities have overwhelmed traditional policy frameworks. They have failed to perceive how the new economy has devalued their institutions. They have failed to recognize that to get to global success, they must first move beyond the boundaries of customary cause and effect.

In *Breaking Boundaries*, I explore the many ways in which existing rules, policies, and strategies have lost their economic relevance and, in doing so, expose the powerful antiglobal bias built into many aspects of contemporary government and business. If a detailed solution to every problem examined in these pages is not set forth, it is because we are still moving at breakneck speed along the global learning curve. But the most important step in finding solutions is recognizing the problem. America's competitiveness dilemma is not so much about the weakness of

American enterprise as it is about obsolete frames of reference competing with new global realities.

No nation is beaten by other nations in the new economy, but only by itself. There is no more certain way to subordinate the American economy to the rest of the world than by relying on traditional institutions to meet the very untraditional challenges of the global economy. The sooner the policymakers who guide those institutions understand that they are not able to remold the new economic realities to fit their former bases of power, the sooner America can get on with applying its vast entrepreneurial talent to reap the unprecedented opportunities of the new economy.

Joseph E. Pattison

FALLING OFF THE FLAT EARTH

Ask technologists to identify the most important development of the twentieth century, and most will unhesitatingly point to quantum theory and its offspring, the semiconductor and microprocessor. The quantum concept has opened vast new realms of knowledge and liberated human endeavor in ways never imagined. Yet those who nurtured it harbor great frustration over the tortuous efforts of business and government to exploit the concept. The most important breakthroughs for development of the microchip were made thirty and forty years before resources could be focused sufficiently to introduce the technology to the world. Some quantum scientists speak with haunted tones of the irretrievable decades when the world could have been empowered by the microchip but ignored it.

The reason? The world, including the greater community of scientists and those who controlled vital resources, could not fathom the concept. Traditional analysis showed it to be illogical. Those at the helm of government and business looked for a machine in the quantum concept, for mechanical functions. They wasted years by approaching it according to traditional criteria, by judging it in terms of the clockwork motion of Newton's universe. In other words, what severely retarded acceptance and use of the idea was the analytical framework applied to it. For years business and government leaders stubbornly tried to fit monkey wrenches to microchips. If anyone would make sense of the new concept of the semiconductor, traditionalists assumed it would be the leading American vacuum-tube producers—GE, RCA, and GTE-Sylvania—and the industrial-policy managers who resided in the Pentagon and the

White House. They all tried, and they all failed. Minicomputers would still be the stuff of science fiction but for the dogged efforts of a few dedicated theorists and venture-capital pioneers who were bold enough to disregard conventional wisdom.

Today the global economy has brought an equally revolutionary change to the broader stage of industry and government, and an equal degree of misunderstanding is undermining the institutions that must adapt to it. Like the physicists who lost many valuable years trying to fit nonmaterial quantum energy into a framework designed for the material world, companies and governments around the planet are inflicting great harm on themselves by trying to fit the realities of today's global economy into a policy and strategy framework designed for a world that no longer exists.

The rise of quantum theory has been described as the greatest advance in understanding the universe since Copernicus shattered the notion that the sun rotated around the earth. In much the same way, the emerging global economy is the most important development for economic enterprise since the industrial age emerged 200 years ago. But that reality has yet to penetrate the consciousness of most policymakers in government and business. Until it does, the measures so urgently needed for the transition of enterprise and government to the new economy will be stalled. Failure to make that transition soon will mean enormous social costs for governments. The penalty for enterprises that cling to obsolete strategies is even greater—they are on the same path as the stegosaurus nearing the end of the Cretaceous period.

Judging from the rhetoric of change that dominates much policymaking in the halls of government and corporate management, one might easily assume that the global adjustment is well under way. Look at the massive restructuring by firms during the past decade. Look at the 611 separate pieces of legislation for American "competitiveness" considered in the last Congress. Look at the shiny new corporate outposts being opened in Brussels, Tokyo, London, and even Moscow. Look at the legions of officials in the industrial nations assigned to study competitiveness and the blue-ribbon panels overflowing with advice on industrial policy. Look at the ambitious new World Trade Organization and the laborious Uruguay Round of negotiations that launched it. Look at the firms that have declared themselves to be globalized. In September 1995, while French nuns and Greek fishermen told American television audiences how global IBM was, a team of IBM executives informed a U.S. customer that their structure made it impossible for them to provide a global technical support agreement, that such an agreement would have to be negotiated piecemeal on each continent. The CEO at another Fortune 200 company recently gave a 15-minute speech to shareholders in which he used the word "global" twenty-seven times to describe his firm and its strategies—although his board has no non–U.S. members and more than 95 percent of his production, research, and employees are based within U.S. borders.

Such efforts and words are starkly reminiscent of the activity surrounding quantum theory when its unorthodox applications were first broached decades ago. The high-profile, often costly response was not only disconnected from reality, it was profoundly damaging to the quantum transition. Confusion and unfulfilled promises seemed to rule as the world pretended that electrons behaved like pinballs or bedsprings.

The response of government and business to the global economy is similarly mired in self-delusion. The misconception held by many that America can still "go it alone" at the end of the twentieth century is only the most obvious part of the problem. Much more subtle and profound are the implications of this new economy for the way we think about basic tenets of strategy and policy. Most policymakers conduct themselves, for example, as though the primary value in our economy is still created by combining labor, energy, and materials; as though the resulting value always carries a flag with it; as though technology grows by keeping it in a closet shielded from the world; as though international commerce exists because nations have innate but disparate advantages. They consider that global issues are merely geographic in nature and that the main credential for a global manager is a foreign-language skill. They approach every international economic challenge from the mind-sets of the trading economy. Such views are as obsolete and counterproductive as those that kept the minicomputer from medical research, space exploration, and energy development for decades.

Far too many officials and managers treat global issues as little more than a fad, like one-minute management, quality circles, or other concepts-of-the-month. Their efforts are akin to the reengineering frenzy that swept through firms in the U.S. and Europe during the early 1990s. Many firms boasted of being revolutionized after having computerized traditional functions. Often they missed the real message: They should have challenged the basic tenets of their functions, not recycled them onto software. "Going global" is chronically misinterpreted in the same fashion—i.e., a mandate to apply old practices and concepts to a new format. Thus has been born an entire genre of sham globalization in which organizations declare themselves leaders in the new economy by virtue of offshore acquisitions, advertising set in exotic venues, or the

3

dog-eared passports of staff. Such efforts vastly underestimate the process of adapting to the new economy. They build a dangerously false comfort, like remodeling offices in a skyscraper whose foundation has been fractured by earthquake.

AMERICA'S WAR OF THE WORLDS

America has not adapted to the global economy. It has collided with it. A decade ago, when the global economy began to emerge, the results of America's inattention to it were merely embarrassing, even humorous, like watching the antics of a Westerner trying to cope with chopsticks for the first time. But today the inability of American government and many American enterprises to cope with the global economy is a sober reality that is undermining the economic life of all Americans.

"Can America Compete?" query headlines not only in Wichita but in Singapore, Perth, and Milan. Indeed, all across the planet we hear not so much about the global economy as about "competitiveness"—and in America, when we read about competitiveness in the media we have been trained to brace ourselves for bad news. Competitiveness gurus are quick to remind us, for example, that:

- Twenty years ago, U.S. firms dominated the list of the world's fifty largest companies; today the number of U.S. entries is only seventeen.

- Of the top ten worldwide producers of electronic goods, only one is based in the United States.

- Since 1950, the U.S. share of world trade has plummeted 50 percent

- The entire export production of the United States is equivalent to the output of only one midsize state, such as Illinois.

- Of the top twenty banks in the world, none are based in the United States, and in the last ten years the international market share of U.S. banks has slumped by 50 percent.

- The United States has lost its world leadership in many of the technologies designated as "critical" by Washington.

- In 1960, U.S. firms made one half of all the cars in the world—today they make one fifth; since 1967 the United States has gone from an auto-export surplus to an auto-import deficit of $60 billion.

4

- In 1965, the United States produced one fourth of the world's steel; today it produces one eighth.

Many days it is difficult to pick up a newspaper without finding a similarly dismal report. Such reports are so pervasive that "declinism" seems to have become a fashion among America's pundits. With the twisted logic that often seems to characterize such mentalities, the global economy is frequently blamed for these disturbing realities—after all, if we didn't have to compete, then we wouldn't have competitive problems. Ralph Nader has followed similar logic in declaring to American audiences that "international competitiveness" is "a strategy by global corporations to reduce our rights and standards of living to the levels of the Koreans."

America's plight has not come about *because* of the global economy but *in spite* of it. American government and American enterprise have problems in the global economy because they have not adapted to that new economy—and they can't adapt until they abandon their obsolete way of looking at the world. They cannot find the answers because they do not understand what questions to ask. The data of declinism is itself a perfect example. Entering the context of competitiveness with concerns about deficits in merchandise movements or the flags on finished products is like entering an ice hockey game equipped for tennis. There *is* disturbing data about America's status in the global economy, but it is not the data of traditional measures. Policymakers take comfort, for example, in reports that the United States in most recent years has shown comparative advantage in all the industries that the Organization of Economic Cooperation and Development (OECD) characterizes as high tech. Yet if we look behind that data, we find that in half of those sectors—which are the critical sources of growth for every industrial nation—U.S. producers have experienced a steadily eroding global position.

In many years during the past two decades, the United States has been the only major industrial nation in which high-tech export growth lagged behind that of manufactured goods generally.[1] Indeed, the National Science Foundation reports that the portion of high-tech content in U.S. shipments offshore has sharply contracted in the past five years.[2] In essence the United States has had the advantage in high-tech industries, but it still has not been competitive. That reality should be a clarion call for policymakers: Something is seriously amiss in the way the United States treats those industries that represent the best jobs, the best products, and the primary path to future prosperity. But the disturbing questions cannot stop there. Why have real (i.e., inflation-adjusted) average earnings in the United States fallen an average of 1 percent a year since 1974 while they have risen in many other countries?[3] Why is the globalization of American firms in many sectors on the decline while that of firms in other industrial nations is sharply rising? Why has the contribution of international firms to the U.S. GDP declined significantly since the 1970s? Why are U.S. firms losing ground to their foreign competitors in research and development investment?[4]

The answers to all these questions can be found in the fact that so many officials and managers behave as though the American economy ends at the Atlantic and Pacific continental shelves, as though there were nothing but an economic abyss beyond the continent. They represent a mentality that has played a major role in defining the contemporary role of American enterprise on the planet. Tokyo has also established policies that have shaped the role of Japanese business internationally. In an earlier decade those efforts were sweepingly characterized as "Japan Inc.," a term that conjures up, often inaccurately, visions of a global juggernaut staffed by adept internationalists. Only one corresponding caption could realistically capture the policy machine operated by the managers and officials who deny today's global realities: "Flat Earth Incorporated."

In their actions, in their speeches, in their investments and their regulations, Flat Earth thinkers seem unable to shake the notion that the economic mass of America is defined solely by the land mass of America. As the global economy has firmly established itself, the Flat Earth regulators of Washington, with a regularity that would be appreciated by students of thermodynamics, have exhibited an equal and opposite reaction at nearly every stage of its ascendancy. As a greater, more unrestricted flow of goods has been needed, Washington has expanded many of its restrictions on that flow. As more widespread operations on multiple continents have been demanded for the success of global enterprise, resulting in a cross-border evolution of jobs, American policymakers have acted as though terrified, equating the international allocation of labor with defeat for the American worker.

Their antiglobal prejudice extends far beyond those arenas traditionally identified as international into a broad spectrum of competition, communications, banking, securities, technology, tax, and other policies. As alliances or mergers are offered to help U.S. firms compete globally, Washington has blocked many with the use of antitrust laws drafted in the last century. Robert Mercer was the chairman of Goodyear who had to painfully watch as Washington bureaucrats invoked such laws to devastate his company's strategic global position. "Our favorite government doesn't understand we are in a global marketplace," Mercer bitterly noted after Washington preempted his strategy of offsetting the size of his foreign competitors by combining with one of his domestic competitors. "Foreign companies are allowed to merge with American companies when other American companies are not." Not only in the context of mergers has antitrust policy hit American competitiveness: Again and again Washington purports to protect U.S. "competition" by imposing restrictions on the overseas activities of American firms.

As more cross-border capital has been needed, Washington's misunderstanding of new global capital flows has effectively restricted the capital pipeline. As other industrial nations create new tax structures to promote globally focused operations, Washington doggedly pursues international tax policies based on concepts laid out seventy years ago, when flows of capital and revenues were dramatically different. As more management-labor team-building has been needed for the unorthodox corporate structures and manufacturing systems of the global economy, Washington has invoked a 1935 law to declare many such structures in violation of workers' rights. As cross-border synergies in research have mushroomed, Washington has confounded scientists with its controls on cross-border research exchanges, not infrequently even blocking visits by foreign scientists to America or American scientists overseas.

For five crucial years in the 1980s, while international telecommunications markets experienced meteoric growth, federal laws were applied to prevent the American Baby Bells from investing outside the United States, allowing offshore competitors to obtain vital beachheads in those new markets. As greater sensitivity to the transnational enterprise has been required, many policymakers seem to become more and more insular. "Why should I worry about international business?" asked a Midwestern senator and erstwhile presidential candidate when pressed to support legislation to facilitate operations of U.S. companies overseas. "I've got enough trouble right here at home."

FLAT EARTH BOARDROOMS

Although its influence on decisions to build factories, ship goods, recruit workers, commit capital, and conduct research is far greater than many believe, Washington does not itself usually make such decisions. Unfortunately, however, the Flat Earth mentality also flourishes in the private sector. As the global economy draws more and more firms into it from other countries, those U.S. firms that choose to be involved in cross-border activity remain a negligible fraction of American businesses. Year after year, one fourth to one third of all U.S. exports are made by a scant fifty firms. In a nation with scores of thousands of manufacturing companies, *85 percent* of all exports are made by only *250* firms. American managers seem hell-bent on ignoring the fact that 95 percent of the world's consumers live outside the United States.

Business observers everywhere tell us we live in the age of globalization for American enterprise. But by objective standards, that trend is not so clear. The Center for Transnational Corporations, for example, reports that foreign direct investment by U.S. firms dropped from 60 percent of all foreign investment in 1970, when the U.S. accounted for 36 percent of world GDP, to slightly more than 19 percent today, when it accounts for 26 percent of GDP. Foreign investment by U.S. firms as a percent of total assets peaked over twenty years ago—about the time that Congress began to posture foreign investment as a political issue. The center reports that Germany today—with one third the U.S. population—has more than twice as many multinational firms as the United States,[5] and it has concluded that the "transnationalization" of U.S. firms peaked before 1975, which was approximately when the first hints of global competition appeared in many industries.[6]

The number of Americans working offshore for U.S. firms declined by 25 percent during the 1980s. In many recent years European firms have been annually investing in the U.S. as much as *ten times* the amount that U.S. firms invest in Europe. Washington has been far from helpful on this critical point: A major plank in the successful 1992 Democratic presidential platform, for example, was an attack on investment by U.S. firms offshore.

These trends are not confined to investment. One fact depicts the hollowness of globalization in America better than any other: Today there are fewer foreign directors on the boards of U.S. companies than in 1980. In a Conference Board study of 589 large American firms, only 24 percent of manufacturing firms, 14 percent of financial firms, and 9 percent of service firms had a non–U.S. national on their boards. A broader survey by the newsletter *Directorship* found that of 4,863 board seats in major U.S. companies, only 104, or 2.1 percent, were held by non–U.S. nationals.[7]

Obviously, many managers don't take the time to meaningfully consider the issues of the global economy. Even those who embrace globalization often do so by simply extrapolating homegrown practices, policies, and attitudes offshore. Hussain Abudawood, a Jeddah-based industrialist, watched in disbelief as American firms surrendered their majority market shares in Saudi Arabia to Japanese and European firms. The problem? They stubbornly refused to adapt their organizations and products to local needs as the markets grew more competitive. "The American attitude," complained Abudawood, "is 'we like ketchup, what's wrong with you?' "[8]

"If you don't like ketchup, you're not important" would have been the perfect slogan for new managers at RJR Nabisco who found an all-too-easy solution for early payment of debt after the high-profile takeover engineered by Kohlberg Kravis Roberts. When they looked overseas they didn't see the painstakingly created strategic global network developed by their predecessors at Nabisco; they saw cash. As Wall Street applauded, they liquidated the firm's international assets— selling off food companies in India, Scandinavia, France, Italy, Great Britain, Spain, and Portugal in the first eight months, turning the one-time global leader into a provincial North American entity. Two years later operational managers apparently recognized the mistake: They began the laborious, expensive process of rebuilding the firm's international portfolio.

For many managers, the global economy is a topic properly reserved for consultants, professors, and diplomats. They are too busy dealing with traditional business or, increasingly, with the turmoil that seems to have struck their traditional businesses. They are trying to understand why, for example, giant industrial firms, including some of the largest companies in the United States, Europe, and Japan, are being brought to their knees by smaller competitors that were unknown a decade ago. They are confused by the appearance of new organizations that defy categorization: Their structures won't fit into traditional niches, and their managers can't be described with normal job titles. They puzzle over why the majority of international joint ventures are considered failures by their participants. Unknown firms materialize from across the ocean and secure deals with the speed and precision of a commercial blitzkrieg. To the consternation of industrial firms sitting on substantial brick-and-mortar liabilities strewn across the midlands of America and Europe, more and more business is lost to competitors who don't even seem to own factories.

The irony, of course, is that these developments are all driven by the global economy, by the emerging cross-border realities that are redefining industries and reconfiguring the ways enterprises create value.

Flat Earth managers are counting the leaves on the trees in their backyard while the global economy is not merely leveling the forest but restructuring the entire landscape.

THE NINETY-TRILLION-DOLLAR PLEBISCITE

The biggest task in leaving the Flat Earth behind is understanding these changes, a daunting task made all the more difficult by the fact that there exists no ready framework for explaining the new economy, no simple paradigm that can be substituted for that of the old world. Leading traditional experts to the new economy is like leading blind men to the proverbial elephant. We hear it described in terms of information, government, personnel, transportation, organization, technology, communication, legal architecture, or automation, depending on the discipline of the observer. None of these perspectives is entirely wrong. But each by itself is grossly misleading. During the 1980s General Motors let its first efforts at globalization be led by automation experts; it threw away over $50 billion on redesigned plants—and declared the largest loss in corporate history—before it realized it was looking at only one of the elephant's legs. Federal Express lost over $2 billion in its globalization by assuming that it could simply focus on transportation and communication challenges.

Scores of companies have slammed into costly dead ends after being convinced that going global was simply a function of organizational structure or obtaining introductions to the right government officials. AT&T spent $347 million in consulting fees in 1993, most of which the company said went to global reorganization experts, then two years later abruptly discarded its structure and split into three companies. Digital Equipment went global with a complex matrix structure, only to announce a $1 billion write-off in 1994 to abandon the structure.

The only paradigm of the new economy is its lack of paradigm. It is too dynamic, too multidimensional to be reduced to a formula. It cannot be distilled to a single discipline taught in business schools or the learn-it-all-in-a-day seminars to which many managers seem addicted.

Yet at the heart of the global revolution lies one simple reality that is available to anyone who walks through a shopping mall with both eyes open: *The tyranny of production that ruled the old economy has been replaced with a tyranny of consumption.* The global economy was not launched from some ivory tower or created by Swiss gnomes. It was created by consumption, by the relentless, endless search by consumers on every continent for something better, by the daily global plebiscite conducted by the billions of individuals with disposable income who are now dispersed around the planet.

Like a light at the end of the tunnel, that plebiscite must be kept in focus as Flat Earth handicaps are identified and shed, for in the end it explains everything. Its most basic element is the simple reality that its participants buy on the basis of value, not flags. Demand by today's consumers and the organizations that directly serve them is unprecedented not only in its scope, intensity, knowledge, and wealth; it is revolutionary also in the processes by which it seeks and extracts value, meaning the scope and process of innovation itself has been revolutionized. The new ascendance of market forces requires rethinking of the process of going global, which has long been stereotyped as a process of factories chasing low production costs. It is why new companies in many industries must be launched on a global stage—must be born global—if they are to survive. It is why going global is not an elective for many firms and why many firms fail to perceive the global stakes in their "local" business. Ninety-plus advertising agencies were serving the local needs of Nestlé around the planet until the company began a rationalization; only five of those agencies survived, based not on size or location so much as an ability to adapt to multicultural challenges.

The dynamics of the new plebiscite also require rethinking of fundamental regulatory premises. It is the new consumption, not government subsidies or controls, that controls the flow of world-class innovation. It is the new consumption, not protective tariffs, that grows jobs. Industries are no longer defined by patterns of production but by patterns of consumption—which, as discussed later, has rendered traditional antitrust analysis obsolete. The new borderless consumption is also the key to understanding the consequences of policymakers' misplaced obsession with trade—i.e., merchandise sales between nations—as the centerpiece for global action. Most basic of all is the plebiscite's role in overwhelming the concept implicit in all Flat Earth policy: that economic regulation deals with captive markets. In the old economy, enterprises had to take the regulation dealt to them, and its costs were inevitably absorbed. Today they can leave it. Regulation suddenly must be cost-effective—or it can be rejected.

From 1990 to 1995, telecommunications companies based in the United States spent $6.5 billion of their capital outside the United States.

That vast sum did not go offshore because there was no need for investment in the United States—the members of the global plebiscite residing in the United States were as eager as their offshore counterparts, if not more so, for the state-of-the-art telecom systems built by that money. Some of the money would have inevitably gone offshore to preserve strategic positions, but most of the capital went to serve non–U.S. segments of the plebiscite because comparisons were made between opportunities overseas and the costs of an unstable, byzantine telecom regulatory system at home. The United States lost that money because communications and antitrust regulators could not perceive that they were no longer controlling domestic industries but instead bludgeoning U.S. participants in a global industry, participants who could select the host for their capital.

Flat Earth thinkers chronically confuse the global economy with the traditional trading economy. Four trillion dollars is one of their oft-quoted figures. Four trillion dollars is the value of the merchandise that flows across borders every year, a figure frequently cited as supposed proof of the health of the trading economy and, implicitly, the role of trade as the key to the health of the global economy. But ignored by most decision makers are far more compelling figures that tell the real story of the new economy: One third of that $4 trillion in trade is generated in related-party transactions between over 250,000 affiliates of more than 40,000 multinational firms, transactions that are not "imports" or "exports" in the traditional sense. Another *$6 trillion*, unreported because it is "domestic" business, is generated from sales by those affiliates within their host countries—representing cumulative value-added from domestic networks of international enterprise. And even that sum is almost incidental to the ultimate power of the new economy: the *$80 trillion* that annually moves across borders unattached to merchandise,[9] driven by the members of the global plebiscite and the brokers and bankers who represent them. These flows capture the essence of the new economy, yet Flat Earth policymakers have utterly failed to grasp their significance. Those trillions have buried trade. Merchandise trade as the primary driver of the international economy is dead.

BEYOND THE REACH OF GOVERNMENT

For most of the twentieth century, governments were able to exercise control over financial flows with an array of monetary and capital control tools. But innovations in telecommunications and in financial markets have so increased global financial flows—since 1980 the global stock of financial assets has grown 250 percent faster than the combined GDP of the largest industrial countries—that those traditional policy tools have been rendered almost impotent:

- When the industrial nations agreed fifty years ago with John Maynard Keynes's proposal to form the International Monetary Fund as a means of controlling the world monetary system, Keynes specified that to be effective the IMF should control resources equal to 50 percent of global merchandise imports. Today the IMF controls resources equal to 2 percent of such trade—which in itself represents a small fraction of global financial flows.

- Traditional central bank reserves provided the most significant lever for stabilizing exchange rates. In 1983 the ratio of central bank reserves in key industrial countries to daily foreign exchange turnover was 3.5 to 1. By 1995 the ratio had dropped to less than 0.45 to 1.

- At its June 1995 summit in Halifax, the Group of Seven (G-7) key industrial nations decided to expand the emergency financing funds used to offset financial instability, such as the 1994 financial implosion in Mexico. The expanded fund equals $60 billion, which would have been more than enough in 1982 when daily foreign exchange trading, for example, was $10 to $20 billion. But in 1995 $60 billion was equal to *two days* of cross-border trading in securities, *seven hours* of global turnover in government bonds, and less than *90 minutes* of world forex trading.

The most dramatic evidence of all came in 1992, when private market forces—consisting largely of George Soros and his Quantum fund—took money out of exchange markets as fast as governments could pump it in, obtaining $1 billion in profits and pushing the pound sterling out of Europe's Exchange Rate Mechanism. During the 1960s, Prime Minister Harold Wilson fought market forces for three years before finally devaluing the pound. In 1992 the same process took only a few days.

IN SEARCH OF THE NEW ADVANTAGE

The implications of this tsunami of transactions reach beyond the imagination of tradition-bound policymakers. By focusing on merchandise movements, the traditional assumptions about trade that underlie the entire spectrum of economic policy have always directed attention to the factors of production, the inherent endowments that historically defined each nation's manufacturing niche, giving it a predictable, natural, and *national* value to be added as its role in the international economy. But those endowments have been overwhelmed by the new international exchanges *within* borders and nonmerchandise values exchanged across borders. Software, financial data, pharmaceutical formulas, marketing services, clinical research reports, legal advice, blueprints, engineering, management consultation services, royalties, advertising copy, insurance, dividends, licenses, bonds, payroll systems, futures contracts, computer memory designs, and a thousand more processes, services, and other value-addeds have become the most significant elements moving across borders today.

The old economy characterized those elements as mere "invisibles" that followed the movement of hard goods; they were footnotes to real business. But today they are the heart of business, the essence of the new plebiscite. They move far more efficiently than traditional trade and, as a multiplier of economic activity, with vastly greater economic consequence. These new mobile sources of advantage have rendered the traditional concepts of native endowments obsolete. They have proved that no nation can claim innate advantage in the new economy, for *they* embody the advantage that drives competition today. They do not follow trade; they lead trade. They follow only the global plebiscite, which does not spend its trillions according to flags or the national endowments that traditionally drove trade. Advantage no longer derives from places or things, i.e., geography or merchandise.

The fact that eight of the top ten global computer companies are American has nothing to do with natural endowments of the United States. Silicon is as cheap in Siberia or Nigeria as it is in California, and the technology that puts it to work in a personal computer cannot be characterized as native to or belonging to the United States or any other country. Yet corporate and government leaders repeatedly jeopardize U.S. leadership in the industry by addressing the industry's international issues from trade mind-sets—meaning the zero-sum, export-obsessed mentalities described in the next chapter. When those preoccupied with trade look to the global economy, they focus on the $4 trillion in merchandise trade, a mere footnote to the $90 trillion in total international exchanges, ignoring entirely the most vigorous elements of that economy and thereby missing the fact that today competitive advantage resides nowhere permanently—it takes up residency where and for as long as it is nurtured. Trade mind-sets are blinded to the vast opportunities available in supporting the new processes by which advantage moves about the planet. Attracting, or creating, those processes—and supporting their constant evolution—is how enterprise and nations win in the new economy.

Understanding the global plebiscite and the way it has severed comparative advantage from geography is the foundation needed to build such winners. But to build upon that foundation requires a fresh perspective on two fundamental concepts. The global plebiscite owes much of its power to the fact that people, money, and ideas move far more freely and faster than ever before, a process that can be captured by a new use of an old term, *liquidity*. This liquidity means these elements combine for economic growth at a pace and in ways unknown in the old economy. From the outset of the Industrial Revolution, it took Great Britain nearly sixty years to double its per capita income; China has just accomplished the same in less than a decade.

The most important dimension of this process, however, is not speed. The new cross-border movements have given a vast significance to *diversity* in its broadest sense: The new liquidity makes it possible to identify and extract the value from the new and the different like never before. The meltdown of the Iron Curtain not only thrust a billion consumers into the new economy, it also engendered unorthodox new approaches to telecommunications and power transmission as late twentieth-century technology collided with what were often nineteenth-century infrastructures, approaches that were judged bizarre by Western standards but that have not only proven successful in Russia and Eastern Europe but valuable for opening new markets in Asia and Latin America.

At least 600 million new phones will be installed in Asia within the next five to seven years, enough to support thirty new companies the size of AT&T. Those who succeed in the fierce battles that will be fought over such a prize will be those who have grasped this lesson, who understand that the biggest advantages in telecommunications will not relate to traditional telecommunications but to wringing value out of diversity. They will have mastered new skills in applying time, nontraditional uses of technology, organization, and multicultural differences as sources of advantage—and they will have recognized that in the economic sense, issues of geography have been replaced with issues of diversity. Motorola has obtained a big edge—having sold $1.8 billion in personal communications equipment in China already—by combining equipment made in Malaysia with marketing crossbred in China and the United States and an unorthodox push to substitute pagers for telephones.

American computer firms have grown to dominate their industry, placing a personal computer in one of every three American homes, not due to enlightened government policy but because global capital, steered by the relentless plebiscite, sought and connected a network that would have been unimaginable ten years ago: Those computers are made possible by networks that link, for example, a talented lode of software programmers in Bangalore, India (a city that contains more trained programmers than Boston), to disk-drive technology residing in factories scattered across Southeast Asia and semiconductor research carried on in Japan, France, and a small town in Vermont.

Such networks underscore the awesome power funneled by the new liquidity and diversity into *relationships*—another vital theme of the global economy. But relationships as an end or a goal are not what is discussed in these pages. Much distraction has been caused by looking at joint ventures and alliances as entities, treating them as organizational issues. Ask managers to identify the challenges of their joint ventures, and they will typically speak about reporting structures, operating controls, and voting rights. When public policymakers examine such ventures, they preoccupy themselves with issues of tax allocations, prices in and out of the venture "box," and the competition-law dilemmas involved in trying to decide if a venture is a "competitor" or a "conspirator."

To get to the global lessons of relationships, however, they must be viewed as a process; for it is the ever-evolving process of relationships that explains another of the vitally important features of the new economy, the phenomenon of *interdependent competition*. The secret of Nike's industry leadership: It has substituted relationships for capital. The firm has 75,000 workers in forty countries making shoes for its global distribution system. Not a single one is on Nike's payroll; these workers are tied to the firm through a network of contractual links with companies that traditional views would characterize as competitors. The astronomical growth of computer-workstation giant Sun Microsystems has been achieved by adroit structuring of links with firms that conventionally would have been categorized as arch-rivals: Sun built its empire using chips from Toshiba and NEC of Japan; outsourced microprocessor production to Fujitsu; bought chips made by several American firms in Scotland, Singapore, Japan, and the Philippines with equipment made in Germany, Great Britain, the Netherlands, and Switzerland; and called on TEL of Japan to market its products in Asia.

Bitter, highly politicized battles have embroiled the photography industry for years—but the new-generation Advanced Photo System that is expected to revolutionize the industry is the result of behind-the-scenes joint efforts by those seemingly acrimonious rivals Kodak, Fuji, Canon, and Minolta. The costly failures of Cable and Wireless, for generations the world leader in international telecommunications, are in a very real sense failures of interdependence. The company doggedly pursued a go-it-alone strategy that deprived it of the diversity—represented by access to other firms' innovations—and the liquidity—represented by access to new markets—of the alliances enjoyed by all of its competitors. There was no firm on the planet better situated to take advantage of globalization in telecommunications. But Cable and Wireless has been overtaken by companies that didn't even exist fifteen years ago.

In both the public and private sectors, many have utterly failed to grasp the revolutionary implications of the new interdependence, resulting in misdirected antitrust policy, painful missteps in bilateral government relations, and costly misjudgments in competitive strategy. Much of the reform required to leave the Flat Earth behind involves supporting the new interdependent competition and empowering the liquidity and diversity that drive it.

FALLING OFF THE FLAT EARTH

Navigating out of the Flat Earth is not achieved by simply hitching a ride on a bold new concept into a glittering future. The long-standing structures that embody Flat Earth mentalities must be dismantled. To do so requires identifying those structures and casting those mentalities into the harsh glare of new realities. Most conspicuous are the mind-sets of trade discussed in the following chapter and the protectionism that has evolved from such mind-sets, discussed in Chapter Three. The modern-day equivalents of the Luddites who destroyed factories during the Industrial Revolution are those who insist on locking obsolete assets in place through protectionism. Yet today over one third of all goods entering the United States are restricted in a significant way through quotas, special tariffs, or other specific protectionist controls—a higher percentage than existed twenty years ago. The story of American protectionism is a tale of waste on a vast scale and one of bitter irony. Fighting shipments from Taiwan, or Asia generally, is an easy red-white-and-blue exercise for members of Congress—so long as they ignore the fact that General Electric is Taiwan's biggest exporter or that two thirds of the U.S. trade deficit with Asia consists of vital capital equipment and production components shipped to American factories— equipment that cannot be competitively obtained in the United States.

Government policymakers seem to instinctively want to protect their "trading" organizations. But such compulsions lead to schizophrenia in the global economy. Whom should they protect? Some of the most important exporters from the United States, accounting for billions in goods annually, are Japanese trading companies. When legislators clamor to restrict shipments from Japan, they pay no heed to the realities of the new interdependent competition, such as the fact that IBM is one of Japan's biggest exporters and in many years pays more in taxes in Japan than its giant global competitor Fujitsu. Honda is more likely to spend a dollar of its income in the United States than Ford, and judging by its proportions of workers and sales, it is more "American" than "Japanese." The most advanced computer chips are being built in California and sent into global markets as American products—by firms funded with foreign capital. Televisions purchased in Denmark may be made in a San Diego factory by a company "based" in Osaka. Affixing the country-of-origin labels on which trade regulation depends has become an arbitrary—and misleading—exercise in every global industry.

For all the damage caused by timeworn trade policies, the biggest pitfalls for American firms striving to maintain competitiveness in the global economy often are not in what has traditionally been considered the trade arena. Chapter Four examines a hidden aspect of American protectionism—the walls built around American technology by long-standing policies and strategies, walls that constrain that diversity and liquidity that create innovation and that therefore constrain the competitive advantage of American firms. When placed in the context of the new dynamics of innovation, American antitrust policy takes on markedly antiglobal, antigrowth dimensions. Chapter Five looks at the costly consequences of applying century-old competition concepts to the new dynamics of global industry.

Gary Hufbauer, senior fellow at the Institute for International Economics, recently tried to send a wake-up call with his *U.S. Taxation of International Income: Blueprint for Reform.* As Hufbauer explained, one of the most fundamental problems for America's globalization is intransigence among tax policymakers:

> Despite sea changes in the world economy, the intellectual underpinnings of the U.S. approach to taxing international business have changed little in seven decades.[10]

The Internal Revenue Code is written with discrimination against U.S. companies doing business overseas or tapping innovation from foreign sources. Chapter Six examines the effect of such outdated policies on global flows of capital. Myriad laws, orders, and regulations, surprising in breadth and number, have been targeted by Washington at cross-border movements of investment, royalties, dividend funds, insurance services, and banking services.

Similar reliance on the anachronistic concepts discussed in Chapter Seven has made fighting foreign investment in the United States easy for politicians invoking protection for American workers—so long as they ignore the fact that nearly half of the new American manufacturing jobs in recent years have been created by foreign investors and that judging by the criteria of pay and training, the best manufacturing jobs in America are being created in these foreign investment plants.

Some of the Flat Earth constraints described in these pages are conspicuous already to those active in global enterprise. Many corporate executives, for example, have complained for years about the difficulty of obtaining clearances for foreign managers to work in the United States. But even experienced managers frequently accept traditional policy or practices so unquestioningly that they are blind to their cross-border implications. Executives are often unaware that in many industries the global leader owes its success to tax, competition, technology, and other policies that are far more attuned to the global economy than those of Washington.

In the most insidious regions of the Flat Earth, policies lie like hidden land mines, difficult to perceive, and by their near invisibility reach truly treacherous dimensions. These are the measures that on their face have little or nothing to do with events outside American borders—meaning that their connection to the global economy is lost on most decision makers. They include, for example, the antitrust policies that have repeatedly served up U.S. firms to foreign acquirers while denying other U.S. firms the same acquisition opportunity, sacrificing the global competitiveness of the U.S. industry for the sake of an anachronistic notion of domestic competition. These are the federal communications policies that turned over several major U.S. film studios to foreign owners without permitting U.S. competitors to even enter the bidding. These are the arcane competition and telecommunications rules that ignore the instantly connected realities of the new economy and thereby exile much of America's best technology, forcing domestic telecommunications firms to offer the fruits of U.S. research to foreign markets first because Washington blocks their use at home. These are the "domestic" pharmaceutical policies that unduly restrict U.S. firms from bringing their products to global markets. These are the efforts, which can be delineated almost on an industry-by-industry basis, by which policies wrongly focused on obsolete concepts have restricted American participation in the innovation and capital flowing through the global economy.

19

HANDCUFFING AMERICAN TELECOMMUNICATIONS

Recent visitors to the United Kingdom have been surprised at the advanced telecommunications options available in many British neighborhoods. Global telecommunications firms have been pumping cutting-edge technology and billions in capital into new personal communications networks and mixed-media phone services that are the most advanced on the planet. The same technology and capital have bypassed Americans due to the combined effect of century-old antitrust laws and 60-year-old investment rules designed to prevent foreign enemies from infiltrating the U.S. communication system.

While regulators elsewhere are scrambling to accommodate the new combinations of French, Japanese, British, Swiss, Dutch, Swedish, and *American* firms that are leading these advances overseas, Washington blocks many such alliances by stubbornly preserving an anachronistic 25 percent cap on foreign stakes in U.S. telecommunications firms. As billions in telecommunications capital moves across borders, building solid global positions for non–U.S. firms, American regulators bicker over whether unorthodox new shared-investment structures constitute the permitted 25 percent ownership or the prohibited 25.1 percent, blindly defending policies crafted when television consisted of a handful of channels and radios were huge cabinets stuffed with vacuum tubes.

In the late 1980s, in the name of national security, these regulators forced Mexican investors out of television stations in the Southwest. In 1994 they attacked the underpinnings of the Fox television network on the grounds that the owner was formerly an Australian citizen. Ignoring the fact that in the age of 500-channel television, technology makes it impossible for anyone to seize the American airwaves, they use vacuum-tube notions of national security to force American firms to focus many of their telecommunications alliances outside the United States and abstain from equity-swapping deals that are driving industry leadership. MCI and Sprint, for example, were effectively "maxed out" after foreign investment in them by British Telecom (MCI) and Deutsche Telekom and France Telecom (Sprint), subject to the mercy of the FCC and its seldom-used discretion to grant foreign equity exemptions based on competitive conditions overseas and the public interest.

When foreign investment is not in play, regulators often restrict new technology by invoking competition laws. State-of-the-art phone networks in Liverpool and Birmingham were built by American firms whose first choice was to provide such systems in the United States; federal regulators refused to allow the alliances necessary to operate them at home. When a regional U.S. telephone company asked for permission to form a joint venture with a British firm to build a fiber-optic transatlantic cable system for state-of-the-art international video voice and data systems, Washington denied the request, citing concern over what it considered a dangerous precedent: It did not want the U.S. firm using U.S. revenue to fund international expansion.

REDISCOVERING COMPETITIVENESS

One of the greatest ironies of the Flat Earth is the fact that reform of its policies is repeatedly blocked by officials waving the banner of American competitiveness. The countless blue-ribbon panels and commissions convened to remedy American competitiveness are unable to find answers because they are looking in the wrong places. Many of those most prominently involved in America's chronic competitiveness debate suffer acutely from the Flat Earth syndrome. Their answers call for mimicking the trading activities of other nations, managing trade by decree, expanding existing protection programs, and marshaling traditional resources that have lost significance in the new economy.

This high-profile search for an industrial policy is mortally flawed by its failure to recognize that America already has an industrial policy. If a country has taxes, tariffs, subsidies, and commercial regulation, then it has an industrial policy. America's industrial policy may not have been formulated in a particularly integrated fashion, but it has unmistakable themes: It is skewed to concentration of manufacturing, to sheltering technology, to a preeminence of hard goods and fixed assets, to controlling capital, to zero-sum notions of merchandise trade, to maintaining the industrial status quo. In other words, it is an industrial policy designed to support the factors of production that dominated traditional trade, a policy that is at war with the forces of the global economy. A war against those forces is one that no nation, however mighty, can ever win.

Those waging that war misunderstand not only their targets but the tools available to them. For many in government, the only international economic tools are the hammers forged in the era of steam-engine trade, used to pound imports, defend exports, and chip away at exchange rates. Since such hammers are the only tools they have ever known, every problem becomes a nail to be driven down. Washington must learn why its hammers have become obsolete, why global opportunities cannot be exploited when policymakers' primary reaction to every global challenge is to fend off all "intruders." Only then can they begin to understand the revolutionary lessons for government offered by the global economy.

Vast effort is likewise wasted by those who treat competitiveness as a partisan issue. The Flat Earth landscape was not created by any single political movement—but partisan politics are responsible for its most egregious features. The Republicans were once avid tariff protectionists, and the Democrats stood for the principle of free trade. As the GOP shifted from that position, the Democrats moved to fill what they saw as a political vacuum and for much of the 1980s and early 1990s were responsible for the strong protectionist slant of Congress. The Republicans were once active defenders of an unrestricted open-door policy for foreign investment. Yet in the 1980s they created the most rigorous framework of disincentives for foreign investment that ever existed in this country. Such shifts, of course, underscore part of the problem: American global economic interests have become political footballs, often taken seriously only for their political symbolism.[11]

In the heat of elections, encouraged by an electorate that itself is woefully uninformed about its own global underpinnings, incumbents routinely offer Flat Earth promises that America can ill afford to keep. Former Congressman Tony Coelho, as head of the Democratic Congressional Campaign Committee, identified protection from imports as the "Democratic macho issue" that should be tapped to rally support for the party. Writing for *Foreign Policy*, I. M. Destler studied the Japan-bashing that often dominates Congressional electioneering and found one Senate aide who captured the ironic truth: "You don't understand," the aide complained to those who pressed for the substance of the claims. "The target isn't the Japanese; it's the White House." Destler's study on American protectionism concluded that "the system's main result was not protection for industry but protection for Congress."

Complicating any reform effort is the stark reality that the global plebiscite has billions of constituents, but no one represents it politically. The pain associated with the changes of the global economy is localized and easily used as a political lightning rod. The benefits of those changes, though many times greater than the pain, are dispersed across broad populations. Those constituents, moreover, do not carry flags—at least not for economic purposes. Their plebiscite has demonstrated that for economic purposes, the only maps of significance today are not those depicting nations selling to nations but those showing concentrations of consumers and concentrations of ideas. The new economic process is all about connecting such concentrations—a process different for every industry. And as difficult as it may be for regulators to admit, it is industries, not governments or nations, that are the new units of competition. Obviously nations have the power to restrict this process, to restrain liquidity and diversity, and have used such powers extensively. But each restraint is a restraint on a nation's own prosperity.

Also obscuring the vision of many policymakers has been the belief that their policies have been validated by their triumph over Communism. Ultimately this, too, is a Flat Earth perspective: The policies

22

of the West may have allowed the West to endure, but it was the new economy that destroyed the Communist systems. It was the global economy that brought incontrovertible evidence of the West's better living standard to homes from Minsk to Murmansk. It was the global economy that sent representatives of Western firms into the East, by their very presence nurturing the seeds of doubt. It was the global economy that put the actions of dictators under a planetary lens. It was the global economy that gave conspicuously failing grades to the performance of the Soviet economic system. What is lost on those policymakers is that the global economy has not simply overthrown Karl Marx; it has also overthrown much of the wisdom associated with Adam Smith and John Maynard Keynes.

When, in quiet off-duty moments, foreign government officials and corporate executives outside the United States can be cajoled into expounding on the future, many express a common fear—that of American enterprises unleashed from Washington's current policies. "The only thing that gives us a fighting chance in competing with America," a French manager with a global telecommunications firm confided to me, "is your government. If Washington were able to understand what firms need to compete, *then* I would be worried." So far, Washington has given such offshore competitors little to fear. Few were fooled when a recent Congress, amid great fanfare, enacted one of its competitiveness solutions: a joint resolution directing that in the future the United States shall "remain the strongest and greatest nation on earth."

THE LOST DECADE

In 1986 the leading lights of government convened to set the world economy on a new course. After a now-famous meeting in Uruguay, Washington announced that it would invigorate America by bringing home a larger share of world growth; with a nod to the future, it even promised to attack barriers to investment, technology, and services. The Uruguay Round was to be a benchmark, the beginning of a new age of policy firmly rooted in the global future. But ultimately the Round deteriorated into nearly a decade of bickering over the last few percentage points of existing merchandise tariffs[12] and other minor impediments to hard-good shipments. The negotiations that preoccupied international economic efforts for so many years offered at their conclusion a gain of a mere 1 percent of world GDP, not immediately but sometime in the next century.[13] Left begging were the far greater opportunities for growth available through supporting the new diversity and liquidity and removing impediments to cross-border relationships and barriers to movements of technology and capital.

At the outset of the Uruguay Round, Washington was at a crossroads. It had the opportunity to set its course according to the new global plebiscite and thereby begin the long overdue reform of its Flat Earth machinery. It could have committed, for example, to dismantling the confusing framework for cross-border investment caused by over 900 different investment treaties or consolidating the hundreds of inconsistent financial, labor, and technology standards that handicap the operations of cross-border enterprise. Instead it paid lip service to such goals, then allowed century-old mind-sets to sweep it toward the trade path, toward the far smaller stakes of the old world. The Round's impact on investment, technology, and services was negligible. The Uruguay Round did indeed become a benchmark, but it was a benchmark of Flat Earth behavior. Washington led the planet in building new policies around merchandise and maps, a process akin to designing new machines based on steam power to compete with nuclear fusion. By focusing on the biggest Flat Earth barriers for American enterprise—those existing within the United States—Washington could easily have achieved for the U.S. economy alone an amount surpassing the entire global gain claimed by Uruguay Round negotiators.[14]

The biggest barriers to adapting to the global economy are the answers developed for yesterday's problems. It is impossible for policymakers—whether they be Uruguay Round negotiators, members of Congress, or executives in Omaha—to tap the full power of that economy until they break through the boundaries of traditional trade-bound thinking.

Applying the tried-and-true methods of past decades to the strategic problems of the new economy is an invitation to catastrophe. Martin F. Klingenberg, a Washington-based merger and acquisition expert who has been managing international investment negotiations for twenty-five years, today starts every deal by preparing his U.S. and European clients for the unexpected. "The single biggest challenge is leaving traditional dealmaking behind," notes Klingenberg. "Forget the old techniques for valuation. Forget the checklists taught in classrooms. Forget the neatly laid strategic structures. The proven techniques of fifteen years ago are being proven wrong today. The entire context of dealmaking seems to have changed."

The context is indeed changing—for dealmaking, for strategy, for law, and for policy. The entire context of enterprise has shifted. Those ready to address that shifting context, those ready to listen to the new message of the globe, can exploit a vital new reality: There has never been a force as effective as global competition for exposing obsolete regulation and strategy. Yet most policymakers act as though they still inhabited the executive suites of the '60s and '70s. Not only are they unprepared to cope with the seismic changes that are quietly realigning the foundations of their institutions, but most have not even recognized those changes. They are blindly waiting for a future that has already arrived, expecting robots in their kitchens while vastly more important developments are unfolding around them.

THE DEATH OF TRADE

Getting to the
Global View

It is extraordinarily difficult for most policymakers and managers to think of the global economy in terms other than geographic. Executives consider themselves globalized by acquiring passports. Companies announce they are global after signing offshore office leases or translating product brochures into the languages of distant markets. Governments convince themselves that global competitiveness is attained by mimicking the policies of capitals across the ocean. Global prowess is measured by transoceanic phone calls and six-digit mileage in frequent-flier accounts. "Just wait 'til they get those hypersonic planes in service—New York to Tokyo in three hours," a petroleum industry executive proclaimed at a recent foreign-investment symposium. "Then we'll really see the start of global companies."

Going global is not a linear progression across borders. It is not a matter of geographically extrapolating homegrown knowledge and skills or of borrowing people and policies with foreign accents. But that is precisely how American policymakers have been taught to understand it. For them international business has always consisted of moving hard goods across borders, filling boxes with "our" value and extracting payment for it from "them." In other words, international business has always been defined in the polarized terms of trade.

The implications of always approaching global economic issues as trade issues are seldom considered by policymakers. Yet trade is far more than a mechanical movement of boxes across oceans. It is a way of thinking about business and economics that has long been institutionalized in public policy and management structures. It is a mind-set that not only determines reactions to import-export issues but that has also distorted technology, manufacturing, investment, and organizational issues as they have increasingly assumed international dimensions. It is the reason so many Americans believe that being global is about being more "foreign," about becoming more like "them" and less like "us."

The trade mentality is the perfect example of why the idiom "tried-and-true" has itself become outdated in the new economy. The biggest handicap for global success isn't that portion of the population who inevitably will never think internationally: It is those who insist that the key to America's global future lies in moving U.S.–made semiconductors to foreign markets, balancing merchandise accounts, and bickering with foreign governments over America's "fair share" of world production. They do not understand the extinction of trade.

THE FLAGS OF ADVANTAGE

Obviously, merchandise still moves across borders in the global economy, and for most of the population the most visible evidence of that economy continues to be packing labels from distant lands and harbors filled with container ships. But the new economy has irreversibly altered the significance of those boxes and labels—and of the claims that government and enterprise can make on them. No one wins in the global economy without understanding these changes, without breaking through the boundaries of trade.

Adam Smith's *Wealth of Nations*, published in 1776, and David Ricardo's *Principles of Political Economy and Taxation*, published in 1817, first articulated the concepts of trade and comparative advantage. Trade revolved around "natural" efficiencies, Ricardo explained, derived from each nation's peculiar natural endowments in the primary factors of production. In Ricardo's classic example, because England had endowments that gave it more efficient woolen mills and Portugal had endowments for more efficient wineries, England would trade cloth for port wine. By specializing in sectors in which, due to its natural endowments, it had the highest productivity, a country increased its revenues and living standards.

Ricardo and Smith laid the foundation for the way governments and economists have viewed the international economy ever since. National mercantile rivalries were inevitably interwoven with such views for the simple reason that goods in the trading world always had flags. Port wine was from Portugal; wool, coal, and locomotives were from England. Sewing machines, grain, and harvesting equipment were from America. International business could easily and logically be reduced to columns of imports and exports.

In this trading world, to the extent that taxpayers' monies were directed to support international business, they have always gone to support the classic factors of production—labor, capital, and natural resources in simplest form—for export activity. To the extent that the government funded jobs to support international commerce, they were allocated to control, promote, or process imports and exports. To the extent that Congress passed laws aimed at international commerce, they were antidumping, antisubsidy, and other laws for "relief" of home-country factories from imports or authorizations for financing and other promotion of exports.

Production of merchandise did not become paramount in the traditional economy solely for reasons of trade, of course, but the mentalities of trade were inextricably entwined with such production. Tax, patent, labor, investment, technology, and natural resource policies were heavily skewed to favor massing of fixed assets and the construction of large manufacturing facilities built for economies of scale—with every factory in effect a ship in the country's sovereign navy.

OUR MYTHOLOGY OF TRADE

Out of the simple structures of the trading economy grew concepts and perspectives with far-reaching implications for government and enterprise. These implications are complex and subtle, ranging from the painfully destructive—like the high-tech plants exiled by American protectionism—to the merely ridiculous—like Washington's peanut quotas, which restrict each American to an average consumption of two foreign peanuts a year. But their most significant aspects can be reduced to a handful of common denominators. In a conceptual sense, all of them are variations on two themes: geography—involving issues of conflict, sovereignty, and national rivalry—and merchandise—involving manufacturing and the application of labor to fixed assets and natural resources.

The most harmful elements of the trade mentality can be described even more simply: They are all part of the export obsession, typified by three myths.

Export Myth Number One: The only good international business is export business.

For many in the private and public sectors, exports have long been the primary evidence of international activity and therefore the primary benchmark of international competitiveness. How is America faring in the global economy? Check the trade balance. If we have an export surplus, we are winning. If we have more imports than exports, we are losing. Some policymakers cite as proof positive of America's isolation and unfair treatment in the world economy the fact that American exports constitute a much lower percentage of GDP than do exports of other industrial nations. A corollary favored by a new cadre of antiglobal commentators: Our economy is not global because ratios of exports to GDP have changed little in 50 years. Such views conspicuously ignore the powerful roles played by cross-border investment, international technology transfers, international sourcing networks, and the intangible value-added transfers that comprise most of the $90 trillion annually moving across borders.

Today U.S. firms active in the global economy sell *five times* more through foreign subsidiaries to third parties than they export from the United States. The value of U.S. production within Japan in most years exceeds the amount of the U.S. trade deficit with Japan. To the trading mentality, such facts represent a defeat. The offshore operations of American enterprise are liabilities in this mind-set, which considers that such sales have stolen U.S. jobs. Managers of such firms would quickly point out, however, that it is those extraterritorial operations that keep them competitive. Bringing those sales "home," closing the international door, is a treacherously naive Flat Earth concept. Even if it were possible, it would drive such firms out of their industry leadership positions and often out of the ranks of competitive global enterprise.

The venues of knowledge and capital—and those who manage knowledge and capital—are vastly more significant than the venue of final assembly. In 1989, Japan's Canon Inc. was blasted by the Japanese media and government over its announced plan for becoming more competitive: The company declared that it was going to sharply cut its exports and sharply increase its imports of components. The company is much stronger today as a result. American companies that lead their global industries today, like GE, Intel, or Hewlett-Packard, were less vocal about their plans than Canon, but they learned the same lesson early on their path to success. Exports are not viable measures of success or competitiveness today.

Export Myth Number Two: Exports make jobs, imports take jobs.

This is the school that anticipates a "giant sucking sound" in the American workplace each time the country moves toward closer integration in the global economy. This is the credo of those who insist that the only workers who win from the global economy are those who manufacture exports, and of those for whom the only international issue is jobs. The trading economy taught us that factories add jobs to make exports, and imports displace jobs, based on the simplistic reasoning that if a pot, a basket, or a television set used in America had not been made overseas, it certainly would have been made at home. Import dependence, moreover, represented U.S. vulnerability. Trade policy was thus the simplest of political reflexes: Fight imports and promote exports. The only beneficial connection any American could have with the international economy was producing and selling exports. But those who understand the new economy know how false such premises have become.

One of the most remarkable pieces of Flat Earth legerdemain of the 1980s was the conclusion, often cited on Capitol Hill, that the trade deficit (i.e., an imbalance favoring imports) had cost America 3 million jobs. The basis for the calculation, scorned by serious economists but cited quite soberly by many legislators, was that since the trade deficit represented 3 percent of GDP and employment was approximately 100 million, the deficit must have cost 3 million jobs,[1] all caused by disloyal Americans becoming addicted to imports. To such perspectives, competitiveness simply equates to a full employment and export surplus; we would be competitive if we just shut our borders to imports and concentrated on producing soybeans and wheat for the world.

Such facile logic ignores basic issues like productivity, the quality of jobs, and the standard of living sought by Americans. A favorite ploy in recent years has been to expand exports through weakening of the dollar, an effect that appeals to trading mentalities as job-enhancing but that only undermines our standard of living. American workers—and American competitiveness—are the biggest victims of such devices. Exchange-rate manipulation and other favored export subsidies of the

Flat Earth bolster low-paying, low-skill jobs but ignore a new global fact that is anathema to Flat Earth thinking: Imports are vital to the health of American enterprise.

Imports can be as helpful to employment and competitiveness as exports. Today, more jobs in America rely on imports than exports. Nearly 90 percent of American manufacturers utilize imported materials or components in their production.[2] Scores of thousands of jobs would disappear overnight if imports were cut off—but millions more would be affected more gradually as enterprises grew less and less competitive. Such links do not represent vulnerability, only good competitive sense. We often hear that U.S. firms would collapse without their "fix" of imports. What we never hear is that thousands of firms in Asia and Europe would collapse without their own "fix" of American inputs. Trading models of the world economy leave no room for the most important source of employment in that economy: not the production of end-use products but the movement of value-added across borders. But policymakers cling to the fiction that protecting jobs from global competition is good for America, as though the size of the employment base were the key determinant of competitiveness. Competitiveness is not based on the number of jobs claimed by a country—in which case China would always be number one—but by the value added by jobs. The most important new jobs being created in *every* country are those generated by the global economy—including many that do not directly generate exports.

Statistically speaking, moreover, increases in merchandise deficits are actually linked with higher American employment. Throughout the heavy trade-deficit years of the 1980s, U.S. employment grew by millions, while in Europe, with a negligible trade deficit, it was stagnant. Indeed, Europe, whose merchandise trade balance and industrial planning are often looked at jealously in Washington, has created no net private-sector jobs since 1970.[3] While Congress complained about the theoretical 3 million job loss due to imports, the reality was that 7 million jobs had been added to the U.S. economy. In 1995, as the country was at what was widely considered to be full employment, the deficit kept rising. To Flat Earth thinking, such trends are anomalies. But the global economy easily explains them. Increased wage earnings pump more money into the global plebiscite, attracting more goods from global ("foreign") sources. Imports themselves have become engines of growth as American firms become integrated in added-value chains across borders—and every barrier to imports has become a barrier to exports.

31

Export Myth Number Three: The battles of global competition are battles for cheap factories.

Those giants that dominated the trading economy did so with huge manufacturing facilities, crushing their opponents with economies of scale. Inevitably, managers learned that international business competition was all about efficiency in the tasks of producing, packaging, and shipping goods across borders. In the Flat Earth, therefore, when manufacturing plants are built, bigger is always better. To such minds, international manufacturing is simply a game of factories chasing inexpensive labor—meaning their perception of the sources of competitive advantage is rooted in the old economy. One of the most popular Flat Earth specters of the new economy is that of the next generation of Americans working as waiters in restaurants owned by a foreign industrialists.

Ignored in such views is the simple reality that differences in wages also reflect differences in productivity—low wages always accompany low productivity.[4] International firms are not in the business of chasing low productivity around the world. Indeed, what they are chasing is improved productivity—and the most important gains to be made in productivity today are derived off the factory floor. Those who worship factories as the be-all and end-all of international competition are blind to the vast new opportunities that are available by leaving traditional manufacturing behind. Today some global "manufacturing" firms have no factories, some have factories that seem to move about from continent to continent as though on a massive boat, some have factories that turn out different products every week, some have factories that behave more like R&D centers than production lines. The very concept of fixed costs is being rendered obsolete by such global producers.

The primary value added in today's economy no longer derives from manufacturing or processing of goods. Economies of scale are disappearing as production becomes increasingly specialized and technology-intensive in the global economy. Scale economies have become the golden fleece of globalization, distractions from much more important goals; as painfully learned in the automotive and consumer electronics industries, huge factories churning out the same product in vast quantities are not the kind of factories demanded by the global plebiscite. Economies of innovation are the key—which is the shorthand way of saying that efficiencies of diversity and liquidity are paramount.

Despite loud pronouncements to the contrary by many leading Flat Earth thinkers, the movements of global firms and their production sites have very little to do with relative wage rates. Were international business all about chasing low wages, workers employed by U.S. multinationals in developing countries would account for much more than the 8 percent of total employment that they currently represent at such firms, and U.S. investments by developing-country firms—like the huge new memory-device facility being built by Korea's Samsung in California—would never happen. If the world economy were indeed ruled by those with low labor rates and the highest concentrations of natural resources, America's competitive stagnation or the economies of countries like Israel, Japan, and Holland should not exist. But today such nations have shown that mobile, intangible resources of technology and capital are vastly more important than the natural resources that drove traditional trade.

Long gone are the days when America could expect to be the leading builder of ships because it had the best supplies of timber and iron ore. Yet the primary international tools wielded by policymakers are mired in such a premise. Pushing exports by pushing a weak dollar or restricting the use of capital through penalizing taxes is terrific for those who export wood and soybeans but can be disastrous for the high value-added, globally interdependent industries on which competitiveness depends. The enterprises that lead the global economy are not those with control over hard assets like mines and buildings but those whose primary resources—and the primary value in their products—are intangible, like the computer firms that create vast new wealth by combining buckets of sand and truckloads of ideas.

■

These myths could just as easily be called the myths of globalization, for they represent the outdated perceptions and false assumptions that are applied to argue against either the benefits or realities of globalization. But such global myths go beyond worn-out presumptions about exports and imports; the trade mentality permeates much broader policy views and philosophies, all of which are equally anachronistic and equally damaging. At first glance some of these views may seem absurdly simple, even harmless. But when the relentless light of the new economy is cast upon them, we can see the profound way they have shaped our view of the world:

International business is a zero-sum, either/or proposition.

This is the pendulum aspect of the Flat Earth mentality: International business always has only two elements—outbound and inbound, production and consumption, home and foreign, us versus them. The trading economy taught policymakers to look at international commerce in terms of a struggle between geographic units, in terms of political confrontation and patriotic duty. What is the image of the global economy presented to the average citizen by most politicians and the media today? Floods of imports. Invasions of foreign investors. Seizures of American market shares. Foreign labels on high-visibility consumer goods. Bumper stickers stating "Hungry? Eat Your Toyota."

Although international business has evolved into complex interchanges of added value, to Washington it has always been a zero-sum contest in which governments competed, scoring through imports and exports—a game in which there always has to be a loser for every winner, in which nations were thought to compete in the same way that enterprises compete. Washington's policies for international business—today or fifty years ago—could have been written by the nineteenth-century Japanese philosopher/economist Rimei Honda, who declared nearly two centuries ago that "foreign trade is a war in which each party seeks to extract wealth from the other." Robert Hormats, vice-chairman of Goldman Sachs International, frequently speaks to American audiences on international issues. He often polls his audiences to ask which of two scenarios they prefer: one in which the U.S. economy grows at 5 percent a year and Japan grows at 10 percent or one in which both countries grow at only 2 percent. Their consistent choice is for the low-growth option in which America is not "beaten."

The analytical framework on which Washington relies for formulating international policy continues to be embedded in this bifurcated world, in which one "gets" something internationally only by "giving up" something to foreign interests. Accounting standards, SEC reporting, investment analysis, and nearly every set of data available to international decision makers in the public and private sectors are based on this rigid dichotomy, as are the regulatory frameworks used to address international issues. In assessing America's international competitiveness shortcomings, policymakers look to their trade data and conclude that America's problems are caused by Japan, Europe, or any other country or region that happens to be shipping more into the United States than it is receiving. If Japan sells more semiconductors to American users than it buys from American makers, then Washington must declare a duel, sending diplomats armed with retaliatory American laws—the contemporary equivalent of gunboats—to demand a quantitative balance.

An inevitable consequence of zero-sum thinking is that international economic policies are based on merchandise country of origin. If the "us" column shows a shortfall in sales, the answer lies in retaliation against "them"—and outdated country-of-origin concepts turn every such battle into a bilateral battle. When the economy was driven by commodity shipments, trade weapons could be wielded effectively on a bilateral terrain: When British woolens were targeted by prohibitive tariffs in 1828, all the casualties suffered were British, i.e., all the value in the wool was of British origin, and all the pain of sanctions was felt in Britain. But such absolutes have disappeared today. The import declared to be made in Britain—or Singapore or Italy—today may have as little as 15 or 20 percent content from the declared country of origin; the remaining value (in the form of technology, components, materials, marketing, packaging, and capital) could easily be from five other countries, including the United States, all of which have a stake in the import—but traditional reporting structures render that stake invisible. Even crude oil arriving on U.S. shores is likely to have been produced with the assistance of U.S. technology and U.S. capital shifted through the complex webs of joint ventures that drive today's oil industry.

Yet bilateral mind-sets still dominate international policy. Consider the reaction when complaints arrive in Washington about shipments of low-cost computer motherboards made in Asia. Initiate an antidumping proceeding against the imports to block their entry into the U.S market. Reassure workers they will not be cheated out of their jobs by unfair Asian workers. But those boards represent better technology—created by research in California and funded by Holland, England, and Japan—and more efficient production—as a result of the same global innovation networks—and they are utilized to keep half a dozen U.S. computer producers competitive.

Country of origin as a foundation for policy is the height of absurdity today. "Origin" of product is a counterproductive concept in a world where products represent value-added from two, or five, or ten countries.[5] The global plebiscite has utterly rejected geographic origin as a criteria for spending its trillions. But if all you understand about the international economy is the import and export of "national" goods, then all your policymaking will revolve around country of origin.

Business across borders is a convenience, not a necessity, for American enterprise.

In 1993 one of the foes of the North American Free Trade Agreement received national media attention by announcing, "If we just stopped trading with the rest of the world, we'd be $100 billion ahead."[6] This most simplistic of Flat Earth perspectives, echoed with alarming frequency in the halls of government, considers that international business is merely incremental, that it gives away too much to non-Americans, that the country would be better off shutting its doors. The United States can claim 25 percent of the world's economic activity today *because* of its connections to offshore sources of advantage. Slamming the door would not preserve those riches for Americans only; it would impoverish Americans. Washington already tried such an experiment once: The Smoot-Hawley tariffs of sixty years ago effectively ended trade for several years and played a significant role—some economists say the major role—in the economic implosion that was later dubbed the Great Depression.

While the most extreme isolationist views represent a tiny minority, the sentiment that international business is only supplemental, that it is not as important as "real" business, permeates much policy in the public and private sectors. As will be seen later in these pages, tax laws are written with a bias against international business that would never be tolerated in the context of "internal" U.S. business. Arcane but significant restrictions are crafted against cross-border investment and technology movements, far from the spotlight that is cast upon policymaking in "domestic" matters. Regulators often refer to the "privilege" of conducting trade—and threaten to block the international business of enterprises that do not meet their standards. Managers at many firms still earn bonuses for building U.S. sales, and only U.S. sales, and are warned not to be distracted by offshore markets. Others give lip service to global business, then delegate non-U.S. affairs to subordinates treated as "foreigners."

LOOKING AT THE WORLD THROUGH THE TRADING LENS

The battles waged by Washington against foreign governments in the name of American competitiveness are based on concepts and viewpoints developed decades ago. The data they receive from their trade-oriented statistical machinery steer them inexorably toward Flat Earth conclusions:

What Policymakers See	The New Reality
The United States ships far fewer semiconductors to Japan than Japanese firms ship to the United States. *Conclusion:* The United States has been defeated in this critical segment of the computer industry and must impose quotas on the flow of chips.	Several U.S. firms, like Texas Instruments, make semiconductors in Japan for Japanese computer firms that are missed by trade data. Chip quotas imposed by Washington cost 11,000 high-tech U.S. jobs, pushed computer production offshore, and ultimately protected Japanese

U.S. imports steadily outstrip U.S. exports, and U.S. firms export far less than their foreign competitors. *Conclusion:* The competitiveness of U.S. firms is in steady decline.

The United States suffers a chronic deficit in merchandise shipments between the United States and Japan. *Conclusion:* Japan perennially "beats" the United States in the global economy.

Foreign investors have flooded the United States, buying up assets that have always been, and should be, "American." *Conclusion:* Foreign investors are eroding the American economy and "stealing" jobs and assets from Americans.

Imports cost U.S. jobs by competing with production jobs. *Conclusion:* Restriction of imports builds the American production base.

production. American innovation drives the global industry and provides America with the biggest proportion of global value-added.

U.S. firms sell five times more through foreign subsidiaries than they export from the United States. Sales of Opels in Germany don't appear in U.S. trade data but play a big role in keeping GM competitive. If such offshore sales were integrated into trade accounts data, the chronic U.S. trade deficits would be large surpluses.

In most years, the value of U.S.-owned production within Japan exceeds the U.S. trade deficit with Japan. The deficit figure does not take into account the value of services, licenses of intellectual property, goods manufactured by U.S. firms in Japan, or goods manufactured by U.S. firms in other countries and sold to Japan. Including such value would show that the amount of American goods and services bought by the Japanese is four times greater than the amount of Japanese goods and services bought by Americans.

Foreign investors own a tiny fraction of U.S. assets—and the operations they have taken over enjoy higher pay, higher benefits, higher skills, and, typically, higher productivity. Today they directly account for over 4 million high-skill American jobs and for approximately one fourth of American exports.

In some respects, imports have become as important as exports to American competitiveness. Nearly 90 percent of U.S. manufacturing firms rely on imported components. Many imports are critical elements of the global value-added networks that firms need for global success. One dollar directly saved by a firm as a result of current federal protection programs costs downstream firms $90. Import restrictions directly cost the U.S. economy as much as $70 billion every year.

37

The record shows that U.S. firms with international operations fight against an endless array of unfair barriers. *Conclusion:* U.S. firms are better off staying at home.

U.S. firms with international operations enjoy twice the rate of growth of firms without such operations.

Merchandise trade as a percentage of U.S. GDP is only slightly larger than a century ago. *Conclusion:* The global economy is a myth.

The significance of merchandise trade has been eclipsed by foreign investment, cross-border alliances, technology transfers, and networks of value-added, which have rendered trade meaningless as a benchmark of economic integration.

Trade and competitiveness must be dealt with in sovereign frameworks.

Economic policies in the trading economy were always built around national industries. Study the debate on the international economy of recent years and you'll find that much of it has been preoccupied with far-ranging battles between the "Japanese," "European," and "American" car "industries," the "American" and "European" steel "industries," or the "European" and "Japanese" consumer electronics "industries." In 1989 government policymakers chastised steel importers looking for fewer import barriers with the reminder that Washington had already "contributed" a substantial part of the "American" industry to foreign producers. In 1994 Washington spread turmoil throughout the aviation industry by announcing its intention to pursue new standards whereby international airline routes would be sovereign assets directly owned by the U.S. government. International economic policy is the simplest of political exercises in an economy based on such concepts: When officials "own" an industry—either literally or politically—the answer to every overseas challenge to the industry is to protect it.

Vast political and business dynasties have been built around the concept that nations compete like enterprises and the notion that competitiveness can be won by protecting "national" industries, thereby avoiding competition. But today the concept of "sovereign" competitiveness or national industries is nothing more than a political construction. Fifteen years ago, if an automobile came from Detroit we knew it was American. It was made with American technology, American designs, and American labor. Today a car from one of Detroit's Big Three may have as much or more foreign content than one sold by Honda, Toyota, or Nissan. There is only one automotive industry—not separate industries on each continent—an industry whose players are global companies with historic roots in geographic regions. The comeback of the "American" auto industry in the last five years has been driven by products developed in Europe and Japan—by the "American" industry and its "foreign" affiliates.

Nothing captures the essence of the Flat Earth mentality better than the campaign launched in the early 1990s—and strongly supported by scores of Washington's policymakers—to require that cars made by American workers in American factories owned by foreign investors be treated as imports and thereby subjected to steep duties. Those "foreign" factories in America brought better and smarter jobs, introducing to North America the systems that were responsible for turning around the Detroit producers by the mid-1990s.

Is Schwinn no longer an American bike because it is assembled in Taiwan? The answer isn't yes or no; the answer is that for the producer, the marketer, the distributor, the banker, the designer, and the consumer, it just doesn't matter. They are simply involved in the global plebiscite, the fundamental process of the new economy: providing and obtaining the maximum product for the best value, without regard to political borders.

Insisting that they had to nurture the "U.S." industry, lawmakers refused to include non-U.S. producers in Sematech, the government-subsidized semiconductor equipment consortium, despite the fact that such producers had precisely the new technology and new ideas needed by U.S. firms. European officials made the same misjudgments when they excluded Europe's biggest computer company, IBM, from JESSI, the European Union's corresponding consortium, because it was not "European," and when they later moved to eject ICL, the British computer firm, as soon as it was acquired by Fujitsu.

Viewing industries and technology in such a lockstep national fashion has even blinded many to a broader new reality: The significance of "industries" as a basis for policy has changed. Even the way industries evolve has changed—a fact that has eroded much of America's competition policy and distorted debates over competitive decline. "Competitiveness" programs centered on government intervention in a "national" industry like Sematech or JESSI became sinkholes for taxpayer funds precisely because the underlying concepts of sovereign national industry and technology are not only illogical, they are counterproductive. Vast energy and resources have been wasted by linking issues of competitiveness to the question of how America competes with Japan or Europe, when the real issues are how GM competes with Nissan, IBM competes with Toshiba, Motorola competes with Philips, and AT&T competes with Alcatel.

International competitors are foreigners.

For all too many, the "us versus them" syndrome is a vehicle for prejudice. In the traditional economy, those who stood in the way of international success were intruders who were by definition un-American. Flat Earth thinkers give the term *foreigner* a pejorative sense that is at best uncharitable and at worse highly destructive of enlightened policymaking. Such mentalities have given rise to some of the ugliest aspects of international policymaking and also, unfortunately, some of its most conspicuous—especially in election years. If they're foreign, the sloganeers want us to believe, then they must be wrong, stupid, unfair, or all three. A group called Help Save America for Our Kids' Future disseminates mass mailings preaching that "Japanism" has replaced Communism as the biggest threat facing the United States.[7]

The economic jingoism that grows from such sentiments creeps into much of the public debate when international economic issues are at stake—as poignantly demonstrated during the advocacy of the protectionism discussed in the next chapter. This is the quarter of demagogues who seek to evade the challenges of the new economy by evoking fear and doom and bashing foreign-built radios on the marble steps of government edifices. Identifying "foreign competition" as the cause of competitive decline may be a convenient excuse for such leaders, but it is certainly no strategy for success.

International challenges are all overseas.

Those blinded by trade demagoguery fail to see the simple reality that the challenges of international competition cannot be avoided by ignoring them. They are not across the Atlantic or the Rio Grande. They are down the street. Again and again the new economy has demonstrated that the biggest obstacles to global success are not offshore but right here at home. A favorite tenet of Flat Earth philosophy is that the global economy is outside the United States, and therefore those who don't wish to venture offshore don't need to worry about it. In machine tools, steel, consumer electronics, and many other industries, many American companies have been wiped out because they refused to recognize the effect of global competition on their domestic business franchise. But they'd better worry if their "local" competitor is venturing offshore:

Studies show that sales for firms with no offshore activities grow at half the rate of firms with offshore presence.[8]

In industry after industry, companies that refrain from meeting their competition on global terms have eventually paid for their failure to do so at home. In the words of Ken Morse, a director of Cambridge-based Aspen Technology, "If we have to fight them on the beaches of California, it will be too late."[9] If a company's first "international" experience is finding an offshore competitor building a facility down the road, that company is not likely to survive. There is no place to hide in the global economy.

Global industries are the playground of a handful of giant firms.

As recently as eight or nine years ago, everyone could make confident predictions about who would dominate the global computer, automotive, consumer electronics, and banking industries. Firms like IBM, Hitachi, GM, Philips, and Citibank were destined to rule their global industries well into the next century. In the trading economy, size was almost a guarantee of success. So long as manufacturing was king, as firms got bigger they got better. But the innovations of the new economy have overthrown the reign of economies of size. Settling on a core technology and pouring mountains of capital into it is no longer the path to domination in any industry. Empires built on mass production and mass marketing have become acutely vulnerable to smaller competitors who can more easily adapt to the realities of the new economy and who, thanks to the new global capital markets, can raise money as easily as their far-larger competitors. A daunting challenge faces the leading companies of yesterday: how to be successful despite being big. The new economy favors giant-killers. Small and midsize firms in the United States lag far behind their counterparts overseas in integrating themselves into the new economy. Sixty percent of Japan's foreign equity investments are by small companies. Germany's international success has long been led by its *Mittlestand*, its 200,000-plus small and midsize firms. In the list of the 1,000 biggest international businesses, there are ten times more U.S. firms than German firms despite the fact that Germany has many more multinational firms than the United States. The reason? Hundreds of *Mittelstanders* with low-profile but shrewd strategies have become the leaders in niche markets around the planet. Similarly sized American firms account for a mere 3 percent of America's foreign direct investment.[10] When America's small firms do venture overseas, their record is spectacular: U.S.-based international firms with sales under $100 million grew at the astounding pace of 67 percent per year—with a 35 percent return on equity—from 1986 to 1991,[11] the last year for which figures are available.

Foreign investment destabilizes national economies.

Many mid-twentieth-century theorists posited a product-cycle explanation of trade, built on the concept that firms exported during the early stages of product development, then established foreign investment for production as profit margins dropped. Since in the minds of many policymakers the United States had to be *the* maker of advanced goods and *the* center for high technology, inbound foreign investment was insidious. It meant American production had to be shared with "them." Prejudices against foreign investment by U.S. firms likewise crept into U.S. policy on the premise that such offshore investors were somehow "cheating" America, that they were dishonest, disloyal offspring using their U.S.–bred endowments to fill foreign bank accounts by displacing American workers and exploiting foreign workers.

The global plebiscite has ripped apart the foundation for such views. Today, demand for new products is driven by consumers around the globe. No single country can claim exclusivity for a product for long—either parallel technology is found elsewhere for competing products or a new generation of products is launched, which renders the exclusivity meaningless. Foreign investment also displaces far fewer workers at home than traditionally thought: Over half of all foreign investment in developing countries, for example, is for services or natural resource development that simply cannot be performed at "home," and much of the remainder is driven by freight costs or local barriers that mandate local investment. Foreign investment is not a necessary evil; it is an indispensable tool for keeping the competitive edge in every global industry. Studies of the new flows of capital are demonstrating that foreign investment has become the most important single force in improving a host country's productivity.

FLAT EARTH STANDARDS OF SUCCESS

The prototypical enterprise of the trading economy was the steel producer: Value was derived from the manipulation of natural resources and labor. Massive investment in fixed assets was required. Markets were constant in the sense of being easily identified and relatively predictable. As the central cog in a huge mining, manufacturing, and construction employment machine, steel mills were vital sovereign assets. Some nations acknowledged this by placing them under government ownership. In other nations, like the United States, where private ownership was supported, the sovereign nature of such firms was less conspicuous than in other countries, but government remained a vital stakeholder, giving such enterprises as much government protection—meaning subsidies from taxpayers and consumers—as was necessary to keep them in business. Investment decisions were centered on expanding and refining existing plants. Profitability hinged largely on controlling production costs and government protection.

By the terms of traditional trade policy, one of the great success stories should be the partnership of government and steel around the planet. But the new economy has condemned such partnerships to economic backwaters. The successful producers are those whose products are filled with ideas, not with iron ore and taxpayer subsidies. A transformed industry is being led by producers like Nucor Corporation and Chaparral Steel, who repudiate government assistance or protection and focus instead on continual innovation from sources around the globe. Today, while larger traditional producers still seek political attention by complaining bitterly about unfair foreign producers, the lowest-cost, high-quality steel in the world is being *exported from the United States* by the new generation of American steel firms. Those firms are exporting 7 million tons a year and are inventing profitable new global roles like that of Inland Steel, which has based a successful international comeback on innovative global distribution systems.

By traditional standards, one of the great American failures has been the computer industry: As policymakers bitterly complain, many critical component parts are not made in the United States at all. The majority of the world's semiconductor chips are made by Japanese firms. Between 60 and 70 percent of the hardware used in American personal computers is imported from Asia, creating large trade deficits in computer products between the United States and Asia. By traditional standards, the computer industry is import-addicted, dominated by foreigners.

But anyone close to the industry knows otherwise. U.S. firms control over half the global market for computer peripherals and are the acknowledged leaders in other segments of the industry. By leveraging low-cost commodity producers offshore with innovation in design and applications, U.S. firms add vast new value to imported components and control the evolution of their global industry. Many offshore sources, moreover, are owned or controlled by American firms; nearly all the disk-drive makers in Asia, for example, are owned by U.S. companies and employ U.S.-originated technology. U.S. firms attained global leadership without government assistance—and in spite of Washington's ill-fated management of key materials like semiconductor chips and active matrix screens.

The best international corporate structure is an expanded version of that used at home.

The rigid structures of the trading mentality were built around home-country organizations that exported not only goods but also organizational clones, creating far-flung colonial empires for the home-country parent. The mission of offshore subsidiaries in such structures is in essence to send tribute home, just as India once sent to Britain or subsidiary factories in Scotland sent to Singer, the first U.S. multinational, over 120 years ago.[12] Such trade-based structures are still keeping many companies from global success, imposing control where empowerment is needed, homogeneity where diversity is needed, and constriction of information where liquidity of ideas is needed. Indeed, a new generation of such structures has arrived in which companies have misapplied the model of decentralized global management, used so successfully by global leaders like ABB Asea Brown Boveri, to create new regional fiefdoms that bear strong resemblance to the colonial structures of old.

■

Ultimately, a permutation of the trading mentality could be found underlying every Flat Earth policy and strategy—many more specific ones are discussed later in these pages. But those set forth above capture the broadest and most treacherous features of that mentality. Twenty years ago such tenets could be defended, or their roots could at least be empirically traced to economic reality. But today the demise of trade as the energizing force of cross-border business has rendered them more myth than reality, and the mythology they perpetuate is grossly distorting the processes of policy and planning.

Imprisoned by trading mind-sets, policymakers misunderstand the structure of new global industries and convert the global leverage points that pump value through those industries into American choke points that constrain American growth in those industries. They are blinded to the revolutionary changes in the nature of capital that have been introduced by the new economy. And they fail to perceive that they must look at maps in ways they never did before.

TRADING DOWN: THE DESTRUCTIVE POWER OF TRADITION

In 1991 the United States was poised to capture a large share of the rapidly expanding laptop-computer industry within its borders. Already a

$4 billion global business in 1991, the industry has been projected by Arthur D. Little to reach $52 billion by the end of the century. Apple Computer had constructed a factory in Fountain, Colorado, to build its units. Toshiba was pouring capital into a new laptop facility in Irvine, California. IBM was beginning to spend substantial research sums in support of the new laptop design and production network developing in the United States, hoping to soon build its own plant. Zenith and Compaq were planning to build high-value businesses around U.S.–produced laptops, all relying on sophisticated active-matrix screens imported from Japan.

But suddenly, on the eve of this U.S. victory, a handful of small firms that had manufactured low-quality screens for the U.S. military appeared in the office of trade policymakers in Washington, arguing that they could make the commercial-quality active-matrix display screens that Zenith, IBM, and Apple could not—if only they were given the favor of protection against the "unfair" Japanese imports. Despite the fact that they had never built a commercial-quality screen themselves, they easily swayed Washington. At their request, the Commerce Department imposed a 62.7 percent tariff on screen imports.

To the trading mentality, the decision was a model of wisdom. The United States had broken an unhealthy concentration in screen manufacturing. We had ended an unnecessary dependence on a foreign source of supply. We had expanded American manufacturing. We had assured new technology advances within the United States. We had beaten the Japanese. Sovereign intervention had achieved what could not have been accomplished by the private sector alone.

But the global economy judged the decision a disaster. Every one of its justifications was obsolete:

We had broken an unhealthy concentration in screen manufacturing. The computer industry could not support another of the vastly expensive production bases required to make the high-quality screens demanded by the global plebiscite. The existing screen production represented an investment of over $1 billion by Sharp Corporation, with a supporting investment of several hundred million more by Toshiba, Epson, and NEC, who had worked together to develop the complex technology required for the screens. The market would have condemned anyone irrational enough to spend another $1 billion for a redundant factory in the United States, using untested new "American" technology. Sharp did not represent an unhealthy concentration; its factory, like hundreds of others in global industries, represents the way companies stay competitive, investing today to occupy a niche, always temporarily, in support of a broader web of customers *and* competitors who in turn support the relentless investment necessary to maintain the industry. Sharp had carved out its role in the global division of capital that energized the industry, and American-based enterprises had assumed another, higher-value role: providing leadership in the end-use market with innovative design, assembly of components, marketing, and technical support for customers.

We had broken an unnecessary dependence on a foreign source of supply. The dependence of Apple and Toshiba in the United States on the supply from Sharp in Japan was necessary. It was fundamental to the industry, just as fundamental as the technology shared by American firms that kept Sharp competitive in other sectors. The supply of screens from Asia did not represent some insidious addiction to foreign supply; it represented a vital interdependence. That supply structure was integral to the competitiveness of American laptop-computer firms: By interfering with that interdependence, Washington may not have destroyed the leadership position of those firms, but it sharply limited the benefits accruing to Americans as a result of that position.

We had expanded American manufacturing. American manufacturing contracted as a result of Washington's decision. Washington slammed the door shut on the only viable component available to producers. Apple and Toshiba/California could not sell products with the poorer-quality screens made in the United States. Washington gave them no choice. Apple closed its month-old factory in Colorado and moved production to Ireland, where imported components faced no import barriers. Toshiba announced that it could no longer produce laptops in the United States and moved production to Japan.

We had assured new technology advances within the United States. There was a technology hemorrhage, not a technology gain, as a result of the decision. America never controlled the sophisticated technology used for the screens. Prior to the new import barriers, the Pentagon had pumped scores of millions into display-screen research by defense contractors without the glimmer of a new competitive product. The loss of the laptop factories, however, meant a loss of the U.S. expertise that would have been developed to integrate the screens into end products and the loss of the experts who would have been operating the plants—Apple and Toshiba sent their technology offshore. IBM shifted $100 million in development funds to Japan for a screen joint venture with Toshiba.

We had beaten the Japanese. Washington did not punish the Japanese with its decision. It "beat" the Japanese-funded jobs in the

California facility that closed. It punished the Colorado workers who were to build laptop units for Apple. It punished the workers of suppliers who would have been supporting those factories. We didn't beat anyone but ourselves. The winners were the Japanese members of the industry and Japan itself, which garnished a much larger share of display-screen research and production as a direct result of Washington's actions.

Sovereign intervention had achieved what could not have been accomplished by the private sector. This much was true, although not in the sense Washington intended. No one but Washington could have slammed the import door shut. It gutted American participation in the industry in a way the global economy would never have devised. Left alone, the global economy would have allocated the United States a leadership position in the industry.

Three years later, when the original petitioners for protection still had not built the hoped-for "American" flat screen, trade policymakers puzzled over the failure of their prior decision. Unable to admit defeat, they announced the offer of up to $587 million in matching taxpayer funds to subsidize new screen factories in America as part of a new National Flat Panel Display Initiative. The expected rush of applicants from the global industry never materialized. The lack of enthusiasm by the industry's global players reflected recognition of realities that Washington, in its preoccupation with new manufacturing jobs and "sovereign" technology, had ignored. Whether or not Washington insisted, the industry could never justify a redundant American production base.

In the time since Washington had first intervened, moreover, screen technology had already entered its third generation. Massive investments in new plasma-based liquid crystal screens—again, the only ones the industry could afford—were already under way in Japan. The earlier screens attacked by Washington as "unfair" imports and targeted with new federal subsidies were already being produced in commodity factories in Korea, using the earlier Japanese technology. In September 1995, a start-up venture asked for some of Washington's funding—not for the new factory intended by Washington but for the fourth-generation technology that would inevitably replace the current generation. Other firms—such as Raytheon and a joint venture between Motorola and In-Focus Systems Inc.—proceeded with independent research into completely different flat-panel technology. The U.S. firms were right to second-guess Washington: They knew the global industry, not trade officials, would make the fourth-generation decision.

■

Similar stories of the trading mentality contaminating international strategies and policy can be found in virtually every industry with global connections. Charles and Maurice Saatchi set out to build the first global marketing firm, spending $500 million to acquire operations in every major market around the planet. They achieved their goal—for a moment. Their empire quickly collapsed—the market capitalization of their firm plummeted to the level it was at before the global campaign—because it was based on the notion that they could simply export what they did so well at home, that being global was simply a function of exporting their homegrown cachet to advertising agencies around the world. Citibank suffered much the same problem when it expanded around the planet during the 1980s; by 1990 it had to write off a billion dollars spent in global expansion. Ultimately such stories are about barriers to *liquidity* and *diversity* and the complex dynamics by which they energize an industry, meaning barriers to interdependence. They are all stories about failure to understand the sources of advantage in the new economy.

America's high-tech anomaly was discussed in Chapter One: Despite being the most significant source of new technology, the United States has a chronic problem in growing its high-tech industries. Much of that anomaly is explained by Washington's interference with the interdependence that is the lifeblood of such industries. In 1966, 39 percent of high-tech materials entering the United States—including vital subassemblies and components—faced barriers at the border in the form of quotas, special import-relief duties, or other special measures; twenty-five years later the figure had increased to 62 percent. The liquidity and diversity of high-tech materials and the ideas embodied in them were sharply restricted. To gain global advantage, America's high-tech sectors have to be nurtured from a global base. Washington restricts that process or, as in the case of the early generations of display screens, completely prevents it.

Learning about the new economy in its most important aspects means learning about the new mobile sources of advantage that nurture global firms. Integrating those lessons into policymaking, however, requires casting out assumptions about traditional comparative advantage and integrating those new sources into policymaking. The new dynamics of competition have undermined every policy and every analytical structure based on the "permanent" natural endowments of the trading economy. They have not invalidated Ricardo's basic concept of comparative advantage; the trading models built around his concept grew old and died, but the concept itself was not wrong, nor was it capable of growing stale. It has, however, lost considerable utility to policymakers for the simple reason that its dynamics no longer correspond to their jurisdictions—the competitive structures it applies to are not nations but industries. When all the familiar *venues* (i.e., national economies) and *sources* (i.e., nationally focused production assets) of advantage have dried up, the concept seems less enlightening than it was in Economics 101 a generation ago. Obviously, comparative advantage for any product or service resides somewhere at any particular time, but where it resides is in concentrations of people and knowledge structures that are not bound to geography. In its essence, comparative advantage equates to comparative productivity, and advantage in productivity—meaning advantage in the knowledge needed for cost-effective creation of a product or service—can, and does, shift with awesome speed.

Clusters of production facilities for many computer components and peripherals have shifted over the past dozen years from the United States to Japan and Singapore, then to Taiwan, Korea, and Malaysia. The shift of assembly operations to China has already begun. Such shifts do not mean that American firms have lost their advantage in the computer industry to Asia—those firms are directing many of these shifts. What the shifts mean is that these Asian countries are capturing advantage in certain aspects of manufacturing and assembly, advantage that accrues both to their citizens and the American enterprises they serve. Every effort to interfere with that process—to block shifts of lower-skill, value-added activities to the locales where they can be performed most cost-effectively, to force those low-skill activities back to America— amounts to trading down the productivity of the U.S. economy. If sustained, such efforts invite those Asian countries to leapfrog the United States into high-skill sectors, relegating the United States to the role of a low-value supplier whose productivity and standard of living will continue to move in a downward spiral.

A PARADOX OF POLICY

The industrial nation-state as the paradigm for policy is meaningless in an economy where "industrial" itself is outdated. But Washington stubbornly defines international success in terms of hard assets, national resources, technological ownership, exchange rates, market shares for end-use products, labor protection, and export promotion—meaning that it defines competition in terms of the trading economy and its tradition of industrial production. Confronted with international economic issues, politicians want to talk about trade. They want to talk about exports and balancing accounts and bashing Asian computers or televisions. In other words, they want to talk about economic history. By focusing on what is irrelevant, they make themselves irrelevant. As they console each other with worn-out complaints over "fair" shares of trade, electronic pulses are shifting billions in capital across oceans, and entrepreneurs are busy transferring components, schematics, financial risk-sharing devices, supply contracts, skills, and interdependent relationships that do not compute in Flat Earth frameworks.

It is painful for many to acknowledge that the answers for dealing with the new economy are not made in America. They are not found in the corridors of Washington or the executive suites of traditional industry leaders. But they are also not made in Japan, Germany, France, England, or Singapore. Locating them on a map is a futile exercise—and they will not be found anywhere by decision makers who cling to the myths of trade. For such individuals, globalization is a rallying cry to expand traditional programs and policies.

As discussed in the following chapters, in matters of antitrust, capital, investment, technology, export control, tax, import relief, corporate organization, and monetary policy, these traditionalists are entrenching the country further in the Flat Earth. Yet far from recognizing that point, many policymakers actually interpret globalization as a mandate to colonize their own anachronistic policies overseas, pushing many developing nations to adopt U.S.–style legislation. Some observers have labeled such efforts intellectually arrogant or culturally naive. Others have suggested that they reek of imperialism. The global economy, of course, is indifferent to such labels. The legacy of anachronistic strategy and concepts is a huge burden, but those who pay the heaviest penalty are those who cling to that legacy. Companies and countries that pretend they can prevail today by antiquated trade-based measures will simply be bypassed by the fruits of that economy—for in the new economy, the legacy of trade is no longer wealth but failure.

PROTECTION FROM PRODUCTIVITY

America's Burden of Managed Trade

C hina is the worse nightmare of the Flat Earth. Assembly and processing plants for industrial-country markets are being opened at a rate exceeding one a day. It ships far more to the United States than the United States ships to it. Over fifty separate antidumping proceedings have been convened in Washington to combat unfair pricing of Chinese products. It has taken over production of most American toys. Congressional critics regularly call for the door to be slammed on Chinese imports. U.S. Trade Representative Mickey Kantor targeted China for special attention in September 1995 due to a $30 billion imbalance in trade with Beijing. The country's GDP is expanding at a rate nearly triple that of America's own growth. Flat Earth voices warn that eventually China will produce everything for America and other richer countries, putting the citizens of those countries out of work.

But China is a perfect example of the global economic process: Liberalization in its economy has allowed it to capitalize on the current comparative advantage it offers in many industries, that of a low-skill,

51

labor-intensive production venue for goods entering global markets. That role sends out inevitable ripples into the economies of America and the industrial world. Washington may have reason for concern over certain political issues in the Chinese context, such as human rights and regional security, but it has no reason to rebel against those economic ripples.

Without question, Chinese imports reduce the value of competing domestic goods—or, more importantly, those imports reduce the income of the low-skilled labor that makes the competing domestic product. But that is the essence of economic progress. It is not far removed from the process by which modern dairies devalued the role of the milk cow and butter churn in every household; low-skilled labor, organized by innovative systems, allowed those dairies to offer a product whose "import" into the home was more attractive than devoting the time of household members to low-skill efforts for the same result.

The cumulative effect of such imports into the domestic environment—also including milled lumber, prebaked bread, canned vegetables, woven cloth, mass-produced clothing, oil, coal, and electricity—was the liberation of Americans for higher education and the pursuit of still greater innovation and increased standards of living. Today, the erosion in the value of low-skilled workers from the introduction of low-skilled labor from outside the domestic environment (Chinese labor imports) combined with innovative systems (the production and distribution knowledge of global firms) pushes resources into more highly skilled applications, which provides more revenue, smarter and better jobs, and a greater share of global wealth for Americans.[1] Many such imports—like the components made by Motorola in Tianjin, China—also increasingly serve as materials for higher-value American goods purchased around the planet.

Tradition-bound policymakers, however, focus not on the vital pro-growth nature of this process but on its inherent shifting of jobs. More specifically, they don't see the jobs gained—new jobs make few demands on government—but instead focus on the jobs lost, which always makes at least temporary demands on government. They demand protection for such jobs and obtain it: In the name of helping the American economy, for example, they have protected makers of ship towels, paint brushes, nails, candles, hats, sparklers, paper clips, pencils, lock washers, and pans from the dangers of Chinese imports. They don't need to pause over the alarming implications of such actions—that they are forcing Americans to substitute for low-skill Chinese workers, that each such action pushes productivity toward Chinese levels—because Washington's protectionist tradition says it is the right thing to do.

WASHINGTON'S WAR WITH PRODUCTIVITY

Washington's most conspicuous—and most costly in terms of readily quantifiable expense—collision with the new economy lies in such direct management of international business. By wielding an arsenal of tariffs, quotas, antidumping duties, and other protective devices promulgated over the past century, Washington restricts the number of cars made available to consumers from offshore factories and keeps high-quality foreign steel from producers who need to be competitive globally. It manages the prices paid by American consumers to thousands of offshore suppliers. It controls the precise number of foreign socks, shirts, and shoes sold in America. It regulates the flow of foreign pizzas and painstakingly counts the number of Polish wool dresses crossing the U.S. border—no more than 24,408 a year are allowed.

This framework of protection was erected on the foundations of conventional trade. As those foundations have crumbled, that framework has become economically disastrous. Yet, in what is frequently blasted as American hypocrisy overseas, U.S. negotiators bloody their foreign counterparts to open offshore markets while Washington has in many respects grown steadily more protectionist.

It is rare to find unanimity among economists on any topic, but there is one issue on which even conservative and liberal economists concur. Milton Friedman and Paul Samuelson, for example, often disagree on fundamental points of economic theory, but they find common ground in condemning protectionism. It does not save jobs. It does not create more productive enterprises. As economics it is irrational. As public policy it is destructive. It erodes American productivity. It distorts the decisions that must be made for enterprises to be competitive. It reduces incentives to invest in technology development. It obscures the real issues of the new economy.

Just when we need to be considering the revolutionary new policies and strategies for capital, technology, and investment that are demanded by that economy, we are led to believe that our international problems can be addressed by automobile quotas, computer-chip price controls, or subsidies for sugar beets. Until there is a more rational debate among all the stakeholders in the issue, there can be little hope of moving on to the bigger economic challenges begging attention from policymakers.

Getting to the Global Reality

In the popular image, protectionism is the result of the struggle between home-market firms and unfair foreign producers. The reality is that protectionism is a struggle between local consumers and local producers, between those who use goods and those who believe themselves entitled to profits solely by virtue of their proximity. Protectionists insist that it is not profits but jobs that are protected. The reality is that protection costs this country vastly more jobs than it saves. Washington has never waged a trade war that netted the country more jobs than it lost—the biggest one ever fought turned into the Great Depression. We are told that intervention by Washington is required to vitalize American enterprise. The reality is that no enterprise or sector has ever attained global leadership through Washington's intervention—although quite a few have lost it. We are told that blocking imports strengthens the American economy. The reality is that it pushes American productivity downward and erodes our standard of living.

Yet many policymakers relentlessly pursue managed trade as the panacea to America's competitiveness problems. The United States remains as sharply protectionist as almost any of the countries it criticizes for protectionism. Not since the greatest experiment in managed trade—the Smoot-Hawley tariffs that caused international business to implode by 70 percent—has Washington been so insistent on intervening in the international flow of goods as it has in the past decade.

One third of all imports currently enter the United States under some form of direct management by Washington. Huge bureaucracies exist to ensure that Jamaica doesn't ship more than 970 gallons of ice cream a year to U.S. ports, to count the buttons on sweaters from Mauritius, and to determine whether containers of liver came from geese or ducks (the tariff on duck liver is sixteen times greater than that of the goose). Taxpayers pay hundreds of millions of dollars to support officials who count foreign hair nets, restrict shoelaces (Customs recently blocked 30,000 tennis shoes from Indonesia because they had double sets of shoelaces), and write rules for objects returned from space (duty-free only if they were originally launched from the United States by U.S. citizens).

A cascading series of protectionist measures for the textile and apparel industries has made multimillionaires of dozens of Asian entrepreneurs, who effectively were granted by Congress what they could not otherwise legally obtain: a guaranteed market share and the "fixing" of higher prices. Yet policymakers still respond to new calls for protection, creating in some industries a chain of increasing protection that seems politically impossible to break.

Few even in Washington appreciate the size and complexity of the protectionist machine. It includes not only traditional tariffs but quotas, "voluntary" restraint agreements, orderly marketing agreements, countervailing duties, antidumping duties, and many measures of intervention phrased as "industrial policy" to avoid the label of protectionism. The Department of Agriculture manages rice and cheese shipments. The Commerce Department restricts entries of raspberries, work gloves, ski suits, urea, flowers, and hundreds of other goods. The International Trade Commission evaluates injury from imports for punitive measures and issues cease-and-desist orders against "unfair" trade. The Customs Service enforces restrictions on shoes, toothpicks, and brooms. The U.S. Trade Representative negotiates management of computer chips, aluminum, steel, and autos. And Congress, as the source of authority for all our managed trade, seems to maintain a peculiarly cyclical contempt for non–U.S. inputs to U.S. enterprise, coinciding neatly with election years.

The targets of managed trade are not blind to the paradox emanating from Washington, which enforces strict, often arbitrary quotas against them while pushing them to open their own markets. Richard Holwill, when he served as Deputy Assistant Secretary of State, was embarrassed by his own government's two-faced policies when his job took him to Latin America to promote the American "system": "It makes us look like damn fools when we go down there and preach free enterprise."

The Federal Reserve Bank has estimated that Washington's import-protection schemes amount to the equivalent of a 23 percent income-tax surcharge for low-income families or 10 percent for the "average" family. The Federal Trade Commission estimates that special tariff protection costs the American economy nearly $90 for each dollar saved by the protected firms. While Congressional subcommittees painfully try to find ways to eliminate $50- or $60-million items from the budget, they assiduously support managed trade programs that carry an annual price tag estimated to be *$50 billion to $70 billion*, paid out of the pockets of American consumers.[2]

FIGHTING FOREIGN FIBERS

If protection is, as many in Washington insist, about national economic security, then judging by the degree of protective regulation, the most dangerous elements of our commerce are socks, shirts, cotton balls, and quilts. Since 1791, when Alexander Hamilton introduced the first clothing tariffs as "temporary" measures to help a fledgling industry, Washington has led the world in controlling the flow of textiles and apparel across borders. Under the Multi-Fiber Arrangement (MFA), orchestrated by the industrial nations with Washington's leadership and extended for another twelve years in 1993,[3] the Department of Commerce (representing the Committee for the Implementation of Textile Agreements) has the authority to restrict any products for which imports have increased at prices less than those prevailing in the U.S. market. Under the MFA, restrictions are administered against 3,000 categories of clothing and textiles from dozens of nations. The Commerce Department issues "calls" for quotas whenever imports from a country exceed 1 percent of U.S. production. The committee then determines whether a quota is necessary to protect American producers—but is required by Congress to report any committee member who votes against imposing new restrictions on the basis of a call. Over 25 percent of all manufacturing exports from developing nations are controlled by the MFA, which reaches not only shirts and pants but anything made of fibers, from backpacks to fishnets, sun blinds to tents, pillows to tampons.

Because poor families must spend a greater percentage of their income on clothing than others and because restrictions are greatest on low-cost synthetic-fiber items, Washington's barriers to clothing and textile imports hit these people hardest. The U.S. Association of Importers of Textiles and Apparel has calculated that the poor pay 8.8 percent of their income for Washington's protection; in other words, they spend 8.8 percent more of their income on clothing than would be the case if Washington didn't interfere with clothing trade. Washington's elimination of separate children's clothing categories in quotas ten years ago established another penalty on low-income families: Foreign producers had little choice but to focus on production of more profitable adult clothing. The average price of children's clothing in the United States has nearly tripled as a result.

Washington's quotas have been great for sales of Mercedes and Rolls Royces in Asia. A whole new class of millionaires was created by Washington as a direct result of the MFA. Many producers actually closed their factories when they discovered they could make more money by simply selling their quota rights. A pair of trousers for the American market cost $7 to make in Hong Kong; the market price for U.S. quota rights in Hong Kong for that pair of trousers, without which the Customs Service would deny it entry, is $8, paid not to the U.S. government but to other Asian entrepreneurs. The average American clothing importer pays over $1.2 million annually in added quota expense and still loses over $2 million in sales disrupted due to quota administration changes and delays. Where does all this cash come from? American consumers. The Institute for International Economics estimates that at the retail level, American consumers pay a premium equivalent to at least $24 billion, and perhaps as much as $40 billion, as a result of Washington's management of the textile and apparel trade.[4] A $40-billion premium amounts to a special federal clothing tax of about $500 on every American family—an effective 50 percent tariff on clothing sold in America.

American consumers have long paid another penalty in addition to high prices. Over 100 years ago, the Reform Club of New York published a study of why American clothing was of such poor quality. The answer: Import restrictions prevented clothing makers from obtaining high-quality textiles.[5] In the nineteenth century, many Americans were forced to wear clothes of recycled rags, known then as "shoddy." Many modern apparel makers are still appalled at the "shoddy" character of their domestic supplies. The quality of American textiles is on average still far below that of imported textiles for the simple reason that domestic producers have no competition to keep them focused on quality. Donald Fisher, chairman and CEO of the GAP Inc., knows from years of frustration that the textile mills protected by Washington are "not as flexible, creative, or as good as their foreign counterparts." The global economy is addressing the problem: American clothing makers are supporting foreign suppliers in establishing plants in the United States. A significant percentage of the cloth that Fisher's firm buys from Hong Kong suppliers is now coming from the higher-quality American plants built by those suppliers.

What do Americans get for their steep clothing tax? Preservation of some of the lowest-paid and least-skilled manufacturing jobs in the country. Textile and apparel workers earn far below the average manufacturing wage—and each of these low-skilled jobs saved by textile and apparel protection costs the American economy $700,000.[6]

Washington's trade bureaucrats argue that protection from foreign imports is required for such workers since they will never find work again due to their poor skills. It would, of course, cost far less simply to pay jobless benefits to every textile worker than to pay for job protection. But even that would be unnecessary: The most comprehensive study on the adaptability of textile workers was done by Washington's own Labor Department; it demonstrated that, in fact, most displaced textile workers found new jobs, and their new jobs paid higher wages.[7] Research by the

Federal Reserve Bank shows that at least one job in a related industry is lost for every textile and apparel job protected by Washington.[8] Clothing producers have finally begun to recognize the disadvantages of protection; the American Apparel Manufacturers Association has begun opposing protection—but Congress still thinks it knows better. Senator Phil Gramm sought to inject some realism into the process by introducing an amendment that would eliminate quotas for any country that was less protectionist than the United States; the proposal was defeated by a wide margin. Another amendment to eliminate protection in any year that textile industry profits exceeded average American manufacturing profits was likewise defeated without serious consideration.

Textile and apparel production in every other industrialized nation has shrunk significantly in recent years, shifting to less-productive venues as those nations move to higher-skilled employment. Thanks to Washington's blind support, the production of domestic firms has grown, pushing more workers into one of America's largest low-skill sectors.

MANAGING THE SMOKESTACKS

Nothing has attracted more attention among Washington's trade managers than the labor-intensive smokestack industries that produce steel, machine tools, and automobiles. Proponents of managed trade long ago convinced themselves that in such basic industries, which are heavily linked to U.S. resources, labor, and markets, managed trade is most needed and most likely to be successful. The global economy has proved them wrong on both counts.

After American consumers shocked Detroit and Washington with their initial receptiveness to Japanese imports, Detroit pleaded for protection to recapture lost market share and modernize its plants. It won the first Voluntary Restraint Agreement with Japan in 1981, and protection has continued ever since, with a sharp increase in the restrictions in 1992. But instead of utilizing the opportunity provided by such quotas to increase their market share to counter the Japanese "invasion," Detroit firms boosted their prices, safe in the knowledge that Washington had effectively forced American consumers to accept the price increases.

Their spending of the resulting windfall profits made business headlines during the 1980s—and had little to do with revitalizing plants. GM spent $8 billion to buy EDS and a defense company, then issued fat executive bonus checks as a reward for their success—not in the market but in Washington. Chrysler bought out a major competitor, American Motors. Ford acquired a huge savings-and-loan network and likewise paid scores of millions to executives. Washington's own International Trade Commission calculated that consumers have paid an additional $5.2 billion for U.S. cars as a direct result of the export-restraint agreement with Japan during the past decade. The Brookings Institution concluded that the net effect of auto restraints has been to "transfer billions of dollars from consumers pockets" into the pockets of the Big Three.

Inevitably, due to the combined effect of Washington's protection and the demands of American consumers, the Japanese firms began investing billions in new American auto factories. Detroit, through limited joint ventures at first, then in massive equity or alliance investments with several Japanese producers, began to perceive the global lessons implicit in the Japanese shift to America. Much of Detroit's turnaround in recent years is owed to those lessons.

But Detroit's link to Washington has been difficult to break. It found a ready audience in 1995 when it asked the Clinton White House to intervene in the Japanese market. It relied heavily on allegations of a monolithic "Japan Inc." alliance between the government of Japan and the Japanese producers, which closed the market to foreigners and kept car prices in the Japanese market artificially high. The allegation fit particularly well with the criteria for the most severe of Washington's trade sanctions, but it did not jibe with reality. As anyone who bothered to study the industry could readily discover, the only intervention Tokyo has made in the auto industry has been that forced on it by Washington in administering American quotas. The Japanese automotive producers are not only fiercely independent of each other but have also actively opposed intervention by Tokyo in the conduct of their business. Honda, one of the most successful global producers, developed its auto business over adamant protests of the Japanese government. With respect to prices in the Japanese market, moreover, several studies, including one by the U.S. Department of Commerce, have shown that Japanese cars sell for the same prices in New York and Tokyo.[9]

Washington turned the market-access issue into one more round of traditional trade brinksmanship, only months after obtaining consensus for the World Trade Organization, by reassuring its allies that it would submit such disputes to multilateral resolution. But as it fought Tokyo with press conferences and headlines, threatening to effectively block shipments of Japanese luxury cars to U.S. dealers, Detroit was quietly completing investments to address the biggest barrier to its sales in Japan, its own failure to meet Japanese market demands. Almost nowhere in the vast media and political thrashing of Japan for its restriction of Detroit was mention made of one simple fact: Japanese drive on the left side of the road, meaning that left-hand-drive U.S. autos cannot be used by Japanese drivers. European producers have been successfully selling right-hand-drive cars in Japan for years and already accounted for nearly 7 percent of Japan's market when Washington began battering Tokyo for lack of market access. In June 1995, as Washington's trade warriors were excoriating Tokyo for its unfair treatment of U.S. car producers, the total number of U.S. car models available in Japan with right-hand drive was *three*. In the United States, the total number of left-hand-drive cars offered by Japanese producers was *190*.[10]

As American producers finally accepted the challenge of making products to fit the Japanese markets, the Japanese quickly began to buy them—Chrysler could not make right-hand-drive Jeep Cherokees fast enough to meet demand. Detroit's solution, however, was one that galled Flat Earth observers in Washington: Of 200,000 cars targeted by Ford for sale in Japan by 2000, half will be made by Mazda, of which Ford owns 25 percent. Of 100,000 cars targeted for sale by GM, many will be Opels made in Germany and others will be U.S. cars sold over Toyota's brand—with production financing provided by the Export-Import Bank of Japan.[11]

Despite its strong comeback in the 1990s, the legacy of Detroit's prior reliance on government to fight global battles is deep-rooted and hard to overcome. Detroit continues to trail its Japanese competitors in productivity. The most productive American auto plants in the United States are those of Nissan and Toyota.[12]

One of the perennial arguments heard in protection pleas from Detroit has been that foreign producers have much-less-expensive materials available, especially for major components such as steel. American steel users have estimated that they pay an average of 25 percent more for a ton of steel than their global competitors in other industrial nations. Steel prices have been so high for so long precisely due to a similar story of protection that can be told for the steel industry.

Complex steel quotas imposed during the 1980s against twenty-nine nations cost steel users up to a million dollars annually for every job saved. Despite the goal of job preservation at the heart of these programs, the Center for the Study of American Business concluded that they temporarily saved 17,000 jobs in the steel industry but forced over

52,000 workers out of their jobs in steel-using industries, whose products were uncompetitive due to the higher cost of steel inputs and, in some cases, the inability to incorporate the high-quality steel formerly obtained from foreign sources. The Federal Trade Commission has estimated that steel protection cost the U.S. economy $25 for every dollar in increased earnings to the steel producers. The Institute for International Economics estimates that steel quotas cost American consumers $6.8 billion a year. More difficult to quantify, but no less real, has been the erosion in competitiveness caused by protection. Critical decisions to upgrade plants, develop new international sourcing networks, and invest in new technology were deferred as competitive pressure from more efficient foreign producers eased.

During the height of the steel-import restrictions imposed during the 1980s, exports of steel-using companies such as appliance and equipment makers plummeted—and imports from their more cost-effective offshore competitors increased. USX and Armco used their protection windfalls not to revitalize their plants but to follow the pattern of the auto industry and diversify—only to ask the U.S. taxpayers and consumers for more protection later.

A three-week period in the early spring of 1992, following expiration of prior import restraints, holds a unique place in annals of the modern steel industry: It was the only period in the past decade during which there was no import protection for the American steel industry. For that brief moment, appliance, truck, and myriad other equipment makers were free of one of the greatest burdens to their competitiveness— expensive and poor-quality American steel. Such steel-using companies in America employ sixty times more workers than U.S. steel-making companies. The Center for the Study of American Business estimates that import restrictions had destroyed three jobs in those steel-using firms for each steel job saved.

But in April 1992 the steel industry filed over 2 million pages comprising eighty-four new petitions for antidumping protection against unfair pricing of imported steel. Steel users who complained to Washington of the disruptive effect on business were countered with the point that the petitions were merely requests for more duties, which would be imposed only after expert analysis of the facts to determine if protection was necessary. Steel-making supporters didn't bother to point out that over 90 percent of all antidumping cases result in new import barriers against foreign producers[13]—one reason policy analyst James Bovard considers antidumping laws to be "one of the greatest threats to U.S. manufacturing." Despite loud complaints by steel users such as

General Motors and the American Institute for International Steel, the new petitions eventually resulted in a 30 percent reduction in imports for several categories of steel and an added cost to steel users of $1 billion a year—giving added emphasis to Bovard's view that "the federal government has succeeded in turning steel into a chokepoint in the American economy."[14]

The machine-tool industry in many ways lies at the heart of the smokestack industries, churning out the machines that build steel, automotive, and other products. Invoking national security, Washington launched a stringent series of restraints on machine-tool imports in the mid-1980s. Machine-tool producers became a *cause celebre* in Washington, providing a rallying point for those lambasting the foreigners who were overwhelming American firms with low-cost, innovative products.

After five years of restrictions, Hurco, an Indianapolis toolmaker, took inventory of their effects. Because its unsolicited patrons in Washington had decreed that U.S. toolmakers would be "competitive" only by obtaining components domestically, Hurco's costs to make a finished product had increased by over 10 percent. For the same reason, the firm had to invest several million dollars for new tool patterns and development of new part sources. A $3 million sale to Taiwan was cancelled in a retaliatory move after Washington blocked shipments from Taiwan to the United States. "The people who want to maintain the restraints are trying to fight a war that is already over," Brian McLaughlin, president of Hurco, explained to *The New York Times*. "Protectionism doesn't work. The only way to revive this industry is to focus on research and development, to develop leading edge technology, and to compete globally."[15] Ray Blakeman, former president of the National Machine Tool Association, fought his own association's endorsement of protection: "We are riding a mule that is crippled and should be put out to pasture," he wrote to the industry in 1991. His "mule" was the traditionally separate "American" industry, a concept that had become obsolete in any meaningful economic sense.

CHIPPING AWAY AT SILICON VALLEY

Washington had not learned its lesson from heavy industries when it embarked ten years ago on its long-term intervention in the global semiconductor chip business. The situation was too tempting for Flat Earth policymakers to resist: The world market was suffering from severe overcapacity. The U.S. firms that developed the original chip technology were losing sales to Japanese firms. America was losing an important piece of sovereign technology, and American firms had to be managed by Washington back to world leadership.

But there was no crisis, only a natural shift in the global industry, affecting not simply U.S. firms but every producer. Producers in Japan were suffering far more than their U.S. counterparts, losing billions of dollars as the industry evolved along lines that were anathema to the way to the Japanese then did business. Most were on the verge of collapse. Washington's solution was to use what the White House characterized as its "crowbar" for opening foreign markets: It coerced a pact over the objections of both Japanese authorities and many U.S. chip producers.

Based on the futile premise that a thoroughly global industry could be bifurcated into U.S. "victims" and Japanese "villains," the semiconductor pact ignored the international forces that had created what was still at its core a dynamic industry. Despite chronic complaints that the Japanese government played too large a role in industry, Washington's solution was to install the Japanese government as manager of Japanese private-sector production in a sector where no such government control had existed before. Washington interposed itself as global industry policeman by setting a minimum price for Japanese chips sold *anywhere* in the world outside Japan and obtaining an acknowledgement from the Japanese government that a 20 percent market share for U.S. producers should be "attainable" in Japan.

The semiconductor pact provided a classic example of how Washington's insistence on treating the ebbs and flows of competitive dynamics in global industries as "trade" problems has not only distorted competition but stifled the innovation that drives such industries. Ironically, the negotiations leading to the accord were even the basis for the best-selling book *Trading Places*, written by former trade negotiator Clyde Prestowitz to extol the virtues of Washington's intervention in industries dominated by non–U.S. firms.

Washington's crowbar turned into a weapon of mass destruction—for American firms. Under its power to set "fair market prices" for imported chips, the Department of Commerce raised chip prices in the United States by as much as 300 percent, leaving domestic producers unable to fill demand and causing a severe disruption of production at the myriad computer, appliance, and other firms that relied on chips for their products. When, after a year, American firms were not able to reach the 20 percent Japanese market-share target, the White House publicly condemned Tokyo as guilty of breaking the pact—even though officials on both sides of the Pacific understood that nowhere in the fine print was there a Japanese guarantee that U.S. firms would have 20 percent of the market.

But Japanese producers could not believe their good fortune. Under Washington's system they quickly became profitable and moved into higher-value products. Market prices outside Japan rose significantly. Yet market prices *inside* Japan plunged; Washington, by its direct actions, temporarily *destroyed* the very market to which U.S. firms had sought access—the access that had originally triggered requests for assistance. The Center for the Study of American Business reported that at least 11,000 high-tech jobs at U.S. firms dependent on chips were lost as a result of Washington's intervention.[16]

Some of the same American firms that had called for Washington's protection against Japan's low prices began calling for the Japanese to lower their prices again. A huge gray market developed, in which American and Japanese couriers began carrying thousands of chips into the United States in briefcases and gym bags to sell at prices uncontrolled by Washington's program. To "close" any gaps in control of the trans-Pacific business, Washington announced a retroactive 2,500 percent increase in the tariffs on computer motherboards—despite protests from the Computer and Business Equipment Manufacturers Association that such interference with their global sourcing would cost U.S. producers hundreds of millions of dollars. The fact that American computer producers had to pay sharply higher prices for their chips and boards left them more vulnerable than ever before to global competitors, eroding America's much more important lead in the end-use computer sector. Several American producers, unable to be competitive in their U.S. plants so long as Washington managed the price of their most vital material, left the United States to set up factories in Asia, where they could source chips without the U.S. restrictions.

The semiconductor pact was extended in 1991 for five years, again with a statement that Japan recognized that Washington "expects that the foreign market share will grow to more than 20 percent of the Japanese market." In March 1993 the foreign share actually attained the 20 percent figure. U.S. Trade Representative Mickey Kantor boasted to industry representatives that the pact was at long last "successful." One month later Kantor testified to Congress that the Japanese market for semiconductors was "closed" to foreigners.

The pact not only saved several Japanese producers from ruin, it entrenched them in a powerful new cartel,[17] since incentives for new entries—also an important driver of global industries—had been destroyed by Washington. When MIT economists studied the detailed price and product effects of the pact, they concluded that Washington's policy had brought an ironic "order" to the market. They found that the pact established a position for seven U.S. primary producers and five Japanese firms. If Tokyo, instead of Washington, had applied the type of trade management it had provided to other sectors in the past, MIT concluded that there would have been six U.S. firms and only three Japanese firms. Without *any* managed trade—the situation existing prior to Washington's intervention—there would have been seven U.S. firms and *no* Japanese firms.

George Gilder studied the evolution of the U.S. semiconductor industry in his book *Microcosm*. Gilder's conclusions about the phenomenal initial success of the early U.S. producers are especially haunting in retrospect, after Washington's intervention decimated the industry:

> We [the United States] won because we went for growth opportunities rather than for trade surpluses. . . . We won because we were not afraid of the international division of labor. We had a global orientation rather than a national industrial policy.[18]

When that national industrial policy eventually surfaced, it was a Flat Earth policy that severely handicapped American participation in global high-tech industries.

SOWING GLOBAL INEFFICIENCY

American agriculture has always bred strange politics, but in the trade context, farm policies reach their most absurd dimensions. Rice from Thailand, for example, competes in foreign markets with American rice. Acting on complaints of unfair subsidies, the Department of Commerce imposed a special duty to offset alleged Thai government subsidies; the Thai government was found to spend approximately $100 a year to support each of its rice growers. But the U.S. Department of Agriculture (USDA) studied the Thai rice industry independently and found that no net subsidy existed—in fact the Thai growers paid a net 5 percent fee to their government for the privilege of exporting. Washington spends approximately $200,000 annually for each full-time rice grower in the United States to subsidize rice prices and exports.

Washington bludgeons Japan over beef quotas, although it maintains its own quotas that are just as strict over beef imports from

Australia and Argentina. The USDA also allows each American on a per capita basis to eat approximately one teaspoon of foreign ice cream per year. The reason is the potentially devastating effect ice cream imports could have on American dairy support programs.

Dry milk, a major target of such programs, is a primary component of many bakery, confectionary, and pet food products, keeping hundreds of factories operating all across America. In 1989 the country's supply of dry milk almost disappeared. The reason? Washington's management of cross-border dairy trade. It limits dry-milk imports to less than a thousand tons a year—and only allows them from Canada and Australia. When, in the late 1980s, dry-milk prices overseas surpassed U.S. prices for the first time in over twenty years, Washington quickly offered fat subsidies that make it possible for American companies to export 370 million pounds of dry milk. The exports created a severe shortage in the domestic market, meaning American producers had no milk to make cakes, crackers, and candy; they sought permission from the managers of their trade to buy dry milk overseas. But Washington refused, stating that it did not intend to "micromanage" the supply of dairy products—this from the same agency that maintains a rule that restricts some countries to shipments of *one kilogram* of blue cheese a year. The Department of Agriculture itself estimates that federal management of dairy trade cost Americans approximately $5 to $7 billion annually.

There are far fewer sugar farmers in the United States than dairy farmers—and they have grown much richer from Washington's management of trade. Intervention in sugar markets consistently keeps U.S. sugar prices higher than world prices. The "sugar program" of the Department of Agriculture is a combination of price supports and import quotas that keep low world prices from eroding the profits of U.S. producers. The program costs American consumers $3 billion a year.

The huge disparity in prices during the 1980s triggered a bizarre chain of events as a result of Washington's intervention. Entrepreneurs began importing products like iced-tea mix that contained sugar but were not included in quotas, for the purpose of extracting the sugar and selling it at Washington's inflated price. Washington discovered the entrepreneurs and went ballistic; stringent new controls were placed on a huge list of imports that contained the slightest trace of sugar, from pickles to croissants, soups to barbecue sauce. Twenty thousand kosher pizzas from Israel were seized because they had a .005 percent sugar content. While the sugar growers were recycling some of their profits into political contributions worth millions—they have been among the most aggressive of campaign contributors—Washington launched Operation Bittersweet to arrest company executives for importing products with sugar content.

The Commerce Department has estimated that at least 9,000 American jobs at candy and bakery companies have been lost because of the sugar-import quotas during the last ten years. Brach Candy alone moved 3,000 jobs to Canada to take advantage of free-market sugar prices. Ten sugar refineries, accounting for 7,000 more jobs, have also been closed in recent years. Total number of sugar farmers in the United States: 11,000.

Washington's finesse in sugar trade has effectively "managed" a number of other agricultural trade sectors. In the Caribbean, where sugar has been efficiently grown for centuries, farmers have been forced to plant wheat and corn, cutting off former export markets for American grain farmers. Buoyed by Washington's subsidies, sugar farmers have been converting acreage to sugar beets from soybeans, traditionally the country's most successful export crop. Of course, American soybean trade had already been hit hard by Washington years ago: As a result of its 1979 temporary prohibition of soybean exports as a measure to stabilize domestic prices, a new competing export industry was created almost overnight in Brazil and other countries, establishing significant competition for American farm exporters where none had existed before.

Grain farmers are the backbone of the agriculture economy in many regions. Left unrestricted, they could easily and profitably feed vast populations at home and abroad. But Washington has lent a bizarre new meaning to "breadbasket of the world." U.S. production of durum wheat plummeted after the new Conservation Resource Program, which paid wheat farmers to shut down production for ten years. Meanwhile, demand for durum, a primary ingredient of pasta, was growing relentlessly, exacerbated by Washington's subsidies for exports of wheat. Washington spends hundreds of millions in taxpayers dollars every year to support such exports—an astounding $700 million in 1993 alone. In 1991 Washington paid a subsidy equal to 78 percent of all the wheat produced in the United States, turning what was once a thriving, self-sufficient industry into a huge burden on the taxpayers. As a result of the export subsidy, foreign food producers can buy U.S. wheat more cheaply than U.S. food producers. Thus U.S. imports of pasta have doubled in the past ten years as foreign producers of pasta use American wheat to make pasta to be imported and consumed by American citizens. What is the most cost-effective means for American pasta makers to compete with foreign wheat? Using imported Canadian wheat.

The General Accounting Office has determined that taxpayers spend $50 to support every $1,000 in agricultural exports. Former USDA

Chief Economist Robert Thompson examined the broader implications for competitiveness of Washington's management of agricultural trade, with Purdue University professors Thomas Hertel and Marinos Tsigas. Their conclusion: The productivity of other American sectors is heavily penalized by Washington's nonmarket (political) allocation of capital to agriculture; they found that farm trade supports cost America $7.5 billion in manufactured exports and $3.4 billion in service exports annually. One study by Kansas State professor Andrew Feltenstein found that a hands-off policy by Washington in the farm sector would increase U.S. exports by $42 billion annually.[19]

DUMPING ON PRODUCTIVITY

In recent years, the most actively used protectionist mechanism in Washington's arsenal has been the antidumping laws promulgated seventy-five years ago to remedy predatory price-cutting by foreign manufacturers. On their face, those laws appear perfectly evenhanded; they authorize the Department of Commerce to impose an offsetting duty against any products sold for less than their fair or normal value, determined by reference to their home-country price. But the definition of fair value for any specific product is left to a large bureaucracy charged with interpreting rules that consume over 100 pages of fine print in the Code of Federal Regulations. Commerce Department regulators are authorized to scrutinize—and challenge—costs of production, costs of sales, prices to third countries, administrative expenses, profit levels, warranty costs, even corporate organization in the course of their investigations to set "fair value." They may interpose their own figures for costs and profits when an exporter's data is "insufficient" for their calculations or the foreign producer fails to permit U.S. government auditors full access to their operations. The complexity of those procedures has spawned an entire antidumping "industry" populated by lawyers, economists, accountants, paralegals, and regulators.

Not surprisingly, the process by which scores of antidumping battles have been fought in recent years is costly and arcane. Raspberry farmers in Canada were penalized with duties when Commerce decided to impute fictional profits as well as wages to family members; an Asian company had its duties increased because it donated television sets to a U.S. charity, on the grounds that a transfer at $0.00 was less than fair value in Japan.

Antidumping duties are not imposed unless the International Trade Commission determines that the domestic industry has been injured by the subject imports. But because Commerce looks at a six-month period to determine dumping and the Commission looks at a three-year period to determine injury, there is no way to accurately determine if industry performance over the injury period has any correlation with dumping by foreign firms. The outcome of any particular pricing or cost issue is wildly unpredictable, although the outcome of proceedings is not; as noted above, 90 percent of cases result in the erection of import barriers.

Despite the reality traditionally accepted by the Department of Justice for antitrust purposes—and well known by managers in many industries—that profitable "real" sales can be made by selling above variable costs, the Department of Commerce rejects such a notion. It penalizes any firm that sells across the U.S. border below fully allocated "total" costs. Many high-tech producers routinely sell just above variable costs, but Commerce insists that if their flow of value-added comes into the United States, it must sell above whole costs, or these producers will have their access to U.S. processing operations or consumers restricted. Similarly, Commerce ignores the reality of forward pricing by which many firms spread capital and research costs over the life of a product; such a practice, used by many international firms, can easily result in pricing that violates Commerce standards. Antidumping laws have become significant impediments to the freedom of international firms to adapt to market conditions or change prices for their own internal cash-flow reasons. They have a sweeping indirect effect, causing firms to refrain from changing prices or from selling in the United States at all.

The shadow of the Commerce Department hovers over executive tables at thousands of international firms, distorting market decisions and disrupting the sourcing networks that empower many global industries. Antidumping orders hit two categories of products: the low-skilled goods that global competition delegates to low-productivity countries and components circulating through international value-added networks. The long list of products supervised by the Department of Commerce includes not only rope, nails, and pencils but also keyboards, partially processed steel, equipment components, optical scanners, thermostats, telephone components, tuners, transformers, and compressors. The decision that exiled laptop computer production from the United States for many years was an antidumping decree.

Critics have frequently pointed out that domestic "dumping" is a practice well rooted in American commerce, reflected in loss-leader sales, pricing tiers based on customer age, after-Christmas sales, even promotional sales for magazines. Economists Richard Boltuck and Seth

Kaplan have succinctly captured the obvious explanation: "That dumping is regarded as unfair only when practiced in international trade suggests that the dumping law reflects the resolution of strong domestic political forces and weak international ones."[20] In the global economy, such disparities only hurt the countries enforcing them. A number of global companies—including Hewlett-Packard and Caterpillar—have pushed for the substantial dilution or elimination of antidumping laws. But Washington has taken the opposite course, entrenching them at home with ever-more complex regulations and abroad with campaigns for mirror-image laws to be adopted by more countries.

A PARADOX OF POLICIES

Washington not only manages to ignore the implications of managed trade in the context of the new economy; it also often ignores it in the context of other international policy initiatives. The White House besieged Bangkok with complaints over market access for American cigarette firms in Thailand despite the fact that through other government initiatives, the Thai government had joined Washington in a vigorous antismoking campaign. No wonder it was confused when Washington, hell-bent on supporting U.S. exports, demanded that the Thais buy more American cigarettes.

Washington made sure all the world knew of its commitment to help the former Soviet Union build a free-market economy; much less conspicuous was its intervention in aluminum sales from Russia, which once represented the brightest economic hope for several regions of the deprived country—in 1993 aluminum exports represented 30 percent of all Russian exports to the United States. But Washington forced Moscow to reinstate central planning in order to obtain quotas on shipments for protection of U.S. producers.[21] As C. Fred Bergsten, director of the Institute for International Economics, explained in the *Wall Street Journal*:

> . . . It was back to business by edict [in Russia] after a few months of trying to establish a market. The only differences are that the new production quotas are maximums rather than minimums and they were imposed by the U.S. rather than by the Communist Party.

Bangladesh was given more than $7 billion in foreign aid during the 1980s in an attempt by the Western governments to help the impoverished country climb up the development ladder. Textile production has always been a key to economic development in countries where workers are not highly skilled; trying to comply with the free-market suggestions of aid donors, Bangladesh funded entrepreneurs for clothing and textile production. From less than twelve firms in 1978, the industry grew to 700 firms by 1985, offering the first real chance at self-sufficiency and pride for hundreds of thousands of workers. Washington slammed the door on their hopes, however, by declaring their imports "disruptive" to the handful of firms that dominate U.S. textile production.

Experience over the past two decades shows that administrations prone to boosting social-welfare programs for the poor are most inclined to protection, citing the need to preserve the low-end jobs that are usually most threatened by import competition—and viewing the added tariff revenues as a way of having foreign countries fund America's social programs. But protection is the most regressive tax of all, brutally hitting the lowest income ranks. Washington's management of trade takes away 32 percent of the purchasing power of the family that is at or just above the poverty level.

The ultimate paradox of protection is that it is invoked to save jobs. The link between *producer* protection and *job* protection has grown spurious. In today's economy, it is sign of vitality that jobs shift, not a sign of defeat. Such shifts reflect an ever-shifting flow of value; ultimately, they reflect the forces of liquidity and diversity at work. Washington's intervention has displaced many more workers than it has saved. The specter of wholesale unemployment from lifting of protection is a related fiction. Workers move out of their jobs for many reasons unconnected to imports. Annually, an estimated 1.8 million workers are dislocated in the U.S. economy. It has been estimated that a lifting of all protection to allow competition to filter low-skill global industry jobs out of the U.S. economy would dislocate another 70,000 workers annually during an adjustment period of five years, an increment of 3.8 percent over normal job movements.[22]

ANTIGLOBAL, ANTIGROWTH

One of the great ironies in a city so preoccupied with competitiveness is that officials on both ends of Pennsylvania Avenue are busy issuing free passes to companies feeling competitive pressures from across the U.S. borders. Applying their well-stocked arsenal of trade management devices, the Commerce Department, the Department of Agriculture, the Customs Service, the U.S. Trade Representative, and, of course, Congress routinely hand out licenses to raise prices, licenses to reduce quality, licenses to reduce technology development, and licenses to give a free ride to unproductive workers—all in the name of American competitiveness.

Those officials have lost touch with economic reality. They relentlessly wage war on a vast category of vital goods components—those that happen to cross an international border; by doing so they wage war on every company that strives to increase its productivity in the global economy. Playing by an outdated rule book, Washington thinks it must accommodate every company with a large factory instead of allowing those factories to squarely meet the challenges, and opportunities, of the global economy. T. J. Rodgers was the president and CEO of Cypress Semiconductor during the turmoil caused by the semiconductor pact. As his own company has proven with its dynamic global base, Rodgers wrote in the *Wall Street Journal*, "the balance of power . . . is shifting away from many of the big established companies toward smaller, nimble companies focused relentlessly on innovation and quality. The old guard continues to rely on the incorrect premises of economics of massive scale and political protection—in manufacturing, in trade laws, and in wasteful litigation" against foreign competitors. As Rodgers has tried to explain to policymakers in asking Washington to abandon its management of the business, ". . . the giants that dominate the debate in Washington are still calling plays from yesterday's playbook."[23]

For many politicians, there is a basic disconnect between supporting the global economy—including the global consumers who drive it—and the structure of American politics. No better reflection of that disconnect exists than an argument made several years ago by a persistent proponent of protection, Senator Fritz Hollings of South Carolina, as he appealed for broader government intervention in international business: "The government must take care of producers. No government was ever organized to get everybody something for a cheap price."[24] The vaunted "producers" in the instance of most protection programs are not those who work in fields and factories but those who own the fields and factories. *Forbes* magazine estimated that U.S. consumers make an "involuntary contribution" to one family in Florida of as much as $52 million a year as a result of sugar protection.[25] And while the government may not do so, the global plebiscite *is* organized to bring everybody *everything* for a cheap price—so long as government doesn't stand in the way.

Proponents of protection behave as though it were a school of economics. But no serious social scientist has been able to justify it from the economic perspective. As Paul Craig Roberts, former Assistant Treasury Secretary and currently a fellow at the Cato Institute, wrote in September 1995, "The government that can hide behind tariffs will have the worse economic policies imaginable."[26] Even in 1930, when President Hoover enacted the catastrophic Smoot-Hawley tariffs, he did so over vigorous protests set forth in a petition signed by 1,028 economists.

Nor is protection a business philosophy, at least not for any business that cares about its customers, employees, and suppliers. Protection is bad policy, policy of the worse kind for a nation in transition, policy for the short-term protection of low-skill jobs, policy against the growth of high-skill jobs and productivity improvements. But it is great politics. The locked and smoke-filled room is largely a thing of the past—except when a problem can be blamed on "foreigners." It is no coincidence that the number of antidumping and other petitions for protection increase dramatically during Presidential election years.

As in other aspects of the trading mentality, stereotypes and ignorance play leading roles in the process. In a public opinion survey in the early 1990s, 60 percent of Americans said that the then–European Community was unfair in its treatment of American goods; in a separate poll, over 60 percent stated they didn't know what the European Community was.

Nothing has ever captured the ugliness of protection politics more vividly than the political frenzy in 1993 over passage of the North American Free Trade Agreement (NAFTA). Two presidential candidates, Ross Perot and Patrick Buchanan, obtained an extra year's worth of media attention by leading opposition to the treaty. In public speeches to unions fearful of adjustments in job ranks, one of them was fond of noting that the Mexicans who wanted to "steal" American jobs "lived like livestock." The other was fond of publicly referring to Mexico as a "pigpen." When the odd coalition of populists and protectionists fighting NAFTA was asked to provide economic data supporting their claim that millions of American jobs would be lost, their response was only that "America must be first." When asked why they thought foreign investors bringing state-of-the-art factories to Mexico would be bad for the Mexican environment, one of their favorite replies was to smugly assert that Mexicans live in tar-paper shacks amidst raw sewage. Economic analysis was confronted with small-minded demagoguery. NAFTA opponents picketed a plant in California that was closing, pointing out that it was a fatality of NAFTA; they didn't bother to talk to its management, who would have explained that production was simply moving to another location in California. A Catholic bishop announced to the national press that free-trade laws harmed the poor, ignoring the overwhelming evidence that international commerce has raised many developing nations from poverty. A St. Louis archdiocese issued a statement that free trade was contrary to the teachings of the Gospel.

MANAGING THE STATUS QUO

Protectionism plays well to crowds of voters because most voters don't like instability and uncertainty. They may have few qualms about voting to change the faces in government, but they hate change in their own lives. As consumers, they may love new technologies, new gadgets, new conveniences. As employees and breadwinners, they understandably abhor clouds over their paychecks.

But the essence of the new economy is change. Whether or not governments and individuals can learn to leverage and benefit from such change, it will continue. It is as inevitable and inexorable as the change in relations between nation-states that came with the invention of gunpowder. In the last century, there were bitter debates over the introduction of cotton gins; they destroyed traditional jobs and threatened a way of life. In England, there was armed resistance to the introduction of modern textile mills; machines were attacked and burned. They were treated like foreign invaders, which in many ways they were—they invaded traditional lifestyles and forced thousands from existing jobs. For individuals, for entire communities, the transition was often painful. But it was as inevitable as the tides and eventually raised the living standards of all.

The rhetoric of today's protectionists may sound more sophisticated. After decades of democratic reform, their political clout has matured. But ultimately what they argue for is the same as that which the Luddites argued for in nineteenth-century Britain. Today they can find eloquent spin doctors to create arguments for them. But they are still arguing for preservation of the status quo.

If *preservation* implies mothballs and mummification, inflexibility and aging, then we would be well served by substituting the term for protection in our public debates. The tale of protection for semiconductors has been the tale of preservation of capacity to make outdated low-value chips and disruption of new international structures needed for leadership in the industry. The tale of protection for steel and autos has been the story of preserving old-style, unprofitable factories and costly delays in competitive adjustment.

But preservation was never so painful as it is today. Until a decade ago, new technology could take a generation or more to permeate an industry, meaning adjustment could often be addressed by attrition. That is no longer true. The new global stakes are higher than ever before, and the pain of adjustment is more immediate than ever. Even after Washington's greatest managed-trade experiment, the Smoot-Hawley tariffs, it took years before the catastrophic effects of President Hoover's actions became apparent—and it was not until the 1970s that world trade reached its previously high level of *1914*. Today Washington's tampering with a global industry can—and does—destroy enterprises within months, not decades. Robert L. Bartley, editor of the *Wall Street Journal*, captured the point perfectly in the title of an essay assailing the protectionist slant of the new administration that took office in 1993: "Baby Boomers Toy with Matches."[27]

The global economy does shift employment, but for any country populated with entrepreneurs it shifts it to higher-value occupations and jobs with greater productivity and knowledge content—provided government does not erect barriers to productivity at the border. The proportion of Americans using a computer at work, for example, leapt from one in four in 1984 to one in three by 1990. Such a process should be celebrated, not feared, even by the union leaders who need to understand that ultimately protectionism jeopardizes their own jobs. John Maynard Keynes tried to explain the point five decades ago when he stated that "a tariff can do nothing against unemployment that an earthquake cannot do better."

Those American firms that lead their global industries have remained sharply more productive than their European or Japanese counterparts precisely because they embrace the constant shifts of the global economy. Robert Allen, chairman of AT&T, has learned the lesson through painful experience at the hands of regulators. "Protectionist barriers," Allen observes, "are to economies what steroids are to athletes—temporary fixes and long-term disasters." Government management of international business builds weakness. It promotes investment in noncompetitive sectors at the expense of potential global winners. It enshrines low-skill workers. It impedes the growth of productivity. It ignores the root causes of noncompetitiveness. It institutionalizes the status quo—and in the global economy, policies focused on the preservation of the status quo are a vast liability to both enterprise and government.

THE NEW PROTECTIONISM

Washington's
War on
Global
Innovation

There is one point on which most policymakers, whether rooted in the Flat Earth or the new economy, will agree: the single most important factor driving competition today is innovation. High-profile speeches, essays, even entire books are written to say little else. When consultant James Moore observed in 1993 that "the only sustainable competitive advantage comes from out-innovating the competition," the editors of the *Harvard Business Review* proclaimed it in large 30-point type.[1] Perhaps such observations are useful as a rallying cry for fiercer competition, but simply recognizing the importance of innovation sheds no light on how to gain its advantage. Declarations about that importance are nothing more than what Joseph Schumpeter and other observers of capitalism have been telling us for decades: that capitalism thrives on change. They do nothing to explain how the new economy has transformed the process of innovation. They do nothing to expose the unexpected chill cast by traditional policies upon that process. They do nothing to explain why we must break the bounds of those traditions if we are to liberate American innovation.

Trade-bound perspectives are punishing American innovation in every sector. We have seen how Washington, pursuing the illusory goal of job preservation, constrains flows of semiconductors, automobiles, steel, and thousands of other items being conveyed by the global plebiscite. But it is not simply hard goods that are being constrained against the forces of the global plebiscite; every product denied entry embodies ideas, concepts, and processes that, if left unrestricted, would build improved ideas, concepts, and processes—meaning more competitive products and services—in the United States. Implicit in every story of import protection is a story of technology obstruction.

Washington also intercedes—with import *and* export barriers—in the name of protecting "national" technology. During most of the past decade, more than 50 percent of all U.S. export categories were subject to federal control to prevent advanced American goods from reaching non–U.S. participants in the global plebiscite. As a result, American producers of telecommunications and computer equipment, for example, had smaller markets and therefore less of a base to fund research than many of their foreign competitors. With minor exceptions, the plebiscite obtained its goods elsewhere, frustrating the intent of the policy and leaving American enterprise less global and less innovative.

Such efforts are built on obsolete premises: Apart from a narrow spectrum of exclusively military technologies, the concept of national technology is as anachronistic as the concept of national industry that has driven so much traditional economic policy. The controls on machine-tool imports that began in 1986 were designed to shield America's national machine-tool technology base. Seventy thousand workers made machine tools. Four *million* used machine tools to make products ranging from automobiles to kitchen appliances; they were relying heavily on Asian imports that were better designed, more efficient, more precise, and capable of innovative functions not available on the U.S. equipment. Washington's controls preserved the American technology—obsolete as it was—and forced American manufacturers into a painful choice: move offshore to obtain the competitive tools or function at lower levels of quality and precision than their foreign competitors.

It is not only such direct intervention in international business, moreover, that constrains America's participation in the global innovation process. The federal government spends $70 billion a year[2] to back research by firms and industries that it has nominated as global winners—without consulting the new realities that determine such winners. Its attempts to thus manipulate technology, based on assumptions that America only benefits from American technology and that "our" best technology must never be given to "them," have brought great handicaps to firms trying to climb the ranks of their industries.

An unintended—and seldom acknowledged—effect of regulatory programs as diverse as tax, immigration, health and safety, and antitrust protection has been a further chill on vital flows of information, the obstruction of the new process of innovation that drives global competition. The world in which those programs were originally crafted—often forty, fifty, even 100 years ago—no longer exists; yet its legacy of regulation rumbles blindly on. America has a vast, unequaled capacity for innovation. But Flat Earth policies are hammering away at the use of that capacity.

GETTING TO THE RIGHT QUESTIONS

Evidence of American technology decline is a favorite fodder for those who advocate government intervention to stimulate competitiveness. They remind us, for example, that in 1987 the United States was surpassed by a foreign country for the first time in the volume of total world patent applications (latest score—for 1993: Japan, 208,347; United States, 57,890) and that in recent years, the U.S. Patent and Trademark Office list of the top ten firms receiving the most U.S. patents has been dominated by firms based outside the United States.[3] Roughly half of all patents being filed in the United States today are from non–U.S. firms. Advocates of government intervention lament the fact that more technology flows *out* of the United States (as measured by royalties) than flows into it, that technology payments by U.S. firms to unaffiliated firms quadrupled since 1980, that the share of U.S. jobs in manufacturing has dropped from 50 percent in 1950 to 20 percent today, that the ratio of Japanese students in the United States is severely "out of balance" with the number of U.S. students in Japan, and even that the per capita use of machine tools in the United States ranks only twentieth in the world, just above Bulgaria.

In 1992 Washington policy spotlights fixed on a General Accounting Office (GAO) benchmark report entitled *High Technology Competitiveness*[4], which further spread alarm over our technology decline. The criteria applied by the GAO in establishing the decline: trade balances in high-tech merchandise, ratios of patents filed by U.S. and foreign companies, nationality of authors of scientific publications, and spending in research labs. At the request of Congress, the GAO also issues reports on the number of foreigners working in U.S. labs—

policymakers complain that the number is unfairly high compared to the number of Americans working in foreign labs.

An entire genre of technology alarmism is based on import data for high-tech materials. Heavily emphasized in the GAO's benchmark study were comparative data on imports over a ten-year period for computers, structural ceramics, consumer electronics, fiber optics, aircraft, and telecommunications equipment. In speaking of America's technology challenges in 1992, the then–Undersecretary of Commerce for Technology invoked America's technology crisis by citing the fact that although industrial robots had been invented in the United States, today we import 75 percent of all robots sold in America. The GAO also emphasized robots, the Potomac's perennial symbol of competitiveness, complaining that more robots were installed in Japan than in the United States.

Such evidence of technology decline is available in abundance from universities, pollsters, and myriad agencies along the Potomac. Their criteria for technology assessment have much in common with those used to support arguments for protection of American manufacturers. Just as in trade protection arguments, heavy emphasis is placed on a pejorative characterization of inputs from offshore, investment in fixed assets, the primacy of pounding steel and turning screws—in other words, it looks at innovation through the lens of the trading economy.

The status of American technology may indeed be in a crisis in some respects, but it is not the crisis described by traditional perspectives. Evidence of patents and robots and cross-border imbalances is gathered according to obsolete frames of reference. It misses the point. It is largely irrelevant to the global economy's process of innovation and provides no guidance for gaining advantage from that process. With true Flat Earth flair, it paints a simplistic image of American technology under siege from abroad, without regard to the new realities of innovation.

Machine-tool use may be down, for example, but it is not due to a decline in innovation; it can be traced in part to the restraints that pushed use offshore and, more importantly, to the simple fact that technology has advanced to the point where the "tools" being used to add value are much more intangible than they were even five years ago. The disproportionate number of foreign students in the United States is a tribute to American knowledge; they have flocked to the U.S. sources of knowledge and proven to be invaluable assets in expanding those sources. Royalties and patents, moreover, are the clumsiest of measures of technology in the new economy, where the primary flow of ideas is not funneled through legalistic forms but embodied and transferred in consulting, management, and informal sharing relationships.

We should not be preoccupied with machine tools or robots when we consider the essential evidence of America's innovation dilemma: National productivity over the past decade has grown more slowly in the United States than in any of the other G-7 industrial nations but one, and privately funded research peaked in 1989, declining significantly since then.[5] The number of robots or other tools—which are merely some of the inputs to innovation—does not explain such decline. It is the result of barriers and weaknesses built into public policy and enterprise strategy, beginning with a widespread failure to understand the new process of innovation.

New criteria for evaluating innovation are desperately needed, and old policies are in dire need of reform or elimination. But neither can be accomplished until the realities that have overwhelmed traditional technology mind-sets are better understood.

KNOWLEDGE WAS POWER

In 1789 the American textile industry was launched when an Englishman named Samuel Slater arrived in Rhode Island and began to build a mill based on his memory of working in British mills. Slater's transfer of technology evolved into new American-bred technology that built a major industrial base, which fueled much American growth in the nineteenth century. Vast empires like that of Du Pont were likewise built on the transfer of expertise from Europe. Many sectors of American industry, from pharmaceuticals to shipbuilding to chemicals, had a strong European flavor in their early days. The process certainly was not one-sided: Isaac Singer's sewing machine and Cyrus McCormick's harvesting technology permanently transformed millions of lives around the planet in the last century. Technology has moved across borders since the earliest days of commerce. The American textile industry may have been built on English technology, but centuries earlier the English industry was built in part around Italian know-how. Italy's own industry was built in part around knowledge brought from Central Asia and China.

But the transfer of technology was never a pillar of the trading economy. The shifting of advantage it represented never played the role of the natural endowments that drove traditional trade. Technology usually moved at a glacial pace. It was a footnote to trade, or, more accurately, it was usually just embodied in trade: A nation's technology was in its products, nurturing the paradigm of national industry and national technology embedded in so much traditional policy. As industrial bases were built within U.S. borders, their technology quickly became entrenched "national" assets. It was only two years after Slater arrived in America that Washington protected its textile industry with steep tariffs. The only important technology was the technology used in the heavy industries, always the focus of the heaviest political protection. Technology centers were production centers. "Innovation" implied little more than evolution of production technology. Technology was developed unilaterally at such centers (i.e., by the "owner") and jealously guarded as it funneled into products, a process that built the "not invented here" mentality by which anything less than autonomy in technology was viewed as a sign of weakness.

To the extent markets for technology developed, it was through the cumbersome process of licenses. The technology license, however, was always more than a mere legal device. It was a concept, the paradigm of how technology moved in the traditional economy. Like goods, technology had one source, one owner, and that owner inevitably had a flag, a sovereignty. It was encapsulated in a bundle of legal controls, usually reduced to a patent blessed by the sovereign "home" government; it was developed unilaterally and moved bilaterally, from the originator to the user.

International transfer of technology, especially from America, had another familiar Flat Earth theme. It was a footnote to the "real" business to be done at home, a way of sharing in markets that did not merit the direct attention of the licenser. The history of international involvements by many American firms during the 1950s, '60s and '70s was a history of patent licenses "discarded" to foreign markets for a few extra royalty dollars.

Within this traditional framework, decision makers could easily reduce issues of technology and technology movement to convenient compartments for policy purposes:

- patents, or placing a "flag" on technology and providing government ratification of the technology and its ownership

- royalties derived from the flow of technology rights, manipulated by taxation and central bank remittance policies

- labs attached to large manufacturing bases, meaning technology assets dedicated to hard-product next-generation breakthroughs in product design

- government funding of such labs, which provided a means for officials to manipulate the content and scope of research

For both public- and private-sector decision makers, these compartments presented structures for control. Whether technology moved internally or externally—in both the geographic and organizational sense—control was always the priority. Research followed the paradigm of the pipeline, the epitome of lockstep control: Labs were given mandates for a stipulated new product; the product eventually emerged from the pipeline into the factory and was ratified and inventoried by the government in patent filings; it generated sales and royalties, generated tax revenues, and provided a platform to secure the research pipelines for the next sequential generation of products. Innovation was evolutionary, not revolutionary.

Ultimately, the entire structure of technology management and technology policy in the trading economy could be summarized in one familiar phrase: Knowledge Is Power. Knowledge was valuable to the extent that no one else knew it. Knowledge was to be hoarded. It was to be contained and controlled and protected. A company's or a nation's knowledge was valuable to the extent others did not share it. The "not invented here" syndrome was as potent a force on the government level as in private enterprise: The country could not be self-sufficient in manufacturing if it was not self-sufficient in technology. Entire regulatory regimes were built around this concept of national technology, most notably the export-control system, which enforces the concept that American ideas must be kept out of the hands and brains of foreigners. It is a concept that has grown dangerously counterproductive.

THE INNOVATION REVOLUTION

The new process of innovation cannot be understood in terms of unilateral flows, sovereign controls, or government-funded white frocks. It can no longer be understood in terms of a single enterprise or even a single industry as a fixed target responding in a fixed manner to a stimulus of funding and protected markets. It cannot be understood in terms of factories, laboratories, or patents. It *must* be understood in terms of movement of knowledge among multiple parties, back and forth in constant interdependent flows across borders of geography, organizations, and industries. In the new economy, the most meaningful focus for technology policy—and policy for supporting innovation generally—is on the liquidity of ideas.

In the new economy, American's best interests are served not by pursuing self-sufficiency in merchandise and technology but in attracting the *best* goods and ideas, without regard to flags, then adding vital new value to them in sectors where American firms lead the world *because* of the global movement of goods and ideas, not in spite of it. One of IBM's most successful products, the laptop computer, was made possible by leveraging the value added from a network of internal and external sources, including an outsource motherboard manufacturer; a research center in Japan; a chip-manufacturing facility in Essones, France; manufacturing and assembly centers in Santa Palomba, Italy, and Boca Raton, Florida, as well as Fujisawa, Japan; a software facility in Santa Teresa, California; a marketing team in New York; and a global distribution facility in Greenford Green, England.

American computer firms delegate the job of manufacturing the motherboards for their personal computers to highly skilled Asian contractors—four out of five motherboards sold today are made in Taiwan, a highly profitable strategy that was made possible by *sharing* technology, not hoarding it. One of the ways Intel keeps command of the microprocessor market is by sharing its specifications with these Asian producers to maximize the number of motherboards that will be compatible with Intel products. When, in October 1995, Intel announced plans to make "American" motherboards, it simply meant that Intel, as an American-based company, was going to vie for leadership in one more sector of its industry by producing the boards in a network of plants under its direct control—in Malaysia, Ireland, Puerto Rico, and Oregon.

Apple Computer took a different course. It toppled from the summit of the personal computer industry by steadfastly refusing, until late 1994, to share its software with third parties, thereby missing the lesson of interdependence that has become so profitable for its competitors. Apple was forced to spend 8 percent of its revenues on research and development. Competitors such as Compaq, which shares its technology, spend 2 percent of revenues on research because sharing technology with firms like Microsoft and Intel allows them to design themselves "into" Compaq's machines, giving them incentives to invest in development of what the world sees as Compaq's product but what is in reality a joint product.

Firms that have become global winners have done so by learning how to glean the best components from around the globe and adding American value—not necessarily *in* America—with respect to design, quality control, assembly, distribution, marketing, and product applications. The computer industry is a powerhouse of American innovation.

But no one would know it who tried to measure it by domestic/foreign patent ratios, origin of components, or investment in traditional American research labs.

Export-control laws, first promulgated in the years of World War I, have become a huge damper on America's participation in such global networks of innovation. U.S. high-tech companies suffered significant competitive disadvantage during the 1980s—the all-important globalization period for many high-tech industries—as a result of Washington's efforts to select their customers by export screening. Faced with an absolute prohibition on sales of many state-of-the-art products incorporating memory chips, personal-computer manufacturers, medical-equipment makers, process-control companies, manufacturing-equipment firms, and many others sat in frustration while competitors from Asia and Europe cornered new markets, unable to compete because Washington did not condone the international distribution of American memory chips. While they futilely tried to explain the new dynamics of high-tech industry to Washington, the same chips, made offshore, were being sold in talking dolls by street vendors in Hong Kong.

Digital Equipment Corporation (DEC) relies heavily on sales outside the United States—65 percent of its revenue comes from offshore. Its efforts to apply its innovations offshore have been repeatedly attacked by the Department of Commerce. In 1991 it was charged with sixty-five separate violations of export-control laws for marketing its "American" computers overseas. The charges supplemented the U.S. Treasury with over $2 million in penalties but did nothing to protect "American" technology or, obviously, to enhance DEC's competitiveness. The equipment involved was already available offshore from non–U.S. producers. In 1993 DEC was forced to remove two important new hardware products, located within the United States, from a global communication network that permitted potential non–U.S. customers to sample their performance from remote locations. The Department of Commerce severed the network connection because the potential customers had not been approved by Washington.

AT&T, U.S. West, and other U.S. telecommunications firms were locked out of vitally important contracts in Russia and China as those countries embarked upon what is forecast to be a $40 billion telecom spending spree by the end of the century. U.S. cellular-phone producers have lost critically important contracts in Europe, Asia, and the Middle East because customers required encrypted signaling software to ensure the privacy of users. American firms had the best encryption technology in the world, but Washington strictly controlled it, although it is, and was, available through many non–U.S. competitors; encryption software can even be downloaded anywhere in the world from the Internet. Global executives often violate the same unrealistic standards when carrying their laptop computers overseas; many have carried encrypted software like Lotus Notes all over the globe without being aware that they would be subject to a fine of up $500,000 for doing so. Foreigners, except those with green cards, technically may not even access such equipment *within* the United States.

The National Academy of Sciences (NAS) has estimated that export controls on U.S. goods and technology that have no connection to national security have reduced American overseas exports by as much as $9 billion a year. In a survey of high-tech firms, the NAS found that 52 percent had lost sales primarily due to restrictions imposed by Washington, 26 percent had deals turned down by customers who rejected being "controlled" by Washington, and 38 percent had customers who had expressly stated their intentions to find alternate non–U.S. suppliers due to U.S. red tape.

Incremental liberalization of these standards occurs periodically. The capacity of controlled supercomputers was raised in 1995. Controls on certain telecommunications equipment were liberalized in 1994, allowing AT&T and U.S. West to at last proceed with contracts in Russia and China. Steps are underway to moderate the encryption controls that have burdened so many computer and telecom firms. But such actions are cause for only limited celebration. No reform is meaningful unless it is long-term legislative reform. The liberalization celebrated in 1994 and 1995 was simply part of a well-established cycle of administrators catching up, years late, with technology. Unless the underlying anachronistic legal regime is transformed, it is inevitable that injury to the same global firms will quickly return. Some firms, moreover, have never recovered from the losses incurred in their global markets during the period of heavy control that dominated the 1980s.

Permanent reform is required that eliminates the authority of bureaucrats to unilaterally block the sale of any commercial products and puts the responsibility for the few controls that may be needed for world security on the only stage where they will be effective—the multilateral stage. This has already been accomplished on a limited basis with the Missile Technology Control Regime.[6] Such reform has been discussed for years; the last three Congresses have received landmark proposals from groups like the National Association of Manufacturers and the Business Roundtable, which would vastly simplify the byzantine rules applied by the Department of Commerce. Every year, such proposals are blocked by those who insist "American" technology must not be compromised.

Reform efforts and the integrity of American computer suppliers were dealt a costly blow in 1993 and 1994 as the White House and law enforcement officials pushed to require a "Clipper Chip" in all U.S.-made equipment, which would allow the U.S. government to electronically eavesdrop on the equipment anywhere in the world after it had been sold. Just as problematic was the Administration's September 1995 proposal to "liberalize" the concept by simply requiring American firms to sell software with encoded "keys," which would be made available to U.S. and foreign governments—a handicap reluctantly accepted by IBM in 1996 as part of a deal to secure Washington's blessing for certain offshore software sales.

As Scott McNealy, CEO of Sun Microsystems, complained in fighting export controls that were keeping his firm from expanding its global base, such "U.S. policy does not restrict high-level technology; it simply hampers U.S. companies from competing in the global marketplace."[7] Cray Research, maker of supercomputers, has frequently reminded policymakers of another impediment caused by controls: To build a global product, companies are often forced to "underdesign" their equipment to satisfy export requirements, in effect requiring them to enter international competition with one hand tied behind their back. The extent of the rules, moreover, is far greater than the casual observer would expect. They apply not only to product shipments but any movement of knowledge. They obstruct the liquidity of ideas in all its forms.

Even a conversation taking place in Kansas between one scientist with a U.S. firm and a non–U.S. colleague employed in a foreign subsidiary is theoretically controlled by the rules. In October 1995, trying to underscore the absurd dimensions of current rules, I mentioned to an export-control official that the rules he applied were so expansive that his office could require government licenses for the video conferences between researchers on different continents that have become common in many global firms. His response, perfectly serious: "Of course we could. Maybe we should get local police more involved."

George Gilder has long scrutinized Washington's obsession with controls on the computer and related industries. His conclusion: "By constantly imposing special export controls for nonsensical national-security concerns and changing policy from month to month in response to utterly spurious emergencies, the U.S. government has become the chief obstacle to U.S. competitiveness in electronics." Export restrictions, notes Scott McNealy, "mean less funding for the research and development that create future products that create new jobs." Export controls have been controls on U.S. innovation.

That the new process of innovation relies so heavily on interdependence and mutuality means that *import* controls can be as disruptive as export restraints. Tariffs have worked to keep innovation out of American health care, for example. In recent years many American hospitals sought urgently to obtain new German lithotripters, machines that destroy kidney stones without the expense and pain of surgery. Although no U.S. producer made competing machines, the Customs Service levied a 7.9 percent tariff on their importation. In order to offer the advanced non–U.S. technology to their patients—and expand the skills of the Americans who would learn to use the German technology—American hospitals had to pay a surcharge of over $189,000 to Washington for each machine.

As discussed in Chapter Three, antidumping laws authorize officials to intervene in the global flow of literally thousands of products. Import restrictions under the laws constrain the flow of large numbers of innovation-intensive products, like cellular telephones, pagers, microwave amplifiers, consumer electronics, transformers, word processors, and computer disks. At no time in the complex process by which antidumping duties are imposed is their effect on American innovation considered.

Seldom has the shadow of managed trade over innovation been more in evidence than in Washington's efforts to intervene in global semiconductor commerce. Trumpeting the interests of American technology, regulators argued that Japanese companies were intruding on a turf claimed by American firms. Left to market forces, they reasoned, the core technology for designing and producing semiconductors would belong to the Japanese. Washington intervened, with disastrous results for American firms. Left out of most accounts of the pact, however, is a vitally important sequel of technology dispersion, an important lesson in how the global plebiscite will always eventually defeat those who seek to manage it by obsolete notions.

By closing the door on foreign-sourced chips, Washington created protected conditions for new investment in U.S. production. New investment arrived, but not from traditional capital sources, which were handicapped by new capital-gains tax disincentives. The investment came from foreign semiconductor and computer firms, most of them Japanese. Washington's pact not only saved several of those Japanese firms from bankruptcy, it effectively paved the way for them to become direct participants in U.S. research. In the months following the launch of the pact designed to protect American producers and their technology, twenty-six foreign companies made investments in U.S. semiconductor firms. Other foreign firms announced plans to start their own production facilities in the United States, employing the same U.S. scientists who had launched the industry. Between October 1988 and October 1992, investors from Asia made investments in 426 U.S.-based high-tech firms, most of them in the semiconductor and computer sectors.[8] Concurrently, as previously discussed, many U.S. firms using chips to make computers and other equipment moved production or sourcing to countries in Asia, which did not fall under the pact—meaning they either took the technology with them or gave significant new funds to new producers in countries like Taiwan and Korea, funds that were aggressively applied to new research.

Washington's misguided attempt to keep American chip technology for Americans only ultimately advanced the global process, accelerating dispersion of both the technology and the value that would have been added in the United States but for Washington's actions. Noted the research head for a Japanese producer who observed the process with amusement: "Anyone who thinks this kind of technology can stay within borders is lying—to himself and everyone else."

The pact also had a painful downstream effect for many American high-tech firms, many of which live or die by keeping up in the race of product cycles; they must sell today's generation of products to fund research for the next generation. A few months' lost time in product introduction can mean the loss of a whole product cycle. And that is what happened: The shortage of chips caused by the pact resulted in severe disruption for many firms. Apple was unable to release its Macintosh SE upgrade and laptop as planned. Hewlett-Packard's Vectra 386 could not be released on time. Compaq's laptop was significantly delayed. Sun Microsystems had to postpone delivery of a new generation of workstations. A huge clog in the innovation pipelines of American computer makers occurred—giving non–U.S. competitors a significant leg up on the next generation of products.

FIGHTING FOR A GLOBAL BASE

The innovators of the new economy are not simply concerned with finding new things to invent; they are equally occupied with finding new ways to invent things. They don't operate through long unilateral pipelines of discovery; they operate through multilateral, contemporaneous interchanges. Liquidity vitalizes them, but their lifeblood is diversity. They work at junctures in vast borderless networks of ideas, accessible instantaneously by telephone, fax, and the 250 million personal computers now networked around the globe. A savvy researcher today can, in the course of a few hours, access a billion bits of information from a thousand locations around the globe and create more value than could be achieved in a year under traditional technology transfer arrangements. The process is creating bold new combinations that defy the wildest expectations. A Danish company mines microbes from lawn clippings to ferment cheese for American gourmands. U.S. and Japanese firms are joining to develop microcircuits from living tissue; other joint ventures are developing piezoelectric materials that change shape when an electric current passes through them.

Almost half of G. D. Searle's revenues come from products that originated from outside the company; one of its most profitable drugs was licensed from a German firm. Japanese and European companies designed tires based on their experience on five continents to produce in their U.S. plants (operating under such familiar names as Firestone, General, Armstrong, and Uniroyal-Goodrich). The process led a European steel-cord firm, N.V. Bekaert, to explore technology developed in Japan, which led it to refine the technology at its facilities in Belgium, which led it to build a $200 million steel-cord plant in Rogers, Arkansas.[9]

Savvy global managers also cultivate technical diversity within their organizations through internal networks that disperse, analyze, and sift information from dozens, hundreds, even thousands of perspectives within the enterprise. Today at Hewlett-Packard, one of the most consistently innovative firms based in the United States, 9,000 researchers around the globe are directly attached to business units, not to a central lab. As Frank Carruba, head of HP's research, explains, each of these research units is encouraged "not to sing from the same sheet of music" so as to push innovation closer to the diversity of their markets. This phenomenon of diversity was anathema to old-world approaches to research, in which information flowed to experts who strictly controlled analysis and use of conclusions, structures that blinded many firms to diverse external sources of innovation. A visiting scientist from Frankfurt or Osaka was there to learn, not to teach. And if Washington chose to get involved, it would be to ensure that the visitor didn't learn too much.

But today, to become global winners, firms must turn innovation *inside out*: Instead of innovating from one headquarters location to reach multiple markets, they must innovate from multiple local viewpoints within key markets around the planet, but with a single global vision. This means their innovation is for naught if they do not understand the peculiar tastes of customers around the planet; understand how their competitors innovate to adapt to local markets; understand the legal and commercial frameworks governing how ideas are commercialized in myriad countries; understand that any one "global" problem might have five different solutions— each of which is perfect for a different market; understand that science, like marketing, can have a cultural context. Japanese firms took facsimile technology global because electronic mail systems did not fit their culture; their complex *kanji* ideograms could not be communicated by keyboards.

TAPPING DIVERSITY IN INNOVATION

The National Science Foundation reports that approximately one half of the postdoctoral science and engineering students in America are from foreign countries and that one third of all science and engineering doctoral students are foreigners. Thousands of non–U.S. nationals conduct research in the United States for U.S. companies, many participating in rotations that put American scientists in company labs overseas. Such diversity represents a vital force of innovation—one third of all American Nobel Prize winners were born overseas. But public policy makes it increasingly difficult to maintain such diversity:

- Recent changes in immigration rules force many foreign students to return to their home countries after graduation.

- U.S. immigration laws (through the H-1B visa program) generally permit foreigners with specialized expertise to work in the United States for no more than six years; in 1995 the Department of Labor requested that this term be reduced to three years.

- Washington imposes numerical limits on the number of foreign professionals in the United States, and debate began in Congress in 1995 to cut the number by more than 50 percent.

- Legislation was introduced in 1995 to require U.S. firms to pay to the U.S. Treasury a one-time fee equal to 30 percent of salary for hiring foreigners and to pay a 10 percent surcharge on salaries paid to foreign professionals employed in the United States.

- The Labor Department began a "crackdown" on the use of foreign professionals in 1995.

- In September 1995 a bipartisan Commission on Immigration Reform recommended to Congress that American companies pay substantial fees to the government for each foreign worker with a college degree they employ.

- In 1995 the Senate Subcommittee on Immigration proposed to slash the number of skill-based immigrants (those with expertise unavailable in the United States) from 140,000 a year to 75,000.
- The Department of Labor spends $60 million annually to certify that each foreign skilled worker does not "displace" a qualified American.

In hailing the 1995 proposals to cut immigration of professionals and skilled workers, the White House declared that the proposals would protect Americans "so we can better compete in the emerging global economy." The senior vice president of the National Association of Manufacturers replied: "Recommending a reduction in the number of foreign workers U.S. companies can hire shows an ignorance of how business operates in today's global markets."

Firms in many innovation-intensive industries have long understood that global access is a *sine qua non* of research: For them, domestic sales are simply not enough to justify their required research. In 1990 the research necessary to launch a new pharmaceutical cost at least $190 million; by 2000 that figure is expected to reach $1 billion for some products. Investments in research for new generations of computers already start at $1 billion and upwards, depending on the complexity of the application.

Such a global focus is never simply a matter of loading sales volume to support research at home. The diversity of innovation derived from a global base is always a major ingredient for leadership in global industries. Long-time Sony chairman Akio Morita spent much of his time in recent years explaining to public and private policymakers how global winners are built. A common theme in his speeches: When he established Sony Corporation of America in 1960, it was with an unshakable commitment to conducting research and engineering activity within the United States. Many of Hitachi Corporation's scores of divisions lead their industry niches with sophisticated, rapidly evolving products. Hitachi is consistently on the list of the top ten firms receiving U.S. patents each year. Six percent of all private-sector research funds spent by Japanese firms is spent by Hitachi. That money is spent not just in Japan but at sprawling labs in Dublin, Ireland; Cambridge, England; and Princeton, New Jersey—as well as at joint research facilities it operates with Hewlett-Packard, GE, and IBM.

The world's largest automotive testing center is in Arizona—funded by Toyota to test vehicles for all its global markets. Toyota launched a $144-million research program in 1990, including new labs in Ann Arbor, Michigan, and Torrance and Newport Beach, California.[10] Squibb is spending $50 million for joint genetics research at the University of Louis Pasteur in France. Chemical and pharmaceutical research in Japan has increased heavily in recent years—primarily at new labs built by U.S. and European firms like Dow, Monsanto, Pfizer, Upjohn, Ciba, Bayer, Du Pont, BASF, Hoechst, and Rhône-Poulenc Rorer. At least seventy-one U.S. organizations have research operations in Japan.[11] Global leader 3M Company has 2,500 technical personnel stationed overseas. Hewlett-Packard's research is guided by the HP Labs Research Board, consisting of eighteen scientists from five nations. The British government's British Technology Group markets technology on behalf of New Jersey-based Johnson and Johnson. Non–U.S. companies spend over $10 billion annually on research in the United States. U.S.–based firms spend over $7 billion on research overseas. They do not do so out of convenience or in quest of cheap Ph.D.'s. They do so out of necessity.

Without its global network of research sharing, the biotech industry would not exist. North Carolina labs receive funding from French companies to improve molecules identified by British researchers for a medicine to be made in Japan and Holland. Many transplant patients owe their lives to cyclosporin, a bioengineered antirejection drug developed by a veritable United Nations of researchers. Two Massachusetts labs, Procept Inc. and Vertex Pharmaceuticals, have led the way in using computers, X-ray crystallography, and nuclear magnetic resonance spectroscopy in revolutionary ways to design new pharmaceuticals— funded by $60 million received from two European firms.[12] Notes one of the senior American researchers who helped bioengineer an important new anti-inflammation drug: "Would the drug exist if we didn't have input from Switzerland and England? No way, at least not in the next five years. No one can afford to be nationalist about technology today." French health organizations applied a "not invented here" standard with tragic results: They rejected advanced blood testing technology developed outside France on the premise that French labs could develop their own tests. The French test was proven to be ineffective only after hemophiliacs all over France became infected with the AIDS virus.

When AT&T launched a massive development effort for its new personal communicating devices, one of its first steps was to find a foreign partner to help fertilize its research, not simply with capital but with ideas; it signed up Matsushita Electric. Liquidity of technology in the automotive industry began with a few technology joint ventures in the 1980s. Today it has become a *sine qua non* of successful operations; the old prototype of auto engineering groups owning a car from start to finish has been overtaken by sharing of parts, designs, factories, and sales systems on a vast scale. It is more than a coincidence that the biggest private-sector petitioners for protection during the 1980s were firms that had declined to push their research onto a global platform. America's automakers and largest steelmakers, for example, until recently had no research programs in Japan despite the technical advances being made there.

Barriers of language, culture, standards, logistics, education, and organization confront American enterprises that seek to nurture such a global technology base. But for many American firms, the biggest barriers are created by their own government.

The release of a research expenditure study by the National Science Foundation (NSF) in 1987 created a storm of protest. By revealing a sudden spurt in international research by Americans—it showed that research spending by U.S. firms overseas was increasing at a rate of 33 percent annually, while domestic spending was increasing by only 6 percent—the NSF tapped a deep-seated resentment among policymakers towards globalization. Policymakers raised the alarm that American firms were selling out American science and American universities. Some called for prohibitions on foreign contributions to American colleges. Others called for new federal clearances to be required for offshore research and even suggested that new laws prohibit the sharing of such research with foreigners. Others demanded reciprocity: Foreign firms should be required to do their "fair share" of research in the United States. But U.S. firms were only fighting to catch up with global competitors from outside the United States, who have much more geographically diverse innovation efforts. Less than 10 percent of patents granted to American firms, for example, are for work done outside the United States; the ratio for European firms is over 30 percent.

This prejudice against offshore research has long been institutionalized in federal policy. Tax rules in particular have been the biggest club wielded by Washington against research across borders. Since 1977 Washington has penalized companies with offshore research operations through a series of tax-allocation rules, beginning with regulations that established that R&D expenses incurred solely to meet requirements of a foreign government could only be offset against income generated within that country. Such measures launched a long process of changing regulatory formulas, all of which had the effect of limiting deductions taken for research conducted overseas.

The most recent permutation dates to 1993: 50 percent of non–U.S. research expenditures have to be allocated only to non–U.S. income.[13] Firms without sufficient income falling within Washington's strict definition of foreign-source income thus take big penalties for responding to the global research dynamics that drive their industries. The rules, which also push U.S. firms to engage in indirect foreign research by supporting foreign companies in their own research, have been heavily criticized by those active in global industries. In responding to a 1995 Treasury Department study supporting continuation of the rules, the U.S. Council for International Business underscored the unique burden these rules place on U.S. firms:

> . . . the Treasury Department's study . . . places too high a priority on finding a precise relationship between U.S. R&D and intangible income from foreign sources and therefore serves as a distraction from the real issue—i.e., keeping U.S. business competitive in an increasingly competitive global marketplace. In other words, the Treasury and the IRS should avoid seeking a technically pure approach where U.S. taxpayers, particularly those at the cutting edge of technology, would suffer burdensome U.S. tax consequences at the expense of their competitive positions vis-à-vis multinationals from other countries of the world. The United States cannot afford for this to happen. Also in this regard it is significant to note that no other country of which we are aware imposes allocation and apportionment rules of the character and degree imposed by these regulations, if indeed such rules are imposed at all.[14]

For many years, U.S. tax rules have punished cross-border research activities by establishing more onerous rules for treatment of "headquarters" research of firms with international operations, for royalties paid from abroad, and for royalties paid to offshore sources of know-how, as well as by withholding taxes for foreign royalties and even requiring payment of "fictitious" royalties for use of home-grown technology by a foreign subsidiary of a U.S. firm.

PUSHING EXPERTISE OFFSHORE

While foreign-source income rules largely penalize U.S. firms for global research networks, in some situations they also inadvertently push those firms to use experts overseas even though they prefer to develop the expertise at home. For U.S. tax purposes, the source of income for services is the nation where services are performed. But many other nations use territorial rules, which tax services where they are used. A U.S. construction and engineering firm thus faces double taxation on projects in such countries for the architectural, engineering, design, accounting, and even legal content of its work. A foreign tax credit will not solve the problem since Washington will not recognize the income from the "U.S." services as having a foreign source. The only answer is for the U.S. firm to use experts outside the United States for performance of its contract.

The Clinton Administration, which won a hard-fought battle for NAFTA in November 1993, confused many international firms with its strenuous endorsement of a tax package that heavily penalized global research. The proposal, endorsed for many years by leading members of Congress, called for limiting the ability of a company to use credits to offset royalty income from "U.S." technology used outside the United States. The Treasury Secretary explained that the plan would eliminate the "unfair" advantage that firms with international operations have over those who kept their technology within the United States. Enthusiasm for the plan began to fade not because the Administration recognized that technology could not be "contained" in the new economy but due to an ironic twist totally unanticipated by Washington: Global companies explained that the plan would force them to expand their building of research facilities offshore and to begin creating and using non–U.S. origin technology in order to avoid the need for any license fees to be paid back to the United States. Policymakers backed off when they realized that their plan intended to build more "American" technology would in reality result in more "foreign" technology.

TECHNOLOGY SQUARED: CYCLES OF SUCCESS

The liquidity of ideas that drives the new process of innovation doesn't simply mean that more ideas flow to innovators, but that more ideas flow *more quickly*. Time has become a vital element of competitive advantage in global industries. Innovation seems to increase geometrically each year in some sectors. Electronics manufacturers have discovered a new rule for technology development in their industry: The first two producers that get a new product generation to market will obtain 80 percent of the market. Seventy percent of the revenues of the computer industry today come from products that didn't exist two years ago. The phenomenon is not confined to computers; 25 percent of 3M's revenues come from products developed in the past five years. In 1980, launching a new tire at Goodyear required 117 weeks; by 1990 it required sixty-five weeks, and today the figure is approaching forty weeks. In the 1980s, AT&T needed at least three years to take its switching computers from concept to production; today it takes less than eighteen months—and defects have been reduced 80 percent in the process. Intel's strategy for leading the microprocessor industry is to introduce new product families every few months. Ultimately, "speed is the only weapon we have," notes CEO Andrew Grove.[15] George Stalk, manufacturing expert at the Boston Consulting Group, agrees: "If you're not faster than your competitor, you're in a tenuous position, and if you're only half as fast, you're terminal."[16]

THE NEW INNOVATION AT WORK

Planetary Design: Ford Motor's new Global Design Studio is not a place, it's a process. In its effort to reduce costs and time in designing future cars, the company has built multimedia, instantly connected computer and video links for 100 designers in Cologne, Germany; Dunton, England; Turin, Italy; Hiroshima, Japan; Melbourne, Australia; Dearborn, Michigan; and Valencia, California. The system allows designers at each location not only to simultaneously look at computerized 3-D images of new products but to manipulate them in real time, making adjustments to the images as they speak, cutting product development time by as much as 40 percent in the process.

Globally Connected Sports Shoes: A new design for Nike shoes starts with team meetings between designers and marketers in Oregon. When consensus is reached on a design, it is relayed by satellite to the CAD/CAM systems of contractors in Taiwan or Korea. Refining the design by real-time satellite link, engineers in Asia develop manufacturing specifications that are then transmitted to manufacturing plants in countries all over Asia. Its instantly connected global network consistently allows Nike to beat its competition to the marketplace with new designs—primarily with workers who don't "work" for Nike.

High—and Fast—Fashion: The Limited, a store that defies trends in its industry by maintaining profits while many competitors stagnate, owes much of its success to a global innovation system *par excellence.* Within minutes of receiving an order from a store for a new style, Limited managers transmit via satellite a visual representation of the style, displayed on their store's favorite model, to Asian manufacturing centers. Ink-jet lithography details a computer design for the production of prototypes in Hong Kong, then manufacturing orders are sent electronically to factories throughout Asia. The company can move a product from the mind of a buyer to the buyer's store in less than seven weeks.

The speed of globalizing new developments, moreover, has sharply underscored the importance of speed in product development itself. After being launched in the United States, black-and-white televisions took approximately twelve years to become as commonplace in Europe and Japan as they were in the United States. When color television arrived, it took half the time to become "globalized" in such markets and video recorders only three years. Compact discs went global in just one year. Today, companies can ignite chain reactions that penetrate global markets almost overnight.

But time also wreaks havoc with global success. Texas Instruments invested millions in developing a magnetic-bubble memory chip; by the time it got the product to market, it was obsolete. In 1985, Motorola, envied globally for its high-quality, state-of-the-art technology, claimed 79 percent of the microprocessors in engineering workstations; by 1991 that figure was down to 28 percent.[17] The reason: The company's commitment to an earlier generation of processors delayed its development of the new RISC chip technology that dominated microprocessing by the early 1990s. Today, Motorola constantly retrains its computer experts on the assumption that a software engineer's half-life is three to five years. Sun Microsystems was one of the firms that leapfrogged Motorola. In its first ten years, Sun introduced eight generations of computers. Notes Sun CEO Scott McNealy: "Miss one development cycle and you are seriously hurt, miss two and you are mortally wounded."[18]

The most competitive of global enterprises constantly battles to keep up with the liquidity of ideas. When regulators first decided to intervene in the electronics industries, their initial step was a campaign for market access for transistors, even though demand for transistors was evaporating due to the advent of semiconductor chips. This misunderstanding of technology cycles manifests itself in myriad ways. The Internal Revenue Service (IRS) requires equipment used in chip production to be depreciated over five years—a period that is typically longer than the effective commercial life of the equipment. Such misunderstanding has turned some agencies into powerful obstacles to global success.

Those active anywhere on the globe in the pharmaceutical industry are familiar with the U.S. Food and Drug Administration (FDA). The agency has the reputation of being one of the most rigorous regulators on the planet. Policymakers take pride in explaining how the agency protects the American pharmaceutical industry and American consumers. But foreign companies have a different perspective: The agency is one their strongest allies in competing with American pharmaceutical and other health-care firms.

The pharmaceutical industry rivals the computer, telecommunication, and consumer electronic sectors in the pace of technical innovation. Along with a handful of other industries, such as the supercomputer and commercial aviation sectors, the pharmaceutical industry must tie up vast sums of capital to develop and launch a product—and cumulative billions are spent on products that never enter the market. No product can generate revenues until it has been approved—and profits often dry up as soon as patent protection expires. When the International Trade Commission examined the competitiveness of American pharmaceutical producers, it discovered that in the United States, new pharmaceuticals on average needed nineteen years to recover the underlying research expense, but due to regulatory delay, the effective patent life for the average new drug was ten years and ten months.[19]

Summit Technology of Waltham, Massachusetts, has revenues of $30 million on sales of its laser technology for the removal of corneal scars; not one cent of those sales have been in the United States, the biggest health-care market in the world. Although thirty-five other countries have approved the technology, Summit has tried in vain for over five years to get the FDA to act on its petition for approval.

ATS Medical of Minneapolis makes sophisticated heart valves. Although the valves are largely made in the United States, the firm ships them to Scotland for final assembly, to be sold in Europe to France, Switzerland, and five other countries. After years of review, the FDA hasn't granted final approval for sale in the United States—making a mockery of official standards requiring the agency to act on applications within 180 days. During 1992 the agency approved only twelve new medical devices for U.S. sale out of scores being developed in the United States, even though the agency's total staffing increased from 7,600 in 1990 to 8,700 by 1993. Medical devices were once a thriving, highly innovative industry in America, serving as a catalyst for related research in micromechanics and biochemistry. But the industry is being eviscerated by the FDA's failure to support such innovation. Notes Daniel Lemaitre, a medical-device industry analyst at Cowen & Co.: "There isn't a company that isn't thinking of moving its research and development, and its manufacturing, overseas."[20] Venture capital needed for research has been steadily abandoning the sector.

Procter & Gamble spent $180 million to develop its Olestra fat substitute, in the course of the effort obtaining four different patents to protect its investment. The patents proved to be of little use: The FDA stalled its approval process for so many years that the patents expired. Although under the Drug Price Competition and Patent Term Restoration

Act of 1984 patent terms were theoretically to be extended for up to five years in such cases, the law's terms were watered down so much in the political process that they gave no meaningful relief for many products. The new effect: Patent protection is often denied at precisely the moment that firms need it the most, when revenues begin to arrive to offset the massive investment in research. In November 1995, at a hearing before the House Subcommittee on Technology, the Health Industry Manufacturers Association testified that the FDA approval process delays introduction of new products by up to three years and sharply contrasted the process to that of Europe, where consumer safety is preserved with a much shorter approval process. The FDA was cited as the primary reason many medical device and biotech firms were relocating to introduce new technologies offshore before attempting to provide them to U.S. consumers.

The Environmental Protection Agency (EPA) has long been notorious for second-guessing innovation. Deeply embedded in its regulations are prescriptions for specific technology (such as catalysts and scrubbers) or "best available technology" standards for remediation, which have constrained companies to focus on one technology and cast aside innovation. Nalco Fuel Technology, a joint venture dedicated to developing new environmental technology for reducing the nitrogen oxide that is a major contributor to smog and acid rain, had a highly cost-effective technology that provided a means for cleanup of utility emissions at a fraction of the cost of conventional scrubber technology. The product languished for years as authorization for its use was delayed at the EPA; it was kept alive only as a result of sales outside the United States to customers in Asia and Europe, in nations where regulators readily adapted to the product.[21] Similar delays at the Federal Communications Commission in setting standards for bandwidth and system interoperability have dramatically slowed down the introduction of telecommunication innovations in U.S. markets. As Roger Meiners, professor of law and economics at Clemson University, notes, such regulatory impasse "reduces incentives to innovate, thereby injuring economic growth and American competitiveness."

PATENTLY OUTDATED

In a world in which hoarding ideas leads to stagnation, the significance of patents inevitably changes. The liquidity of ideas churning through the global economy has overwhelmed the traditional paradigm of control enshrined in patents and licenses. The new process of innovation is driven by interests, not formal rights. Underscoring the move away from strict rights is the simple reality that traditional intellectual property systems cannot accommodate the complexities of trying to fit multisource, multimedia ideas into rigid frameworks of copyrights, patents, and trademarks.

The biotechnology industry has been significantly handicapped by a patent system that is utterly incapable of coping with the complexity of its products and the liquidity of its ideas. Five biotech companies, for example, diverted vast effort in recent years to argue with the patent office over rights to a class of biomolecules known as colony stimulating factors; each spent over $2 million in legal fees trying to establish rights to aspects of the molecules they each independently developed. The traditional system was useless to them. Roger Mathus, executive director of the U.S. Semiconductor Industry Office in Japan, has watched innovation transform his industry many times. "Outright licensing has gone away to a large extent," he explains, replaced by dynamic new mutual exchanges.

Companies on the cutting edge of innovation increasingly find that they must make a choice between the liquidity and diversity of information required for today's innovation and the protection of the traditional systems. The meteoric pace of innovation of software design *can* be interrupted for audit of copyrights, for constant speculation over how static property rights can be attached to rapidly evolving ideas, and for assessment of the slippery boundaries that copyrights and patents provide in such context. But to do so interferes dramatically with the process of innovation. Cygnus Support, a California-based software firm, has found a profitable niche by defying traditional intellectual-property wisdom: Customers like Hitachi and Sun Microsystems are attracted to Cygnus's innovative new products because the firm deliberately refuses to copyright or patent its products. It places no limits on the reproduction or modification of its products. How does it stay in business? It charges fees for the use of its experts—and it requires customers to share with Cygnus all product modifications and improvements made by them. The pace of cross-innovation between Cygnus and its customers keeps those customers reliant on Cygnus and keeps Cygnus at the cutting edge of its industry. The result is an ever-expanding, fast-paced innovation machine—nurtured far from the strictures of patent offices and other regulators.

The traditional patent establishment cheered when efforts to harmonize *existing* patent standards were moderately successful in the

Uruguay Round GATT negotiations. But the measures were many years overdue and ignored the far more important task of conceptual reform. At best, jury-rigged extensions of traditional laws to digital technology can only be viewed as stopgaps. It takes but a quick review of the disputes currently clogging patent courts to see that the intellectual resources of those courts and the legions of highly trained professionals in the patent system need to be turned to fundamental reform. Protracted legal battles, involving millions in legal fees, are being fought over use of computer screen savers, alleged infringements by operators of networks for materials sent by subscribers, and attempts to apply patents to constrain commercial transactions over the Internet.

PICKING GLOBAL WINNERS

Many policymakers in both political parties have a quick answer to all of America's innovation problems: Washington will nurture key industry segments and key technologies to assure that they remain competitive. The premise of technology targeting of this nature is that by nurturing the right firms and "U.S." industries, Washington can propel those firms and industries to the ranks of global winners.

The record of such efforts by governments at home and abroad is dismal. The tales of failed targeting efforts in Europe comprise a virtual alphabet soup of acronyms: Alvey, Antiope, Eureka, Esprit, Jessi, Prestel, Teletext, Informatique, and Silicon Structures are only some of the most conspicuous programs that become sinkholes for European taxpayer funds. The Japanese government's effort to fund twenty-six high technology centers has become a costly embarrassment to Tokyo, as was its Asoka commercial plane and nuclear aircraft projects. By following guidance—and funding—from Japan's Ministry of International Trade and Industry (MITI) to make them "companies of the future," Japanese makers of airplanes, ships, solar panels, and nonferrous metals became companies of the past. Japanese government gurus turned down a request for help from a start-up that later became a household name around the globe—Sony. Over sixty separate sectors have been the beneficiaries of MITI's targeting and intervention; no more than a handful could be termed successes by any objective criteria, and the connection between that success and MITI's aid is nebulous at best.[22]

Multibillion-dollar counterparts to such failures can be identified in America, including Washington's $5 billion breeder-reactor program, supersonic transport, and many less conspicuous programs administered by the Department of Defense, such as its MANTECH program for manufacturing plants. Washington targeted the synfuels business and lost $2.7 billion in taxpayers' money. The European Union spent billions of taxpayers' money in a losing effort to create a viable "European" computer industry. Entire regions like the Ruhr Basin lie devastated by unemployment today after becoming addicted to such subsidies. Brussels continues to pour millions into a HDTV standard that has already become obsolete as a result of privately funded research elsewhere— much of it at labs in the United States funded by companies headquartered in Japan.

Strident calls for matching programs in Washington answered MITI's announcement of its Fifth Generation Computer Project. Flat Earth policymakers spread the alarm that it would be the death knell of U.S. computer production. After nearly fifteen years and a government investment equivalent to hundreds of millions of dollars, the project has produced no marketable products for the participating Japanese firms. On the same day in 1993 that newly elected President Clinton unveiled plans for guiding American firms in the "development, commercialization, and deployment of new technology" to catch up with Japan and Europe, MITI announced its newest program: subsidies for commercial applications of psychic powers.

Washington's intervention in what it considers to be promising areas of technology is increasingly cited as an alternative to protectionism. But it is not an alternative, only a substitute form of protectionism. In many ways it is even worse for our society and our economy than traditional protectionism, which at least had a link to markets in the sense that it was driven by the reality of jobs and industries in transition. The new technology protectionists work from the other end of the political spectrum, developing policy from their own particular view of the new economy that seems to exist on the banks of the Potomac. They are far removed from the forces of liquidity and diversity felt by firms active in the new global process—but they are very close to taxpayers' dollars and the power those dollars provide.

Being elected to office does not anoint them with the gift of prophecy—but it does mean that their own particular view of the economic future will have a lot to do with the way they channel technology funds. Government funding of innovation on every continent persistently reflects a fundamental flaw of technology policy: The enterprises and industries that will rise to become the technology powerhouses of the coming decades, the enterprises upon which policy is theoretically focused, have no lobbyists today. Those who have the political clout are the large firms and industries of today. Not surprisingly, the vision of the future described to industrial policymakers has a lot to do with keeping such firms in business—meaning that when government funds innovation, those funds go to traditional-style research in the existing industrial base.

Murray Weidenbaum, economic adviser to presidents and currently professor at the Center for the Study of American Business at Washington University, has been close to Washington's technology policymaking for many years. He's not impressed with public-policy pundits who feel they can second-guess today's marketplace. "Government—at least in the United States—is not good at choosing which areas of technology to support and which organizations to do the work."

But the tales of past policy failures seem to fall on deaf ears in Washington. In 1993, when it received a request for higher tariffs to assist small, distressed makers of ceramic chips with implanted circuits, the White House pointedly denied that it would react with protectionist measures. Instead it offered intervention to protect a "national" technology: It created a federally funded research center to be run by the Navy, enhanced research funding from the Department of Energy and the National Institute of Standards and Technology, and created an interagency task force intended to help the complaining firms win more government business and increase their efficiency. "The White House decided to ignore the market and support these firms," observed the government affairs director for a major software producer, "even though there was already successful U.S. production of these same chips—at an international firm called IBM." Presented with pleas for import relief, the government chose not to apply protection through tariffs but through subsidies.

Washington's model for such steps has been Sematech, the consortium that targeted semiconductors as a national technology. Sematech did represent a constructive step forward from wholly government-driven technology projects: Its funding came half from Washington and half from industry coffers in a nod toward the need for research to be demand-driven. But many participants quickly grew frustrated at the scale and bureaucracy of the project—and the stubborn refusal of Washington to recognize the importance of diversity within the industry: When it was formed, Sematech refused to invite NEC of Japan, the company building the then-largest and most advanced chip production facility in the country in Rosevalle, California. In 1992, two

103

founding members—LSI Logic and Micron Technology, two of the most innovative firms in the global industry—left the project. On announcing his company's departure, a Micron spokesperson complained that the original purpose of developing new manufacturing processes had been replaced with an emphasis on "strengthening" existing U.S. factories—in other words, the technology-driven project was developing into merely another protection device for existing manufacturing.

Ultimately Sematech, which today is in the process of winding down, claimed victory in enhancing U.S. production of chips. But the industry existing at the outset of Sematech is not that existing today. Memory chips had become a commodity, subject to vastly different economics. There was new production by some of Sematech's smaller members, but it was driven by Intel's decision to exit production of the product, allowing them to justify new capital investment. The new production was not due to "American" innovation at Sematech but was part of the natural evolution of the industry; it had no real connection to the nearly $1.5 billion spent by Sematech.

Leading members of the semiconductor industry passed their own judgment early in Sematech's life. IBM, Toshiba, and Siemens were already involved in ongoing joint development of a new generation of chips, expressly rejecting government assistance in doing so.[23] Even the U.S. partners in Sematech hedged their bets. Nearly all developed separate pacts with foreign counterparts—Motorola with Toshiba, for example, Texas Instruments with Hitachi, and AT&T with NEC. Advanced Micro Devices, one of the original participants in Sematech, was forging an alliance with Sony in semiconductor chips even as Washington was recruiting it to join Sematech. W. J. Sanders III, chairman of Advanced Micro, explained: "To think we're going to be totally independent is naive."

But while such alliances were being formed, many in Washington fumed. A National Research Council report warned that "considerable effort" would be needed to make certain that such alliances did not benefit Japan more than the United States.[24] "It's sheer folly to think you can nurture global winners by excluding the leading global players," notes Umberto Colombo, president of the European Science Foundation. "Picking winners only within one's own borders is doomed."[25] Ironically, Japanese government-funded research projects, so often criticized as unfair, include a large number of foreign participants. Tokyo has acknowledged the borderless nature of most important manufacturing technologies.

FOREIGN FIRMS PARTICIPATING IN JAPANESE GOVERNMENT RESEARCH

Advanced chemical processing: SRI International (United States)

Supersonic/hypersonic transport propulsion: Rolls Royce (United Kingdom), SNECMA(France), United Technologies (United States), General Electric (United States)

Micromachine technology: IS Robotics (United States), SRI International (United States), Royal Melbourne Institute of Technology (Australia)

Nonlinear photonics materials: BASF (Germany)

Molecular assemblies for functional protein: GBF (Germany)

High-performance materials for severe environments: Crucible Materials (United States)

New models for software architecture: SRI International (United States)

Production technology for complex carbohydrates: Pharmacia LKB Biotechnology (Sweden)

Quantum functional devices: Motorola (United States)

Source: Agency for Industrial Science and Technology, Tokyo.

. Flat Earth thinking dies hard. Washington continues to second-guess tomorrow's technology through a major new initiative known as the Advanced Technology Program (ATP). The ATP has become one of the fastest-growing federal programs, with $785 million promised by the White House to develop new commercial technologies for chemical catalysts, auto and truck manufacturing, data storage, video imagery, and refrigeration systems.

In 1993 the leadership of the House of Representatives responded to criticism of intervention into technology development by offering a sweeping new reform package captioned the Federal Technology Commercialization and Credit Enhancement Act. The proposal called for an ambitious new network for dissemination of government patents. Sponsors proudly pointed to the manner in which it would inherently build the U.S. industrial base: Funding for the program was to be achieved by imposing a stiff new tax on imports.[26] In 1994 the effort was repeated with the proposed National Competitiveness Act, which sought to expand the government's role in technology development. A primary element of the act, strongly pushed by the chairman of the House Energy and Commerce Committee: a requirement that any company using government-funded technology had to purchase its components and materials from sources within the United States.

TOO IMPORTANT FOR GOVERNMENT

In an incredibly short period of years, private enterprise has created a vast and intricate network of innovation. Those American enterprises that are succeeding globally have been successful in cultivating that network, reaching out without regard to borders to find the best human talent, the best venues for developing ideas, and the most effective sources of materials to nurture the process. Left unrestrained, many American firms are second to none in their ability to adapt and innovate. In an economy where permanent natural endowments have lost their role in comparative advantage, the closest thing America has to a "natural" endowment is that capacity to innovate. The challenge for Washington and governments everywhere is to find means to promote that capacity without interfering with it, to understand that when government targets a company or industry or second-guesses its innovation, government makes that company or industry an easy target for global competitors.

In the words of Lewis M. Branscomb, former chief scientist at IBM and currently a professor at Harvard University, "Technology policy is too important to leave to policymakers."[27] Branscomb has been close to technology policymaking for much of his career. What drives his conclusion is perhaps the single biggest problem with any government technology intervention: Like protection of trade, it is based on the status quo, current research, and current manufacturing bases.

Marina N. Whitman is vice president for public affairs at General Motors. She has a deep suspicion of innovation intervention by Washington. Any governmental effort to pick global winners is implicitly flawed, she points out, because "it would undermine the right to fail." As Whitman explains, "Placing the burden of failure for noncompetitive decisions on the political process" encourages bureaucrats to "keep high-profile R&D commercialization projects that would otherwise have collapsed alive on expensive life-support systems."[28] The burden of relentless innovation is on private enterprise, not government. Having Washington presume itself a partner in that process can be characterized the same way Helmut Schmidt once characterized Washington's role in international political affairs: "It's like having an elephant in your canoe."

It is no coincidence that the industries in which America has the most successful world-class competitors are those that have the most distaste for technology intervention. Most U.S. computer and software firms swore off Washington's help after witnessing Washington's role in managing semiconductors and display screens. American pharmaceutical firms do not rely on Washington for protection or funding; they spend 15 percent of sales on innovation, and many are in the top ranks of their industry. American chemical firms have proven highly innovative based on their own funding and enjoy billions in global sales. Not only are both industries far removed from government intervention, they also escaped much of the 1980s trade-regulation frenzy that handicapped firms in other industries. It is also more than coincidental that those industries, especially the pharmaceutical sector, benefit from an anomaly in Washington's tight-fisted technology approach: Research conducted by the federal National Institutes of Health is made available to all competitors regardless of nationality.

The technology interventions offered by Washington are Faustian bargains for American enterprise. There is a useful role for Washington in the new process of innovation, but its focus should be on improving basic legal infrastructures and driving the antiglobal prejudice out of existing laws and programs. For many policymakers trying to understand how innovation works in the new economy, the best point of departure may be words penned by Ralph Waldo Emerson over a century ago, simple words that have taken on a compelling new significance today: "If a talent is anywhere born in the world," he said, "the community of nations is enriched."[29]

DINOSAURS ON THE PROWL

Competition Policy in a Changed World

A t the end of the nineteenth century, international business in many industries meant American business. In a wide range of sectors, American firms held much larger international market shares than they do today. Left with those shares, they would have been well positioned to maintain their leadership throughout the twentieth century. But they were not permitted to do so. They were not even permitted to defend their positions against legitimate competitors. They were forced from their international markets under the assortment of social and economic policies that Washington has traditionally combined under the caption "antitrust."

America's first generation of antitrust regulators compelled American tobacco firms to sell their controlling interests in production around the planet.[1] In 1911 they disbanded the massive overseas holdings of Standard Oil, which operated sixty-seven subsidiaries in overseas business. They forced the U.S. managers of Alcoa and Du Pont to disengage from involvement in offshore business. AT&T established American leadership in early telephone and telegraph markets in Asia and Europe but in its earliest bout with antitrust regulators was compelled to divest its foreign operations, not to be allowed overseas again until 1984. The copper, match, sulphur, and other industries all had to withdraw from strong positions offshore under pressure from Washington.

The breakup of American business overseas wasn't simply an ancillary result of actions focused on U.S. markets. The enforcement actions expressly targeted foreign business, and the breakup of foreign operations was demanded because of a perceived international dominance by the U.S. firms. In several cases, Department of Justice and Federal Trade Commission regulators announced that they were protecting consumers and competitors around the world from American multinationals or, alternatively, that they were protecting American consumers by ensuring that they did not "subsidize" international activity by American firms.

There is little point in arguing the merits of such past actions, of asking whether such protection was worth the historic cost to American competitiveness. But vital significance attaches to the future tense of that question: Will today's American enterprise be able to succeed globally under those same competition policies? More specifically, can it succeed in the relentless new competitive environment under policies that restrain them from the relationships that now drive leadership in many industries? Will U.S. enterprise be able to implement effective competitive strategies while being denied opportunities for mergers, acquisitions, and distribution systems available to non–U.S. firms? Can it effectively tap the new advantages of liquidity and diversity under rules built around concepts of stable, homogenous national industry that are no longer valid?

There has never been unanimity of support for America's antitrust laws. More than a few economists, managers, and consumers watched in confusion as Washington destroyed John D. Rockefeller's global petroleum empire. Antitrust folklore, as reflected in the media and more than a few textbooks, tells us that penalties were justified due to Rockefeller's industrial concentration, restraints on the entry of new competitors, and maintenance of artificially high kerosene prices. But the clearly documented facts before the Standard Oil courts were that kerosene prices had dropped by 80 percent during Standard's rise in the industry, and 147 other refiners—many of them entries in more competitive western oil fields— competed with Standard, which had a 64 percent kerosene market share and 9 percent crude production share at the time of the proceeding. The courts upheld the regulators' case against

Standard solely on the grounds that the company had shown an intent to monopolize by the "unreasonable" formation of its holding company.

Thirty years later many observers again watched nonplussed as federal regulators completed another of the "classic" antitrust cases, this time against Alcoa for preempting competition. The words of the final decision ring hollow today, when managers struggle daily to build the type of organization for which Alcoa was condemned:

> . . . we can think of no more effective exclusion [of competitors] than progressively to embrace each new opportunity as it opened, and to face every newcomer with new capacity already geared into a great organization, having the advantage of experience, trade connections and the elite of personnel.[2]

The global photocopier industry was an American preserve until antitrust regulators stepped in and forced Xerox to divest its technology. As head of Bell Laboratories, Nobel Laureate Arno Penzias has watched Washington's management of high-tech competition with deep suspicion. "When you think of what the Federal Trade Commission did to Xerox," complains Penzias, "it said 'Set up foreign competitors.' They wanted Xerox to give up its patents so people could buy from a Japanese competitor."

While there has always been dissent from the theories behind American antitrust rules, never before has there been such a compelling need to reexamine the basic context of those rules. As the global economy has emerged, in industry after industry, the pro-competitive intentions of traditional antitrust regulation are producing anticompetitive results.

WASHINGTON'S RECALCITRANT INDUSTRIAL POLICY

Antitrust policy has become America's most significant industrial policy. Industrial policy, after all, is about government intervention in the allocation of business resources, about steering enterprise toward goals set by government, about setting a hierarchy of government economic judgments over private-sector economic actions. Not only does antitrust policy share all those characteristics, it also has a far greater impact on the course of enterprise than policies more traditionally associated with industrial planning. It reaches virtually every American enterprise.

But if it is ever to be effective, industrial policy must be fluid. It must evolve and adapt to changing circumstances. It will, inevitably, turn counterproductive unless it is a participative process, unless it takes account of changing realities. No better evidence of the industrial planning implicit in competition policy—and the countercompetitive effects when it does not evolve—exists than the telecommunications industry proceeding that began with the AT&T case. No one could characterize the breaking up of twenty-two operating telephone companies, the compulsory restructuring of the American telephone service industry, and the forced transformation of the telecommunications equipment industry as a mere "enforcement" action. The breakup of any monopoly established by government—as AT&T was—is, with few exceptions, in the country's interest. But the process by which a handful of Department of Justice lawyers and one federal judge were able to commandeer one of the country's largest industries by invoking century-old competitive assumptions has *not* been in the country's interest. They exercised legislative powers over the industry far from the scrutiny of the legislative process.[3]

The industry, and American competitiveness, have paid a heavy price not only as a result of the anachronistic assumptions applied by those trustbusters but also because the process has coincided with the globalization of the industry. American telecommunications firms needed to be focused on that globalization, but they were compelled to focus on regulators who considered global facts irrelevant facts.

Those regulators could ignore global realities because they were driven by social and economic judgments made decades ago about what was deemed to be in the best interests of consumers and, implicitly, the dynamics between those interests and the conduct of enterprise. Many members of the Senate Judiciary Committee, including former chairman Joseph Biden, have repeatedly warned against tampering with those judgments, elevating antitrust laws to near-constitutional status in Washington's lawmaking regime. But there was no commandment from the Founding Fathers that industries should not be concentrated, no sacred law that competitors should not join forces, no sacrosanct rule that companies should not become too big or that competition shall be preserved by preserving specific competitors.

Not only has the structure of industries changed since Washington's competitive paradigms were created, but the way industries relate to each other has changed, the power of the individual entrepreneur has changed, the process of innovation has changed, and barriers to entry in every industry have eroded. The global plebiscite, moreover, has empowered consumers in ways never imagined when the framework of competition policy was laid a century ago. On its face, that framework is simplicity itself. It seeks to protect the welfare of American consumers by restraining the effects of industrial concentration and collusion between competitors on pricing, production, and other competitive conduct. America's primary antitrust law, sponsored by Senator John Sherman in 1890, prohibited anticompetitive activity through monopolistic action and agreements in restraint of trade. The Sherman Act remains the principal law regulating relationships between competitors. Price discrimination is prohibited under the Robinson-Patman Act. Other agreements to restrain trade, such as customer allocation or price fixing, are illegal under the Clayton Act or the Federal Trade Commission Act.

From these simple underpinnings, policymakers have created a patchwork of implementing standards and measuring devices that are anything but simple. Understanding what particular enforcers consider to be inimical to consumers could tax the skills of a clairvoyant. Prices, for example, may be too high, or prices may be too low. Prices may be too similar among suppliers. Prices may be too different. Prices may be too stable at successive levels of distribution. Armed with sobering terms like neoclassical microeconomics, supracompetitive, industrial organizational theory, economic determinism, regression analysis, and economic disequilibrium, an army of experts have established lucrative careers deciphering such standards as well as the corollary rules applied by industry agencies like the Federal Communications Commission, the Nuclear Regulatory Commission, and the Federal Aviation Administration.

From the perspective of enforcers, the focus under these laws is either structural, involving the basic relationships and concentrations in an industry, or transactional, involving the specific behavior of enterprises and their managers. Regulators insist, moreover, that these standards are not a burden on American enterprise because so few companies are involved in proceedings. In 1995 only thirty-five lawsuits were filed to block mergers by the FTC and only sixteen mergers were challenged by the Department of Justice.[4]

But from the perspective of enterprise, such figures are misleading. In what veteran merger-and-acquisition negotiator Martin Klingenberg characterizes as the "iceberg effect," vastly more transactions are chilled, or killed, without involvement by the agencies. "For every merger or venture challenged," notes Klingenberg, "five or six more die in the making as a result of antitrust advice. Washington sends people to jail for antitrust violations. That gets the attention of executives. But it also prevents entrepreneurs from pushing the envelope in ways that may be entirely legal. Innovative deals die because many refuse to run the agency gauntlet."

That gauntlet is the process for approving transactions filed with the agencies. The expense alone kills many deals—the process can cost anywhere from $50,000 to over $1 million. Others die from the "intrusion" factor—once an official file is opened, regulators may demand truckloads of internal documents in a review that could consume months of valuable management time.

Managers, moreover, are not concerned about structural or transactional aspects of policy. They see a much more significant bifurcation: Competition policy seeks to restrain *actual* wrongful conduct—a price-fixing conspiracy, for example—or the presumed future wrongful effects of proposed conduct—a proposed merger or joint venture, for example. Business and society understand the first category: It involves wrongful intent that causes actual injury. But the second category reaches a vastly greater spectrum of economic activity, with results that are increasingly difficult to justify within any industry. It is in this category that official action is based on assumptions about the dynamics of enterprise developed a century ago and factual presumptions about the future effects of transactions. As Klingenberg notes, however, "What manager knows where his business is going to be a year from now? But regulators confidently project two, three, even five years into the future and punish companies *today* for what they see in their crystal balls about tomorrow." In the context of global competition, such projections are, at best, speculations—but those speculations have the power of law.

THE FEAR OF FEWNESS

The "core provisions" of antitrust law, the FTC announced in July 1995, "serve as effective tools against the exercise of unrestrained private economic power."[5] Whether the FTC intended the extraordinary implication that all private economic power requires government restraint, the agency undoubtedly intended to convey that private economic power must not be allowed to become too powerful. The corollary to that point is one of the great tenets of traditional antitrust policy: Diluted economic power is preferred over concentrated economic power. To such minds, four convenience stores on a corner are invariably better than three, and five will be better still. And if one antimonopoly law is good, four or five are better still: Washington controls mergers and acquisitions under the Clayton Act, the Sherman Act, the Federal Trade Commission Act, and several industry-specific laws.

Such laws require constant attention in the new economy. It is difficult to find commentary about any industry today without encountering references to industry shakeouts, realignments, restructurings, or consolidations. The mergers, acquisitions, and other combinations denoted by such terms have become a critical aspect of competition. What is lost on many observers, however, is that they are not merely an effect of the new competition; they are a means of competition, a competitive weapon that is creating global winners.

Concentration of competitors is not a desultory effect of industries crossing borders; it is an inextricable element of globalization. A look at the Standard Industrial Classification groupings relied upon by Washington shows, for example, that from 1979 to 1989, as companies rapidly expanded their global reach, the average number of firms competing within each three-digit SIC industry grouping dropped from fifty-three to twenty-eight. Global industry drives "fewness"—but no global manager would consider that globalization has eased competition.

But the deep-rooted assumption that substantial competition requires a substantial number of competitors compels regulators to fill antitrust casebooks with efforts to prevent such fewness. Mergers, acquisitions, and other new interdependent relationships are blocked or limited, not on a showing that the relationship actually lessens competition or creates a harmful monopoly, but simply on a reasonable probability of one of those effects—and Washington's fear of fewness in an industry has made the threshold a low one indeed.

"Are the laws of economics different in the United States too?" asked a British consumer-products manager when he learned why his proposal for a U.S./U.K. merger would not be blessed by Washington. "I thought the ultimate job of every manager is to make his products the most sought after, which means lessening the competition for his products." He was even more confused when shown guidelines for mergers published in 1992; they set forth as a "unifying theme" that "mergers should not be permitted to create or enhance market power or to facilitate its exercise."[6] So that "means only bad mergers are allowed to proceed?" he aptly queried.

Rules governing merger-and-acquisition deals have had a devastating effect on the global competitiveness of many American firms. The standards restraining competitors from consolidating their forces are far more rigorous in the United States than elsewhere in the world. On many occasions the standards have blocked the mergers of U.S. firms with moderate-size market shares on the pretense of avoiding the creation of an unduly strong U.S. competitor, then permitted a foreign competitor with substantial global market share but small U.S. share to acquire one of the firms. The net effect: The U.S. firm left out of the deal has been doomed to either bankruptcy or, as has happened in several industries, being swept up by yet another foreign firm. Antitrust authorities have repeatedly sacrificed American global competitiveness for their own peculiar notion of domestic competition.

In 1980, six American-owned tire producers—Goodyear, Firestone, Armstrong, General Tire, Uniroyal, and Goodrich—were forecasting a decade of harsh competition as their industry was being transformed. Traditionally their labor-intensive businesses had been conducted by simply dropping molten rubber into molds and selling the resulting product in local markets to individual car owners. But the American technology that had launched the industry in the nineteenth century was under siege as a result of chemical innovations. New technology was creating tires that lasted twice as long as their traditional products, meaning consumers bought far fewer replacements and that car producers with highly concentrated buying power were becoming the primary customers. On the crest of that wave of innovation, those auto companies were going global, consolidating operations, including purchasing of components like tires, across borders. Deep-pocketed family-owned tire companies in Europe and Japan were already following home-country carmakers into American territory. The solution was obvious for many American managers: There had to be consolidation within North America to capitalize on the respective strengths of American industry members and create platforms for engaging global rivals. Repeated attempts were made by American producers to join forces by merger. Except for an eventual nod for Uniroyal and Goodrich to join forces—a deal later proven to be too little too late—each proposal was rebuffed by regulators who disfavored the "concentrative" effect it would have within the U.S. industry. Arguments that there was no longer any "U.S." industry—that even when combined, U.S. firms would have only a small share in what was clearly a global sector—fell on deaf ears.

Today the industry that existed in 1980 is history. Instead of a dozen significant producers around the world, there are now six. Only one, Goodyear, is an American-owned firm. Firestone was acquired by

Bridgestone of Japan. Armstrong was purchased by Pirelli of Italy. Continental of Germany took over General Tire. Uniroyal/Goodrich was taken over by Michelin. Many industry analysts believe that the only path to global leadership for Goodyear lies in a joint venture or merger with a European producer—but that path is strewn with American antitrust barriers.

In 1990 Gillette found a way to strengthen its global position in the blade and razor industry by acquiring the operations of Sweden's Wilkinson Sword. Boston-based Gillette was interested primarily in Wilkinson's strong position in non–U.S. markets like Brazil, Australia, New Zealand, and Austria, markets that would give the American firm new advantage in its fight with European competitors. The Department of Justice blocked the transaction on the grounds that it would give Gillette an added 3 percent of the U.S. market and reduce the U.S. wet-shaving "industry" to four competitors.[7] Three years later the Department interfered with Gillette's global plans again by filing suit to block the firm from acquiring Britain's Parker Pen. Gillette held 7 percent of the global pen market. With the acquisition, Gillette would have leapt over France's Societé Bic SA to a leading global share of 15 percent. Eighty percent of Parker's sales were outside the United States. The governments of Great Britain, France, Germany, and Canada approved the sale. But the Department of Justice contended that in what it characterized as the American "premium fountain pen industry," Gillette would have a 40 percent share after the acquisition, an unacceptable concentration of pen power. Only the intervention of a federal judge who did not share the Department's concept of "industry" permitted Gillette to proceed.[8]

Nestlé was blocked in its acquisition of Stouffer Foods on similar grounds: The FTC asserted that Nestlé was a potential competitor in Stouffer's American frozen-food markets, so the merger "restricted" competition. The deal went forward only under a consent decree that required Nestlé's divestiture of a large plant in Wisconsin to a new competitor. The Swiss and American firms paid what some foreign managers have labeled America's "synergy tax"— they were allowed to combine for global synergies only if they surrendered a significant portion of their competitive potential to a third party.

Restricting such combinations due to a perception that they are anticompetitive often makes them uncompetitive. Concentrations don't block competition; they are the only means of competition in most global industries today. By any objective criteria, the computer and software industries, for example, represent a profound American success story.

But not according to traditional antitrust perspectives, which only see a pernicious degree of concentration. Look at the personal computer: Over 85 percent of the 140 million personal computers on the planet have operating systems from one company—Microsoft. Over 80 percent of all personal computers globally contain a microprocessor made by one company—Intel—and over half of Intel's processors are made at one factory in New Mexico. The microprocessor and others chips are encased in ceramic packages, over 70 percent of which are made by Kyocera—which makes over half of its packages at one plant in Kokubu, Japan. Forty-five percent of data-reading heads in the disk drives are made at one factory in Kofu, Japan. Seventy percent of the special saws used to slice the silicon in the chips are made by one company in Asia. Seventy percent of the chips are printed by tools from a single company. Forty percent of the photomasks used to engrave the circuit on the chips are supplied by Dai Nippon Printing. Sixty-five percent of the material used to seal chips in their packages is made at one factory in Asia.[9]

These new concentrations are pro-competitive for the same reason that heavily populated industries were so in the old economy: They create and nurture diversity. Allowing one company or one alliance to concentrate resources on a narrow specialization to be used by multiple firms in multiple applications facilitates innovation, upgrading the value of the entire industry. This new form of interdependent competition allows the huge investments needed for product development to be consolidated while the benefits are shared. Without it, the $2 billion memory-chip facility, the $1 billion pharmaceutical plant, or the $500 million software program does not get made. "This kind of concentration turns out to be efficient," explains G. Dan Hutcheson of the computer think tank VLSI Research. In computers, telecommunications, consumer electronics, chemicals, pharmaceuticals, office equipment, automobiles, and many other sectors, such interdependence is at work: Each industry member is customer, supplier, and competitor to other members of the industry. They have discovered that in the new economy such dependence does not weaken them; rather, these relationships empower them with the kind of flexibility, expertise, and efficient use of capital needed to remain competitive.

But those who view this process through the lens of century-old antitrust policy see oligopoly, collusion, and U.S. market vulnerability. Officials involved in Washington's Sematech consortium and the new flat-panel-screen initiative had their own remedy to what they perceived as the concentration "problem" in the computer industry: make the U.S. players in the industry build redundant capacity in the United States. The

117

same mentality among trade regulators has disrupted global sourcing networks by penalizing the use of cost-effective plants in Asia as supply centers for U.S. production. The predictable result: U.S. plants are removed from such networks.

The global computer industry—and especially its American participants—would be far weaker today were it not for the phenomenal success of Microsoft and Intel, success owed to their "concentrated" powers in research and development. But in 1993 Federal Trade Commission staff recommended strong action against Microsoft for its concentration in operating software. Their attack was aimed at two practices: lower royalties offered to computer producers who loaded the Microsoft system on all their machines and the "unfair" practice of not designing products so that they could be used with competitors' systems—practices that have sharply lowered the cost of personal computers to hardware makers and consumers. Although the FTC refused to accept its staff's recommendation of penalties, the Department of Justice decided to launch its own parallel investigation.

Microsoft won a settlement of that proceeding in 1994, but regulators, seemingly obsessed with the notion that any company with an 85 percent market share (in computer operating systems) had to be punished, still pressed on. When Microsoft announced a $2.3 billion acquisition of Intuit Inc. in 1995, the department rushed to court to block the acquisition on the grounds that the combination of the firms would create an unacceptable future concentration in the network for electronic commerce to be built by the combined firm. After a seven-month battle, Microsoft abandoned its plans, yielding to what antitrust regulators have discovered as a potent new weapon in its cases in technology-intensive industries: time. No companies in such industries—especially those in leadership positions—can afford to let new ventures hang in limbo for months in antitrust litigation over products that have a life cycle of one or two years.

Many industry observers were disappointed: They had been curious to find out how Justice would argue against the realities of electronic commerce. No company, not even a Microsoft, could achieve more than a niche market in electronic transactions when competing with an "industry" owned by the global plebiscite; Microsoft's competition was the Internet and its World Wide Web. The power of that competition was demonstrated in January 1996, when AT&T abandoned its own competing network, surrendering to the Web only a year after paying $50 million for its network assets. Those concerned about the implications of the Microsoft/Intuit case for competition policy were more severely disappointed when the smoke cleared and they realized that what Justice had attempted—and apparently succeeded at—was to shape monopoly standards into a new rule of entry for infant high-tech industries, a step backward for anyone interested in supporting innovation.

THE HANDICAP OF "AMERICAN" COMPETITION

The geographic mind-set of regulators has long been a major obstacle to enlightened competition policymaking. The Federal Trade Commission gutted the global business franchise of Xerox by concluding that "U.S." competition would be enhanced by forcing Xerox to surrender the knowledge comprising its competitive advantage to overseas competitors. Not long afterwards, a number of officials were demanding new barriers to the flood of foreign-made photocopiers entering the United States.

Washington blocked a merger sought by National Steel on the grounds that it would cause competition in the United States to become too concentrated; it evaluated that competition by analyzing the U.S. market shares of U.S. producers without regard to global competitive dynamics, despite the fact that numerous antidumping petitions had been filed at the time to fight the effects of imports.

Emerson Electric was building global strength by acquiring McGill Manufacturing when the Federal Trade Commission intervened in 1990. Because the import share of mounted ball-bearings sales in the United States was only 6 percent, the commission refused to accept arguments from Emerson—and the Department of Commerce—that a global market benchmark should be used. Ignoring global market dynamics, the commission determined that the acquisition would give Emerson an unacceptably high share of the U.S. market and ordered the company to divest the business.[10]

The Fisherman's Marketing Association had been accepted by the antitrust authorities as a joint venture for negotiating the price of seafood sold to processors. Since neither the fish nor the association's customers were confined by national borders, extending the association's membership to include Canadian fishermen seemed a perfectly natural and pro-competitive move in meeting the challenge of new Asian and European competitors. But the Department of Justice disagreed: It told the association that it would declare the entire joint venture invalid if it tried to consolidate the industry by admitting non–U.S. members.

In many industries, the most active "global" competition or the most important global opportunities arise within U.S. borders in situations where a foreign accent is never officially heard. These are the cases, like those in the 1980s tire industry, in which American companies have sought to build enough critical mass to more effectively compete with large non–U.S. global firms but have been restrained by Washington. More recently, when Texaco and Getty wanted to join their businesses to build resources for global competition with bigger U.S. and European firms, they were required to sell 600 U.S. service stations and several U.S. pipelines and refineries before doing so.

Ironically, regulators have shown themselves more than willing to extend their power beyond U.S. borders for protection of what they perceive as the "domestic" industry. Baker Hughes made a $550 million acquisition in the hotly competitive oil field service market to enhance its offshore presence. To protect the domestic drill bit "industry" from a "domestic" competitor with global power, the Department of Justice offered the firm a deal it couldn't refuse: Cancel the acquisition or protect the U.S. market by selling off all its diamond-drill-bit operations around the world, including assets it owned prior to the acquisition. When Baker tried to globally rationalize another line of business by selling its French drilling-rig subsidiary to a Finnish company, Washington had more to say: Over objections of the Finnish government, it filed suit to block the sale on the grounds that it would give the Finnish company too great a concentration in hydraulic rigs.

The FTC took the French company Institut Merieux by surprise when it invoked its interest in the U.S. market to block the firm's acquisition of a vaccine business in Canada—a business, like most pharmaceuticals, requiring pockets of a global scale to sustain the necessary research. After complaining about the firm having "minimal assets in this country to sculpt a remedy," the agency finally agreed to allow Merieux to proceed, but only if it "leased" the Canadian rabies-vaccine business to an FTC-approved third-party competitor for twenty-five years; if Merieux found no such competitor, the FTC vowed to appoint a trustee to find one.[11]

Such offshore attacks give rise to another dimension of Washington's antitrust enforcement. Whether the proceeding involves a U.S. company in an offshore transaction or an offshore transaction with effects in the United States, intervention by Washington is intervention into the affairs of the host country. In October 1995, Sanford Litvack, senior vice president of Walt Disney Co. and former chief antitrust lawyer in the Carter Administration, testified to the FTC that imposing strict U.S. rules on transactions arising offshore puts American firms at "a severe competitive disadvantage."[12] Such intervention invites conflicting outcomes and intrudes in the affairs of the country hosting the transaction. When Hanson Plc. acquired Beazer Plc., both of Great Britain, Washington intervened, blocking the entire global deal until it could obtain concessions concerning operations of the companies in the northern California concrete market. Foreign enforcement agencies have followed Washington's lead. Kimberly Clark's 1995 takeover of Scott Paper was not only reviewed in Washington but also by European antitrust authorities. Some global acquisitions have triggered review in as many as a dozen separate countries, imposing huge costs on the parties as well as disincentives to future cross-border investment.

Attacks by Washington on foreign deals, even those not involving U.S. assets like the Merieux case, are perfectly correct—by the standards bred earlier in the century. Regulators were applying time-honored criteria *against* concentrations within U.S. borders and *for* protection of U.S. consumers. International dimensions aren't any problem to such regulators because such dimensions are all too often viewed as irrelevant to the interests of U.S. consumers. Some regulators have even declared themselves global: The FTC held hearings in the fall of 1995 to address new enforcement methods in light of global competition. Regulators have announced that non–U.S. markets will be considered in market analysis if imports exceed a set threshold, generally 6 percent—a standard that wholly ignores the effect of foreign investment, sourcing networks, and other connections invisible to traditional scrutiny that could make the most global of businesses appear to be "domestic." To such perspectives, taking competition-policy systems global apparently means reaching out overseas to embellish or protect the "national" home industry. To such thinking, including global dimensions in a strategy or regulatory program is nothing more than a simple geographic extension; documents may have to be translated, a few transatlantic air tickets may have to be purchased for enforcers, and protocols need to be negotiated with foreign governments for the flow of documents and information in cross-border enforcement proceedings.

The announcement of new global perspectives in competition offices is of little comfort to the American firms—and their workers—which were denied strategic opportunities in the critical opening stages of their industries' globalization. They also ring hollow to those facing global competition *today*, who still often find no substantive shift from the thinking that has traditionally restrained their competitiveness. In October 1995, Richard Freuhan, director of the Sloan Steel

Industry Study at Carnegie Mellon University, testified that despite such apparent liberalization, American steel firms remained handicapped. To regain a leadership role in a global industry where many non–U.S. producers are larger than U.S. companies, such U.S. firms need to invest $4 to $6 billion in an advanced integrated steel facility. "No single U.S. company could afford this," Freuhan explained. "If such a plant is required to remain competitive, joint ventures of U.S. companies should be allowed for such purposes."[13] The fact that U.S. companies feel intimidated about entering into such ventures is stark testimony to the failure of American competition policy to embrace the new economy.

LEAVING INDUSTRY BEHIND

As in other contexts, the vital message of the global economy for competition policy is not the simple one of geography. Global competition is far too complex, far too dynamic to be captured by simply acknowledging "foreign" competition or integrating non–U.S. data into market analysis. Traditional assumptions about the marketplace must be discarded. The traditional concepts of markets or industry, which have always provided the framework for evaluation of market shares, concentrations, and barriers to entry, must be cast away.

Defining an industry and its market is traditionally the first and often the most important step in assessing a merger or acquisition. In the traditional economy, such definition came easily. Production and markets were national. Consumers reacted with almost mindless regularity. New-product cycles were long and predictable. All new managers "learned" their industry and the lessons lasted for the duration of their career. Officials and managers could depict industries on maps of America using color-coded pins to designate factories, warehouses, and customers. Industries were solid, stable structures that made the jobs of risk managers, like bankers, relatively easy. Industries functioned like clockwork; economists could take them apart and scrutinize each gear to explain how they worked.

Regulators scrupulously utilized such structures, establishing regulatory programs and industry oversight according to tidy industry compartments, each with its proven causes and effects. Barriers to entry like economies of scale, product differentiation, and start-up costs could be readily identified. Officials spoke with scientific precision in projecting how theoretical monopolists would behave—still a common exercise in merger cases. In hundreds of decisions penalizing enterprises for straying from the competitive paradigm Washington developed for their industries, regulators confidently explained future actions of managers and consumers as if the laws they applied were simply the laws of thermodynamics.

Such assumptions today are wholly without support. Not only is the "U.S." gone from most U.S. industries, but the traditional notion of industry is also obsolete. The world of classical segmented industries has been swept away, gone the way of trade and capital that could be controlled by government. Today industries can be, and are, transformed overnight. Markets swell up one day and disappear the next. Innovation wreaks havoc with barriers to entry.

Yet regulators, trapped in old paradigms, judge companies and industries by yesterday's strengths and the last century's causes and effects. Western governments seek to control the structures of their aircraft industries, for example, without factoring in the reality that China is likely to buy 500 new large airliners in the next decade, more than enough to establish several entirely new global competitors and certainly enough to devastate existing industry giants. U.S. regulators chiseled away at the combination of the power generation and transformer businesses of Westinghouse and Asea Brown Boveri, forcing divestiture of key assets without regard to the fact that during the next decade, 45 percent of new orders for the equipment—enough to entirely reshape the industry—will come from emerging markets in Asia. Regulators have also presided over the slow torture of America's general aviation production, invoking outdated concepts of consumer protection to eviscerate American participation while foreign companies absorbed American customers and assumed technology leadership.

Lightning-quick product cycles blitz competitors. An unknown company from the other side of the globe appears and blasts an unprepared local factory out of business. Western regulators smugly plan how to force greater "contribution" to government coffers by traditional Western mineral extraction enterprises without appreciating the scores of nascent mining firms in Russia, Kazakhstan, and other emerging nations dedicated to unseating traditional industry leaders—and often well equipped to do so. An adept manager can open a market in Asia and double the size of his or her factory without a single new sale in the "domestic" industry.

Markets ebb and flow across borders in ways totally beyond the ability of regulators to measure. Mergers and alliances, far from restricting progress, have become vital vehicles for liquidity and diversity, spreading innovation—and with it improved living standards and prosperity—around the globe. Trying to apply Washington's tools for mergers in global industries is a hopeless and counterproductive task.

The traditional Herfindahl Hirschman Index used in merger analysis is obtained by squaring the market shares of existing firms and totaling them to develop an industry "concentration" benchmark; the higher the sum, the more likely it is that an unacceptable concentration is being created. But the index simply does not compute in rapidly evolving markets around the world, where industry dynamics change constantly and today's market share—if embedded in old technology— could be nothing but a burden in tomorrow's market. Two interrelated flaws have turned the index into a counterproductive policy device: It is based on history (i.e., today's market shares as earned yesterday), and it provides no means to cope with the vastly changed significance of barriers of entry (including the powerfully pro-competitive forces of new technology, emerging markets, and deep-pocket "start-up" ventures around the globe).

SECOND-GUESSING TELECOM MARKETS

During the early 1980s, antitrust regulators confidently ripped apart the telecommunications industry within the United States and restructured it according to their own notions of cause and effect. But their notions about the industry in 1982, when they began to restructure the industry, were largely obsolete five years later; they are ancient history today. Technology totally overwhelmed the policy premises that drove Washington's restructuring of AT&T—and that technology, not government fiat, has been the source of white-hot telecommunications competition over the past decade. Telephone calls are made on television cables, the switching stations that occupied an entire building in 1980 can be carried in a briefcase today, and competitive new companies are succeeding in unexpected—but suddenly vital—markets by applying off-the-shelf technology in unorthodox ways. Canadian, British, French, German, and Japanese firms are injecting new telephone technology to be used in homes in Kansas. British Telecom gave its know-how and $1.5 billion to help build a major American cellular operator based in Washington State. Markets in Hungary, New Zealand, and Poland are supporting new telephone investment in Pennsylvania. Scores of new enterprises will be needed to serve the telecommunications needs of Asia in the next decade—and some of them are no doubt being born today in garages in Australia, Malaysia, or Minnesota.

Everywhere on the planet, the phone company that existed in 1960, 1970, and even 1980 is gone. Anyone trying to draw lines around the phone industry today for antitrust or any other purpose better have lots of erasers and a clean sheet to start each day. The "telephone" products that existed ten years ago have been replaced by software, networking systems, satellite links, cellular towers, and television cables. Finding a bright line between the telephone industry and the computer industry is an impossible task. Computer companies are poised to become some of the biggest forces in the telephone sector. And companies that "only" make microprocessors are able to reach out and wreak havoc in *any* sector that uses electronic memory—regardless of whether regulators pretend that they are discrete computer, consumer electronic, communications or data processing "industries."

The biggest foe of this global telecommunications revolution has been Washington—or, more specifically, those in Washington who seek to police the industry according to outdated notions of competition. Were the stakes for American consumers not so high, the gyrations of regulators to control changes in the industry would be laughable. Computers, software, digital compression, fiber optics, wireless satellite "cable," and a dozen more esoteric technologies are destroying any telecommunications monopolies that may have survived the 1980s. But ironically, Washington labors to keep its concepts of monopoly alive, using them to justify new controls on the industry and even giving them sole credit for creating the telecom revolution.[14]

In many ways, its breakup of AT&T and its new campaigns of deregulation and reregulation created more industry restrictions—in terms of constraining global competition by American firms—than ever existed previously. In 1989, a regional telephone operating company asked permission to form a joint venture with a British firm to construct and operate a fiber-optic transatlantic cable system for international video, data, fax, and voice services. The request was denied. In its ruling, Washington expressed grave concern over using the firm's U.S. revenues to fund international expansion and its potential ability to "cross-subsidize" services. Some of the most important telecommunications opportunities of the century have been presented by phone company privatizations around the planet; but U.S. operating companies have been sharply restricted in their participation in those opportunities by Washington's rules.

HANDICAPPING TELECOMMUNICATIONS COMPANIES

Some companies best positioned for American leadership in the global telecommunications sector are its telephone operating companies and long-distance carriers—but Washington insists on second-guessing their global moves. As a result American technology is increasingly being reserved for non-Americans.

- A $472-million investment by Ameritech, the Chicago-based Bell company, in a global data transmission venture with General Electric Information Services was challenged on the grounds that it constituted provision of long-distance services that was not permitted under the telephone company antitrust decree. Ameritech had to structure its contribution as a loan instead of an equity purchase while it started the years-long process of convincing Washington to let it have "ownership" of the global service. Noted Ameritech President Richard Notebaert: "What is frustrating is that [GE Information Services] operates in thirty-one countries and we can operate in thirty of them but not in one—the United States. We can do work for Ford in England, but not here in Detroit."

- Local telephone systems would presumably be extremely well suited to know new equipment needs for the customers they serve. But when a regional operating company sought to become involved in the design of voice equipment and software, Washington slammed the door shut, stating that its outstanding prohibition against such firms manufacturing equipment should be interpreted to mean they could be involved in developing the telecommunications equipment their customers would need.

- Several regional telephone operating companies have sought to participate in privatizations of phone systems in Europe and Asia. Their hands have been tied, however, since obtaining such assets could violate Washington's prohibition against their providing long-distance services. A Washington policy prohibiting the use of "domestic" revenues to fund "foreign" expansion has handicapped many firms that are interested in globalizing. To proceed with their purchase of New Zealand's Telecom Corporation, for example, Ameritech and Bell Atlantic had to obtain a special waiver from Washington.

- Southwestern Bell and Cox Cable have developed state-of-the-art cable/phone "superhighway" networks in Liverpool and Birmingham, England. Their efforts to join forces for similar systems in Phoenix and Atlanta, however, have been frustrated by regulators alarmed over the "competition" implications.

- When Sprint Corporation sought to conclude a $4.5-billion venture with France Telecom and Deutsche Telekom for global telecommunications systems, the Department of Justice filed suit to block the venture because Justice perceived that it would place other American firms at a disadvantage in France and Germany. The venture was given clearance in July 1995 only after the parties committed to a consent decree that barred Sprint from obtaining "favorable" access to its own partners' networks in Europe and required the parties to publish otherwise confidential terms concerning their cooperation in Europe.

The wave of telephone-television mergers launched by the proposed Bell Atlantic/TCI deal announced in 1993 provided some of the most dramatic evidence of the global revolution overwhelming the old structures of the telephone, television, and communications industries. It was American firms that first established commercial systems for sending calls over video lines—but ironically they did so in England, having been prevented by U.S. antitrust authorities from doing so in the United States. The irony continued in 1993, when the Department of Justice weighed how to regulate the new voice and video combinations while, simultaneously, the White House was pushing investment in the new telecommunications configuration popularized as the information superhighway—whose destiny is wholly dependent on such combinations. Meanwhile the then-head of the Senate antitrust subcommittee, Howard Metzenbaum, blasted the Bell Atlantic/TCI merger as a "double whammy for consumers" and called for hearings on the "megamergermania" sweeping America business.

Any need to confront the challenge of applying old standards to the new paradigms presented by the Bell Atlantic/TCI deal was preempted by the FCC. By announcing a new wave of competition rules—requiring, among other things, that each cable firm fill out sixty pages of forms to justify each price for each service and each piece of gear offered to customers—regulators killed the merger by cutting off vital sources of capital for funding the companies' plans. The same rules persuaded Bell Canada to reduce its planned "superhighway" investment with Jones Intercable in the United States; the two firms decided to refocus their investment on new systems for Great Britain.

Meanwhile, another industry has been running pell-mell toward the same products targeted by the telephone and cable industries. Consumer electronics firms like Philips, Sony, and Matsushita had seemed assured of perpetual success as the technology leaders in an industry as closely linked to the global plebiscite as any. They had launched their empires by making exquisite hardware. Sony had gained an edge by adding "software" to its products through the acquisition of entertainment firms like CBS Records. But today, these firms are scrambling to find new strategies on the premise that soon every strategy built only around hardware and software would be obsolete. No one could aspire to leadership without also having positions in distribution systems—positions that antitrust regulators frequently condemn as "vertical" restraints.

While regulators futilely try to second-guess how digital compression or voice-video will affect markets, the global plebiscite reaches its own far more effective judgments, deciding whether to ignite investment blazes under new technology, which builds new markets that attract new investment, thus generating new technology. While regulators continued to micromanage AT&T and its offspring based on their perceptions of "concentrated" power, that plebiscite reached a different verdict: A new AT&T, humbled by global competition, announced the elimination of 40,000 jobs in January 1996. But Washington continues with efforts to assess the dynamics of markets that don't yet exist, using analytical frameworks developed for industries that have already died. The telecommunications legislation passed by Congress in February 1996 began to introduce marketplace realities to Washington's telecom regime, but it did so by building on traditional structures instead of tearing them down. When the legislative smoke cleared, the foreign-investment handicaps in U.S. law were intact, and the FCC was charged with writing more than eighty new federal communications rules.

BARRIERS OF THE OLD PARADIGM

Going after IBM in the old economy may have been a waste of taxpayers' money. In the new economy, going after concentrations in the computer and software sectors—which empower innovation in *every* industry—has far wider negative implications for American competitiveness. It will also ultimately be an exercise in futility, since no one knows what the industry is anymore. This ambiguity is no mere side effect of the new nature of competition: It strikes at the heart of traditional assumptions about barriers to entry, the conceptual linchpins in predicting access to, and competition in, any industry. Concepts built around the barriers to entry that play a prominent role in much merger analysis are inseparable from Washington's paradigm of industry and monopoly.

For those who learn to adeptly apply innovation in financing, contracts, and technology, barriers to entry today can become so small as to be negligible. And as the collapse of sales at companies like Wang and

Leading Edge have shown, large market shares this year provide no assurance of *any* market share next year. Indeed, in many sectors the biggest barriers to entry to next year's market are the entrenched positions in *this* year's market. It is not complacent leadership or entrenched power that keeps any firm in the "powerful" industry positions that regulators so abhor; it is constant renewal. A firm may maintain its industry leadership from one year to the next by competing on overload, keeping its lead by awesome, even painful innovation, but to outward appearances its market share may merely remain static, indicating to traditional analysis that no serious competition exists. Many firms are painfully aware that the greatest barrier to success tomorrow is the power they have entrenched today; in an economy that empowers entrepreneurs to become giant killers, in an economy in which innovation has squeezed product cycles to one or two years, industry leadership is a perilous position. In every innovation-intensive sector, industry leadership today, or industry structure today, has little to do with industry leadership or industry structure four or five years from now.

In the late 1980s, Apple Computer was reigning over a personal computer empire that seemed impenetrable. By the end of 1995, its market share was waning, the company was being referred to as "bruised fruit," and the primary issue for most industry observers was not Apple's monopoly but whether new managers could keep the company alive as a viable, independent entity. The unexpected news in 1995 at Motorola was more positive: The company had taken a new leadership position in the global paging and cellular phone industry, in no small part due to sales in China ($1.78 billion during 1994), a market that didn't exist five years earlier.

Investment in product lines that inevitably will be eclipsed by a new generation rank as the biggest disincentives to radical innovation—the billion-dollar investment in hard copper infrastructure at a telephone company, for example, or the factory for stereo turntables about to be overwhelmed by compact disc technology. Microsoft does not spend $1 billion a year in research to preserve the grip of existing products on the market; it spends the money because it knows that if *it* does not outdate its own technology, someone else will—and they could do it from a college classroom in Bavaria or a dining room table in Brazil. It knows it has to effectively reenter its industry every year or its position will be taken over by one of the estimated 70,000 other software companies around the planet.

The traditional antitrust challenge can take three or more years to resolve. But in any global industry, today's business will not be recognizable in two to three years' time. Consider events in what antitrust regulators characterized as the computer industry during one year, 1992: IBM reported its first operating loss ever. Digital Equipment Corporation's stock market value was surpassed by a company almost unknown a year earlier, Cisco Systems. Industry giants had failed to comprehend the implications of the half-life of memory: Relentless innovation has made the price of a unit of processing power in a chip fall by one half every eighteen months since the invention of the microprocessor twenty years ago. The $550,000 cost of a megabyte of memory twenty-five years ago chilled the entry of many possible computer industry competitors; today that same megabyte costs $38.[15] While IBM, DEC, and other giants stumbled by focusing on traditional systems, new competitors were emerging from unlikely locations, and increasingly sophisticated customers were themselves transforming competitive dynamics by assembling their own networks of hardware and software from multiple suppliers. Prices for many PCs plummeted 50 percent in 1992. Several large producers of PCs and larger machines exited the business. One-time industry giant Wang entered Chapter Eleven bankruptcy.

By the end of 1992, in another industry shift, computer workstation sales had quadrupled from 1987, representing still another massive swing in markets that company strategists—and regulators—had failed to predict. What is the workstation "industry"? At a conference in November 1992, half a dozen workstation company managers were asked to use one word to describe the essence of their industry. "Hardware," said two. "Software," said one. "Communications," said another. Still another, whose focus was database access, said, "Publishing." "Engineering," said the last.

Rapidly moving—and diminished—barriers to entry mean the computer industry itself is an illusion. It has become a convenient caption for workstations, personal computers, mainframes, operating software, networking software, semiconductor production, networking hardware, disk drives, monitors, modems, add-on boards, and printers. Manufacturers of fax machines are working with Microsoft on communications standards for personal computers. The lines have permanently blurred between computers and consumer electronics. Sony makes one fourth of the CD-ROM drives used in American computers. At the prestigious Consumer Electronics Show, the biggest attractions today are the computer booths. Meanwhile, many experts are positing that simple $500 Internet terminals from consumer electronic firms will soon begin replacing far more expensive personal computers, gutting the empires of the large PC makers. Innovation is restrained at any firm that makes distinctions among telephone, television, computer, and transmission technologies—but Washington stubbornly preserves such distinctions.

Great competitive advantages derive today from product differentiation; most global winners have been built around constant innovation driving product evolution. But some old-school regulatory analysts have considered every differentiation to be somehow "unfair"; for them, Detroit's annual change in car models unduly inhibits competition because new entrants can't afford the cost of frequent retooling. While such strident views have usually been in the minority, barriers to entry still carry a pejorative meaning for many regulators: barriers are bad because, intentionally or otherwise, they restrict competition. In such analysis, Intel's introduction of a new microprocessor every two years and Merck's frequent release of refined pharmaceutical formulations are barriers to competition.

Those in sync with the new economy, of course, understand that such measures are actually the *essence* of competition, the source of advantage in that economy. They know that the quest for the next differentiated product is a catalyst for vital innovation—and that as a result of this process innovation has vastly eroded the significance of *every* barrier to entry. By clinging to outmoded concepts of such barriers, by attacking such aspects as anticompetitive, regulators are attacking American innovation. Their failure to understand the shifting nature of barriers of entry and the relentless metamorphosis of industry and markets means that traditional antitrust analysts preserve a paradigm of competition as a force within a fixed universe. The "competition" enshrined by their analysis is, in the words of University of Connecticut economist Dominick Armentano, "a static equilibrium condition" that "assumes homogenous products and preferences, the existence of suppliers already employing the best technology, and the absence of error or surprise."[16] In other words, it enshrines the slow-moving, long-dead economy of thirty years ago.

The new lessons of competition are there for all to see—at least for all not wearing Flat Earth blinders. In most industries globalization does create fewness, and at any particular moment monopolies can be perceived. But these are not the monopolies of yesterday that, in regulators' minds, entrenched themselves to subvert consumers. In the new economy, every monopoly is a temporary monopoly, a transitory position that cannot be protected with traditional barriers to entry and therefore will be, inevitably, surrendered to still better innovation. The potential rewards offered by the global plebiscite, however, are enough to justify the vast expenditures made by such innovators. The billions spent every year in innovation are spent not to preserve today's short-lived monopoly but in the hope of capturing the one that will replace it. Eliminate the chance to do so—as regulators aspire to do—and those billions will dry up overnight.

ASSAULT ON INNOVATION

In their campaigns against monopolies, regulators have, in fact, begun a frontal assault on that innovation process in the form of new efforts to evaluate and manage proposed business combinations on the basis of the parties' capacity for innovation. The policy first materialized in 1990, when the FTC opposed the acquisition by Swiss-based Roche Holdings of California-based Genentech on the grounds that a combination would lessen competition in research; the transaction proceeded only after Roche agreed to divest technology and research assets. The concept of "innovation" as a market was expanded in the 1993 case in which the Department of Justice blocked the merger of the Allison Transmission Division of General Motors with the German transmission maker ZF Friedrichshafen on the grounds that the merger would "blunt innovation"[17] or diminish competition in the worldwide "innovation market" for medium and heavy transmissions. Shortly afterward, Flow International and Ingersoll Rand were prevented from combining their waterjet-cutting operations because, among other things, the merger would restrict waterjet technology.

The FTC continued the trend by applying innovation market analysis in 1994 and 1995 to block or modify acquisitions by Sensormatic Electric Corporation, Montedison Spa. of Italy, American Home Products, Boston Scientific Corporation, Glaxo Plc. of England, and Wright Medical Technology Inc.,[18] using methodology by which an innovation market is defined by the research and development activities of the parties measured by traditional research assets and R&D expenditures. Although the decision in each case also applied traditional evaluation to assess product market effects, the innovation market analysis played a pivotal role: Based on that analysis, research assets were ordered divested as a condition of government approval for each of the transactions.

Observers in global industries have watched innovation market analysis unfold with stunned confusion. Did Washington understand that innovation as a "line of commerce" was a non sequitur? What could be pro-competitive about taking research assets out of the hands of those who best knew how to use them? Who, moreover, was going to identify all the companies and individuals conducting research with an eye on new entry into the product lines under Washington's scrutiny? Did Washington appreciate that its policy would, inevitably, require duplication of research in hotly competitive industries where research dollars are already in short supply?

Many managers also understood another critical fact overlooked by Washington: In many sectors, the very notion of defining innovative capacity by looking to traditional research labs and patent estates—as the agencies did in their case to date—was anachronistic. Others pointed out that "innovation" information might be available in the United States by subpoena if regulators knew where to ask, but the critical innovation competition could as easily be in Japan, France, or Sweden, out of regulators' reach and unlikely to be voluntarily disclosed. Whether found in the United States or elsewhere, the premature disclosure likely in such searches could be disastrous for the potential new entrant's plans—and even have a profound anticompetitive effect in itself. Did Washington understand, moreover, that the vanishing lines between many industries and the constantly shifting lines around others meant that every "innovation" market was a moving target?

"They waved the flag of the future," observes Martin Klingenberg of the innovation market methodology, "then took ten steps backward." Klingenberg watched several European firms shift investments away from the United States after the innovation market cases were announced. "For them, any chance of being forced by government to give up hard-earned research is too big a chance. They had safer investments they could make in Europe." Both Europe and Japan offer laws and policies that *promote* combination of research activities— without forcing firms into the gauntlet of antitrust review.

Innovation market analysis relies on several fundamentally Flat Earth assumptions. It assumes that reduction of research undermines innovation. It assumes that research equates to or encompasses all innovation. At its heart, it assumes that concentration of traditional research assets will reduce the research undertaken. Even in the traditional economy, many economists searched in vain for a link between industry structures and innovation. Today, such a link is utterly illusory.[19]

As described in Chapter Four, innovation in the new economy defies structure and prediction. It cannot be finitely measured—research is only one input to innovation. Whether by merger or otherwise, collaboration—such as combining patents, jointly funding labs, swapping managers across borders, interchanging materials and test results, creating test standards, and creating common software—is a vital catalyst for innovation. Indeed, enterprises increasingly find they must cooperate in such fashion if they are to compete effectively.

The premise that any firm can monopolize innovation today is badly misinformed and defies experience in every global industry. Much research will simply not be done without collaboration; the cost is too great. Du Pont, for example, had a new pharmaceutical unit that made several exciting new discoveries but hadn't the sales mass to support the huge research and development investment needed to develop the products for FDA approval and eventual sale—"the rules of the game have changed, the ante is much higher,"[20] explained Joseph Mollica, a Du Pont vice president—so the unit teamed with industry giant Merck. There is, moreover, vast potential for realizing efficiencies by collaborating on research. In 1995, for example, ninety-eight different companies around the world were doing research on drugs to treat twenty different forms of cancer.[21] To invite government into the process of deciding such efficiency—by dictating who may or may not collaborate—does not merely invite uninformed judgments into the process; it drives collaboration and the value added by it away from U.S. jurisdiction.

ALLYING WITH THE TWENTY-FIRST CENTURY

Washington's competition policy fails to comprehend the new interdependent competition by which unconventional (by U.S. standards) competition groupings are driving global industries. Its tradition-bound reaction to such groupings has been in evidence for years. Anyone who has followed the battle between Washington and Tokyo over respective shares of the global economy, for example, knows that a major—for many policymakers, *the* major—target of Washington has been the *keiretsu* interest groupings. The *keiretsu* operations are families of interest linking manufacturers, suppliers, finance firms, and even customers by cross-ownership of minority shares—often minimal 1 to 4 percent interests. U.S. antitrust regulators have condemned them as illegal monopolies, illegal combinations, and illegal conspiracies. A long series of U.S. Trade Representatives, in both Republican and Democrat administrations, have branded them a "strategic impediment" to commerce between Japan and the United States.

Attacks on the *keiretsu* continue from Washington, largely without regard to the current realities of business. The *keiretsu* have largely left behind the monolithic trading structures for which they were notorious. The trading companies that led most of them for decades stumbled mightily as traditional manufacturing-driven trade began to fade. Some of the trading firms disappeared; others evolved into global investors, accepting the fact that "international trade" is itself no longer a business. Far less conspicuous has been the change inside the *keiretsu* system: Some members of the *keiretsu* groups, recognizing a gradual loss of synergy, have sold their shares and become independent. Remaining members are abandoning much of the old hierarchy and are functioning as teams in mutual design, supply, finance, production, and sales networks. Tokyo's financial downturn that began in 1992 accelerated the process: Relationships became unglued as competition for funds forced firms to recognize the inflexibility built into the system; tied into old-world relationships that did not evolve with the new economy, new competitive pressures from that economy brought more change into the *keiretsu* system than would have been accomplished in decades of antitrust regulation.

Nowhere was this evidenced more forcefully than in the auto industry, where in the past three years auto-parts suppliers once exclusively tied into one of the *keiretsu* of Toyota, Nissan, Mitsubishi, or Isuzu began breaking through the *keiretsu* lines. The floodgates opened, sweeping fundamental change through the ranks of the auto firms. Nissan, Mazda, and Toyota began sharing the same gearbox supplier. The companies even began buying entire vehicle lines from each other, following a competitive practice originating in Detroit.

Regulators dedicated to chastising the Japanese failed to notice the same phenomenon among American-based firms competing on a global stage. They were forming their own interest groups around the world. Such firms began to identify the advantages in reducing their supply, finance, and other "support" relationships to a small core of like-minded firms. Some companies began taking equity positions in strategic suppliers or began asking suppliers and/or customers to participate in new-product design. Motorola's Paging Products Group has won a global market share of more than 50 percent in part by building alliances with its suppliers that improved the quality of its parts and is driving down supply costs at a rate of 8 to 10 percent a year; in stark contrast, its competitor Philips Consumer Electronics has not pursued such alliances and is able to reduce costs at only half that rate.[22] Kodak has invigorated its Asian distribution by taking minority stakes in over fifty suppliers and customers. Some firms are taking ownership shares of firms engaged in promising research. Others have entered into financial arrangements that gave them the advantages of ownership without the formalities of ownership.

On the grounds that the "American" auto industry was too concentrated, Washington maintained stiff opposition to early ventures between Detroit and international competitors that, in Washington's view, would unduly concentrate production technology or management know-how. When GM and Toyota proposed to create NUMMI, the joint production venture for compact cars in California with GM workers under Toyota managers, the FTC strongly reacted to the venture, expressing initial opposition on the grounds that it would inhibit GM from making its own "American" compact cars and that the firms would share too much information on production plans. Commissioners complained that it was unlikely that promised innovations would really arise from the venture and that it was not the "least anticompetitive" way to transfer Toyota management expertise to GM. The FTC wielded its power to extract a highly restrictive consent decree from the partners. They could proceed only if production was limited to 200,000 cars, the venture would terminate in eight years (later extended), and severe restrictions were placed on the flow of information between Toyota and GM.

Despite the restrictions, NUMMI eventually proved a great success. The NUMMI cars quickly became the highest-quality cars in GM's fleet. GM workers labeled unmanageable under the old system proved to be highly productive under the venture's new cooperative management style. GM management began to assimilate Toyota's "continuous improvement" *kaizen* process in its other operations.

The NUMMI venture was a breakthrough event for the competitive structure of the American auto industry. Before NUMMI there were no significant joint ventures between Detroit's automakers. By the early 1990s, several major strategic alliances had been launched. GM, Ford, and Chrysler formed a venture to create composite materials. Chrysler and GM joined to create New Venture Gears for joint production of drivetrain parts. All three firms created a venture to build electric vehicles. With Navistar International, the three firms have joined in a venture for emission-control research. "High-speed multiflexing"— electronic control systems—is the subject of another three-way venture. Five U.S. semiconductor firms joined in a new alliance in 1994 to make chips for another carmaker, Toyota. Washington's General Accounting Office actually reported to policymakers that American companies are increasingly behaving like *keiretsu*.[23]

The term *strategic alliances* is, of course, a favorite buzzword in every competitiveness debate. But its common usage fails to capture the revolutionary nature of these new interdependent relationships. American firms, from a context of too few and poorly focused relationships, and Japanese firms, from a context of "too many" relationships, are converging toward a new global form of *keiretsu*.

Confusion swept through regulatory offices when Cummins announced new owners in 1990. Two hundred fifty million dollars was invested in the Indiana-based company by Japanese competitor Kubota Ltd., truck-engine customer Ford Motor, and tractor-engine customer Tenneco. The deal fit none of Washington's analytical templates. It was a horizontal-vertical, shared technology-sales-management "pretzel." Cummins and Kubota had achieved a concentration without a merger. Tenneco had beaten the barriers to entry that should have kept it out of engine production. Linked to the arrangement, moreover, were plans for Ford to exit the production of midrange engines in favor of Cummins, joint Cummins-Kubota engine production in Europe, and various technology exchanges.[24] Quipped an antitrust lawyer in Washington: "The deal blew out a few circuits" in antitrust offices. But when the smoke cleared, industry observers gave a big nod to the two words used by the Cummins chairman to capture the essence of the deal: "global competitiveness."

Washington regulators claim to be accommodating such changes, pointing to recent policy statements, even minor amendments to the current law, that demonstrate what they call a commitment to alliances. Laws were in fact changed in 1984 and 1993 to provide limited-support joint ventures in research and production. But the fight over *keiretsu* and actual regulatory activity speak far louder than any such rhetoric and minor legislative activity. Washington's attitude toward "combinations" among companies has changed little; American antitrust law still impedes the type of alliances needed for success in new global industries. Limited support for traditional manufacturing and research activity is not nearly enough to empower the bold new relationships demanded by global competition. For many firms, strength may be gained by cooperation, but to old-world antitrust perspectives, cooperation frequently equates to collusion. Many alliances rely on a framework of distribution, resale, or sales-agency restrictions and financial or management links that bring heartburn to traditional regulators. That heartburn, as expressed in speeches by enforcers and industrywide "fishing expedition" investigations, can be as inhibiting as any frontal assault on a firm.

Policymakers bent on protecting what they perceived as the American semiconductor industry were aghast when AT&T entered into a technology-pooling agreement with NEC of Japan so that the American firm could make NEC chips and the firms would cooperate on use of the chips and other production technology. Traditional antitrust regulators shudder over close ties between such giants, especially those involving critical technology. But as Michiyuki Uenohara, former head of research at NEC, has explained, "R&D resources in the world are scarce; even big companies scream for these resources. If we don't collaborate, we can't advance. It's too expensive even for NEC."[25] Similar shock waves were felt in April 1994, when IBM announced that it had entered into an alliance to supply mainframe computer technology and hardware to longtime archrival Hitachi and again in October 1995, when Siemens, Motorola, and Toshiba announced that they would concentrate over $1 billion in resources for development of a new generation of memory chips—at IBM facilities in New York and Vermont.

But company advisers still face conundrums every day in trying to read the minds of regulators with respect to such unorthodox new pairings. Washington has openly encouraged teaming among defense firms for new procurements, for example. But when Alliant Techsystems and Aerojet General did so in 1993, they were penalized $12 million by Washington for creating an "anticompetitive" team.[26]

It is, quite simply, impossible to draw a bright, rational line around some interest groupings and label them illegal while supporting the rest—although Washington continues to try to do so. Washington's big concession to these new realities has been not to change its standards but only to change its penalties. The National Cooperative Research and Production Act of 1993, which received so much fanfare as evidence of a new age for antitrust in America, did nothing more than provide that certain research and production joint ventures would, if challenged under the antitrust laws, be liable only for actual damages instead of the triple damages normally assessed. "So now if they don't like my venture," concluded a disappointed Silicon Valley executive after reviewing the '93 law, "they won't force me into bankruptcy, only take a year or two's profit." Even to qualify for that limited benefit, joint ventures have to notify the details of their ventures to Washington (for public notice), including the nationality of the parties. If the joint venture is involved in production, moreover, the principal production facility of the venture must be in the United States—a limit that to many observers utterly betrayed the promise of the new rule. The alliances generated by the new economy thus were blessed only if they sourced production according to Washington's political dynamics instead of real-world competitive dynamics.

Once again, in the guise of responding to new realities, regulators snatched defeat out of the jaws of victory. The essential value of research and sourcing ventures is their flexibility. Their power lies in liquidity, having full access to diverse ideas and places, being able to surface new techniques and respond to new dynamics wherever and whenever the marketplace demands. Congress took a vital new concept and slammed it into a Flat Earth box.

Nowhere in the underlying debate in passage of the amendments was the obvious question asked: Since enterprises should be judged on their actual effects in their markets, why require the *formation* of ventures to be subject to *any* legal strictures? Washington remains unable to cope with alliances from its old-world framework. "A lot of these ventures are incestuous," a veteran regulator complained to lawyers who came to discuss telecommunications alliances. "How am I supposed to react to the company that wants a venture with competitor A in one region and competitor B in another region for the same subject matter? How can we abide the potential for collusion?" But U.S. West, for example, has a phone/cable venture with Time Warner in the United States and the "same" alliance with Telecommunications Inc. in Britain to be competitive in two different local environments, not to cartelize the world. No small part of U.S. West's patchwork of relationships, moreover, is driven by Washington's long-standing prohibition on manufacturing, interexchange, and information service business by U.S. West and the other AT&T spin-offs.

WASHINGTON'S ANTICOMPETITIVE ANTITRUST SOLUTIONS

In 1993, a Hong Kong venture capitalist was approached by a California firm with a proposal to fund a new company with an exciting new software product for biotechnology applications. Fundamental to the business plan was a series of alliances with computer, chemical, pharmaceutical, and food-processing firms. The Hong Kong investor agreed to do the deal but only on the condition that it would be based outside the United States and be initially focused on European and Asian markets. A confused American manager asked for an explanation. The investor had been involved in several U.S. ventures, he stated, and based on his sour experience with regulators in Washington, said there was "no way I'll invite Washington to second-guess my plans again."

Huge opportunities are being lost by American firms as they try to puzzle out how to become competitive while still meeting the outdated strictures of U.S. antitrust law. The message they hear from antitrust regulators is disheartening. Be bloodthirsty global competitors, they are told, but if you do too good a job we will investigate you. Invest billions in research, but if you strike gold (meaning you are able to preempt the competition for one product cycle), you will be in our sights as a monopolist. Cultivate alliances for sharing ideas and sourcing components, but if you cross over our invisible line, we will attack you for collusion. Build the information superhighway with a route through the telecommunications, television, computer, and consumer electronics industries, but if any of you in those sectors want to cooperate in building it, you better ask our permission.

The original Sherman Act was fashioned to protect consumers. Other laws were added to protect American firms from other firms with "unfair" advantage or to protect the "public" interest. But none of these goals are effectively served by the antitrust laws today. The goals themselves have been overwhelmed by new realities. In an economy where the global consumer is the king, it is ironic indeed that the competitiveness of so many firms is undermined by Washington in the name of helping consumers. In an economy where success often requires concentrated resources, traditional assumptions about concentrated industries are themselves anticompetitive. In an economy where shifting barriers to entry and shifting markets redefine industries every few months, regulatory action based on projections of industry five years—or three years—from now is nonsensical. Such assumptions about cause and effect have become leaps of faith. Entire industries are being held hostage to the speculation of competition regulators.

Ultimately there is no hope for meaningful reform until policymakers understand that the most effective antitrust policy is policy that encourages global competition—meaning policy that embraces global enterprise, maximizes the reach of innovation across borders, and recognizes that the United States is not an island but a region of the global economy. To reach that conclusion, however, they must first understand the implications of a compelling new reality: Traditional antitrust has become one of the most insidious tools of protectionism wielded by Washington. The primary target of modern antitrust policy has become change—through merger, acquisition, new joint ventures, new capital, new technology, and new owners—and barriers to change in the new economy are barriers to innovation and growth. Attacks on the new generation of concentrations and alliances amount to protecting existing old-world industry structures—and there could be no surer antigrowth policy for America than the protection of such structures.

Like dinosaurs trying to learn a new diet, antitrust regulators prowl through emerging global industries. While they lecture new market economies on their need for clones of the American laws, other industrial nations adopt blocking statutes to stop the enforcement of Washington's policies within their own borders. While they cling to old-world paradigms of monopoly, other countries nurture the new interdependent concentrations as engines of innovation. The ultimate solution for Washington's obsolete competition policy is removing it from the realm of speculation—which means ending its role in clearing mergers, acquisitions, and ventures on the basis of presumed future effects. Competition enforcers should be consumer protection enforcers in the strict sense: guardians against pernicious activities such as actual price fixing, false advertising, and direct fraud on consumers. But reform will not come easily. In 1993, Congressman Robert Walker of Pennsylvania, who had pushed unsuccessfully for fundamental reform on the grounds that the antitrust laws were no longer relevant to modern global markets, attached a "Sense of the Congress" statement to a bill for research funding. The statement called for reform of the antitrust laws to remove all barriers to cooperative enterprise. But the head of the House Ways and Means Committee demanded that the statement be removed because it was not relevant to the subject of the bill—which, as stated by the Committee, was the future of American technology.[27]

LOSING ITS PLACE

The New
Global Capital

In the mid-1980s, IBM made an unorthodox decision that attracted harsh criticism from government and industry observers: It chose to refrain from investing several hundred million dollars in a U.S. factory to make DRAM memory components. Although IBM itself had developed much of the underlying technology, it decided to contract production to Japanese firms. Many policymakers in Washington condemned the choice. To them it was wrong in every respect: It represented the loss of manufacturing assets and jobs, the surrender of U.S. technology leadership, and an increase in what they considered our biggest "competitiveness" problem—the trade deficit with Japan. IBM's move triggered calls for controls on foreign investment by U.S. firms, heightened restrictions on sharing American technology, and government intervention in memory-chip markets.

But judged from by criteria of the then-emerging global economy, the decision was a shrewd manipulation of capital that at the time sharply enhanced IBM's competitiveness. It leveraged its competitors' obsession with manufacturing with an innovative contract structure that turned Japanese capital on itself: The Japanese leapt into a race against themselves to invest in fixed assets for new capacity. Their new factories drove down prices to a point where U.S. producers were able to secure DRAMs for less than it would have cost to produce them, giving them a major competitive advantage in global markets while penalizing their

Asian competitors. Ultimately, the frenzy of Japanese investors to invest in hard assets lost them over $3 billion, while subsidizing the development of the next generation of memory chips by U.S. producers.

Flat Earth perspectives would have called for IBM to jealously cling to its technology, to spend hundreds of millions of dollars on a new production fortress in the United States, and to use the resulting product to bludgeon competitors from across the sea—despite the fact that the technological edge would have been fleeting, the factory quickly obsolete, and the ultimate job losses far more numerous at home than abroad. IBM succeeded, at least in that particular battle, by defying traditional wisdom and driving the forces of the new economy to its advantage.

Washington eventually again snatched defeat from the jaws of victory by intervening to manage trade in memory chips, and in the years to come, IBM would stumble mightily as it tried to cope with the effects of the new economy. But its strategic win in early DRAM production was one of the earliest examples of how the new economy has revolutionized the scope, significance, and strategic role of capital.

Fifteen years ago, or 115 years ago, the dynamics of capital were not of strategic or political concern. Capital was a prosaic fact of life, a fixed element of the economic landscape that followed orderly, predictable patterns. Everyone understood what capital was. You obtained it from banks or shareholders. You poured it into the ground and payroll accounts to build products. It presented itself in easily recognizable, decimal-perfect columns in financial statements and annual reports. It was, as any graduate of Economics 101 could tell you, the assets employed in production of more assets, the wealth used to build more wealth. Capital was not, moreover, particularly mobile across borders. International transfers of capital merited mere footnotes in the economic reports of companies and the nation. Capital always moved far less efficiently than goods across borders. Like everything else in the old economy, its characteristics and its markets were overwhelmingly domestic. Here, as elsewhere in the old economy, government could be effective because it regulated captive markets. When the SEC or the Federal Reserve imposed new rules on the management of capital, those who owned the capital might complain, but neither they nor those who used their capital could avoid the rules, meaning the markets controlled by Washington were not particularly sensitive to the burden of regulation.

But that world no longer exists. With an explosion of activity that began a decade ago, capital has become incontrovertibly, irrevocably global. In 1970, cross-border corporate securities transactions involving

U.S. buyers or sellers equated to 3 percent of GDP. In 1980 it was 9 percent. By 1990 it was 93 percent, and in 1993 it was 135 percent. In Japan, such trading was 20 percent of GDP in 1975, 119 percent by 1990. England's cross-border securities transactions soared to 690 percent of GDP by 1990 and to over 1,000 percent by 1993.

In 1985, U.S. investors' *net* purchases of stock in the fourteen primary emerging-country markets was a mere $86 million. By 1992 it was $5.32 billion—a sixty-two-fold increase. The total volume of U.S. securities bought by foreign investors reached $700 billion in 1994, up from $70 billion in 1980. This explosive growth is no mere reflection of the expansion of U.S. securities markets generally: Foreign participation in U.S. securities markets has exceeded market growth overall by more than 50 percent since 1984.[1] In the past five years, new stock exchanges have opened around the planet in such cities as Shanghai, Moscow, Prague, Sofia, Riga, and Budapest; the International Finance Corporation reports that more than sixty exchanges now operate in emerging markets alone.[2] Equity shares of the world's ten largest global companies trade on seventy different exchanges. In 1993, on a global basis, investors purchased a net $159.2 billion in stocks from countries other than their own, up from less than $15 billion in 1987 and $100 billion in 1991. U.S. pension funds, some of the most sophisticated investors on the planet, have led the way: In 1993 they held $262 billion of their capital in foreign securities.[3] During the first half of 1995, foreign buyers bought 86 percent of the new issues of U.S. government debt.[4] Approximately one out of every four stock transfers in the world today is made across national borders.

From 1985 to 1990, flows of direct capital investment from the top five industrial countries grew by 27 percent a year; since 1990 it has grown by another 25 percent. In 1982 the total of outstanding international bonds was $259 billion. At the end of the decade, it was $1.65 trillion. By 1993 the total resources of international financial institutions alone was $14 trillion. Cross-border bank loans increased from $265 billion in 1975 to $4.2 trillion by 1994. The total stock of financial assets traded in world capital markets reached an estimated $35 trillion in 1992, equivalent to 200 percent of the GDP of the OECD countries.[5]

Foreign-exchange transfers are one of the most direct indicators of the global integration of commerce and finance. According to the Bank of International Settlements, foreign-exchange trading was less than $20 billion a day in 1982. By 1986 it had reached $325 billion a day. By 1993 it was just over $1 trillion daily, and today it is $1.3 trillion.[6] The global value of derivatives like options and swaps was $1.1 trillion in 1986. Five years later, it was $6.9 trillion. At the end of 1995, the notational value of outstanding derivatives around the world was $41 trillion.

The increased volume in capital movement doesn't simply mean more of the same, a multiplication of the transactions and strategies applied to capital in the old economy. Here, as elsewhere in the global context, many fall victim to the extrapolation syndrome: Globalized capital is not the capital that we knew in 1970 merely experienced on a larger scale. The very character of capital has been revolutionized. First, of course, it has no flag. Over 200,000 real-time screens operate at trading firms around the globe. Not only does the new global capital have no home today in the sense of traditional sovereign goods, it leaps across oceans in pursuit of new opportunities at a velocity of 9 inches a nanosecond, the speed of an electron through a cable. A report on a technology breakthrough, exchange rates, or other developments from one terminal can spark a billion dollars of trade at another, shifting from one continent to another the capital that competing interests seek for a new factory in Iowa, a new office building in Hokkaido Prefecture, or a new research lab in the Departement de la Rhône. At every hour of every day and night, billions of dollars are being flashed electronically around the globe. In a very real sense, many of these transactions do not occur in a place at all. The new capital has lost its place.

It has not only lost its place geographically. Capital has also changed because its sources have changed, its movements have changed, its uses have changed, the ways it can be managed have changed, its very context for strategy and policy has changed. Inseparable from those changes is the revolution of competition itself: As discussed earlier, the lines defining "industry" have blurred, the sources of leadership have diversified, the very nature of strategic advantage has been altered.

Today's adept global manager can carve out an industry leadership position by replacing millions in capital for a new plant with a few transpacific air tickets or even buying the knowledge that eliminates "production" altogether. He or she can eliminate entire links in the traditional chain of value, turn one link into the source of all an enterprise's value, even reassemble the links into revolutionary new structures. For some firms, the new capital eliminates the need for fixed assets altogether—as can be seen in Nike's global empire, built around 75,000 Asian workers who are all on someone else's payroll. For managers who combined a grasp of technology evolution in their industry with the recognition that Japanese competitors were still preoccupied with typing up capital in hard assets, IBM's decision to shift capital spending on early DRAM production to its competitors was a no-brainer. Managers who understand the new economy are able to array their capital like slight explosive charges that can crack, and eventually destroy, the foundations of industry leaders. With the right timing, investment in a standards writer in Holland, a physicist in Moscow, a software programmer in India, or a product line in Brazil or Bangkok can buy the competitive advantage needed to seize leadership.

Such advantage derives from the dynamics of liquidity and diversity, meaning the essential process of the global economy by which scores of billions of dollars annually seek out diverse knowledge and from it extract value. But contrary to the advice of popular "information age" gurus that the new economy runs on knowledge or even that knowledge *is* the new capital, knowledge alone never creates value. It needs to be connected to markets to derive value, which means it has to be moved through software, engineers, financial systems, product designers, marketers, and hundreds of other possible conduits, both tangible and intangible. It doesn't move spontaneously. It is moved by capital. Capital creates knowledge—by investment in people and the assets empowering people—but value is only created when knowledge has, through the application of capital, been identified, packaged, and applied to a specific problem. Knowledge may have replaced machine tools in the new economy, but, just like machine tools in the old economy, without capital it is useless.

Savvy global managers, however, always prefer to steer capital to knowledge rather than raw materials or factories. Not many years ago, those directing capital in telecommunications-equipment firms arrived at a crossroads. They could invest in new copper-wire systems, or they could venture into bold new knowledge investments. Those able to change their tradition-bound institutions created knowledge-intensive fiber-optic technology, with 12 percent material/energy content. They are rapidly replacing—at a rate of 1,300 miles a day in the United States alone—both the labor-intensive, resource-depleting copper wire (with over 50 percent material/energy content) and the firms that clung to those hard-wire systems. In the old world, iron was smelted to get rid of silicon as an impurity. Those who moved capital to knowledge found vastly greater value in processing silicon to get rid of iron—making semiconductor chips with less than 2 percent material/energy content.

But capital standing still has no power to create such innovation. Without liquidity of capital, the global economic process is frustrated. Without the process of global capital, the awesome churning of money and innovation that gave birth to the software industry would never have been possible. After Bill Gates of Microsoft found the key to powerful new markets by turning computers into personal desktop devices, enough capital converged on the idea from around the planet to create 14,000 new American firms in less than a decade.

Such growth would have been impossible without liquidity of capital. We have irrevocably crossed the threshold of liquidity that makes the global economic process possible. But the awesome volume of capital flowing through global pipelines does not mean that those pipelines are always efficient. The global plebiscite will never allow an opportunity as vast and as obvious as that of personal computers to go unfunded, but many other opportunities are being frustrated by impediments to global liquidity, causing pockets of relative stagnation and disparities of opportunity within industries and between nations.

We are beyond the point where anyone can plausibly deny that international financial flows have been integrated into America's economy. Those flows have become organically subsumed. They have been incorporated into the economic lifeblood of the country, and every impediment to that flow raised by Washington is an impediment to the new configurations of value that drive competitive advantage.

Restricting the flow of capital, moreover, doesn't penalize a few investors. It restricts the exchange of technology. It inhibits the creation of jobs. It handicaps the building of new knowledge assets. It chills the movement of experts—meaning it chills the process of innovation. It discourages risk-taking. It is not incremental opportunity that is thereby lost; it is exponential levels of new enterprise and the leadership of industries. It could be the next generation of Silicon Valley, which may reside in France, Korea, Germany, Britain, or China if the dynamics of global capital are not recognized and supported in the United States.

Obstacles to that new capital are entrenched in decades-old policy—and further obstacles continue to be erected as a result of anachronistic perspectives on what capital is, how it works, and who uses it. By failing to perceive the dramatic ways in which capital has been transformed, regulators clog the plumbing through which financial resources flow. They deny opportunities for precisely those enterprises that are capable of adding the greatest value within the United States. They drive companies to other venues where the plumbing flows more freely. They complain about national capital markets under siege from abroad when in fact the primary siege has been raised by regulators themselves. They posture themselves as global financial police on the assumption that global markets and investors are, or should be, clones of American markets and investors. They grouse about market disparities when in fact many of those disparities are created by their own false perceptions of the scope and content of the new global capital.

Accustomed to dealing with capital issues in terms of regulated financial institutions, they demand new cross-border controls on capital when what the nation desperately needs is a greater opening to global capital. Instead of greeting the awesome new opportunities offered by the globalization of capital, they seem to react with fear and paranoia—for from the Flat Earth perspective, the new global capital is a monster that defies characterization but must be tamed.

OUT OF BALANCE, OUT OF CONTROL

In 1944 John Maynard Keynes spoke to world leaders about a vital premise for the international financial framework being laid at Bretton Woods for the postwar economy:

> We intend to retain control of our domestic rate of interest, so that we can keep it as low as suits our own purposes, without interference from the ebb and flow of international capital movement or flights of hot money . . . Not merely as a feature of the transition, but as a permanent arrangement, the plan accords to every member-government the explicit right to control capital movements.

At the heart of that framework so concisely reflected by Keynes were familiar themes of the trading economy: sovereign control and captive markets. Control over interest rates, control over capital movements, control over "flights" of money, control especially over whatever threatened to undermine sovereignty. The predictable effect of these familiar themes was protectionism. Since perspectives on international capital were bred in policy machines preoccupied with merchandise trade, debate on international financial flows has, not surprisingly, been dominated by talk of national capital balances. There was a widespread impression that balanced accounts or capital "surpluses" were the appropriate goal for policymakers. A Congressman from Texas was recently asked to support a new factory in his state to be funded by Japanese investors. "I gave up trying to stop Americans from buying all their goods, but I'll be damned if we'll become addicted to their capital too," he groused. "What's wrong with American money?"

Among Washington's multitude of Flat Earth concepts, that of balancing capital or "claiming" a fair share of capital is easily one of the most absurd. Protecting capital balances is not merely undesirable in the new economy; it is impossible. Because the balance of payment figures used to benchmark capital flows are net figures, as merchandise sales gaps fall, the apparent flow of capital drops. By definition, a country with a balanced current account has no net flow of capital. Many of the new production, research, and human assets that have invigorated thousands of American companies during the past fifteen years would not have been possible but for capital "imbalances"—i.e., the imported capital from non–U.S. banks and investors that funded them.

Failure to understand the dynamics of capital flows also aggravates our dangerous obsession with merchandise accounts. The dollars used to buy U.S. imports don't disappear: They return to finance more transactions—if not export transactions, then investment transactions. In the always-popular attacks on the "foreigners" who cause our deficits, no one bothers to consider the fact that the amount of the trade deficit is always precisely equal to the amount of capital arriving from offshore to fund economic growth. While the merchandise deficit soared in the 1980s, the United States was enjoying greater growth than any other industrial nation on the planet. It is a mathematical certainty that countries with trade-account surpluses (i.e., more exports than imports) will always have a capital-account deficit.

The "balancing" of accounts was almost invariably appealing to policymakers of another day. But today we know such an effort is meaningless: A balanced account does not mean a country is financially self-sufficient. A balanced account could arise, for example, when a country borrowed heavily offshore and its companies sent their earnings overseas. But the effort is also grossly misleading, since it implies that the books are in order, that regulatory systems are performing as they should, that everything is under control.

Control, after all, was the vital premise of capital policy in the old economy. A recurring theme at official hearings on the financial regulatory system is alarm over the fact that billions of dollars are moving in and out of the country and "we don't know about it" or "we aren't able to control them." As a factual matter, such statements are absolutely correct. As a rallying cry for greater regulation, however, they are dangerously misguided.

CAPITAL PUNISHMENT IN AMERICA

For many active in global industries, the most obvious capital penalties levied by Washington have been administered by the Internal Revenue Service. Perhaps the most notorious arose in 1963, when Washington imposed a 30 percent withholding tax on interest paid on bonds sold in the United States to foreigners. The justification for the tax was a familiar one: It would help balance U.S. capital accounts and dollar bonds were themselves captive and therefore insensitive to regulation. But that assumption was wrong. The market for such bonds migrated to London, creating the Eurobond market through which scores of billions in capital have moved. Although the tax was repealed many years later, the damage was done: The market never returned to New York. By attracting hordes of new customers to the city of London, the move strengthened London's role in foreign exchange trading; today London conducts twice the foreign exchange trading volume of New York.

More subtle but much more sweeping has been the damage done by taxes imposed on gains from capital. It is no coincidence that many of the leaders in global industries come from countries like Germany, Holland, and Switzerland, which promote capital growth by taxing income from growth, not growth itself. Nothing depicts Washington's lack of understanding of this point better than a simple calculation showing the fate of $1 invested over twenty years: In the many industrial nations without capital-gains taxes, $1 in capital that doubles each year through shrewd management and is sold for capital gain will be worth $1 million in two decades. If it is $1 of American capital, however, that same $1 will be worth only $20,000 after twenty years. Capital-gains disparities have sharply defined the direction of many knowledge-intensive (meaning high-tech, capital-intensive) industries. Since 1970 three Swiss companies, for example, have spent $7 billion on American biotechnology companies, amassing what has been characterized as the "largest foreign share ever of an emerging American technology."[7] The three firms, Roche Holdings, Ciba-Geigy, and Sandoz, were able to do so—unlike their American counterparts—because their capital is so much less costly due to the lack of capital-gains taxes and accounting rules that facilitate use of capital in acquisitions. American firms, unable to match the Swiss in amassing vast pools of capital, are often forced to borrow funds for acquisitions, effectively facing double penalties as a result of capital-gains taxes that erode capital accounts and the interest paid for borrowing capital.

Washington distracts itself by looking at capital-gains taxes in terms of "giveaways" to rich Americans, a view that blinds it to the much more profound implications of capital-gains taxes in global growth. Over fifty countries impose no tax on most forms of capital gains. The list with no or very low capital-gains taxes includes many of the nations that have been reaping the greatest bounty from the global economy, such as Japan, Taiwan, Mexico, South Korea, China, Malaysia, and Singapore. It's no coincidence that during the ascendancy of global capital in the late 1980s, those countries with the lowest tax rates enjoyed the highest growth rates. Polyconomics, of Morristown, New Jersey, has conducted one of the most comprehensive of the many studies done on this point, examining the relationship between tax rates and growth in the last half of the 1980s. Leading growth during the period was Hong Kong, with a 97 percent gain in GDP and a composite tax rate of 15.9 percent. At the bottom was Denmark, with 8 percent GDP growth and a 80.2 percent tax rate. With a composite tax rate of 51 percent, the United States had a lackluster 18 percent total growth over the five-year period.

NO LONG-TERM CAPITAL-GAINS TAX

Nations that do not tax individuals on long-term capital gains realized on holdings of corporate securities:

Antigua, Argentina, Austria, Barbados, Belgium, Bermuda, Bolivia, Brunei, Cayman Islands, China, Costa Rica, Cyprus, Dominica, Egypt, Germany, Greece, Grenada, Hong Kong, Isle of Man, Ivory Coast, Jamaica, Kenya, Kuwait, Libya, Macua, Malaysia, Malta, Mauritius, Mexico, Morocco, Namibia, the Netherlands, Netherlands Antilles, New Caledonia, New Zealand, Panama, Papua New Guinea, Paraguay, Peru, Portugal, St. Lucia, Singapore, Solomon Islands, South Africa, South Korea, Swaziland, Switzerland, Taiwan, Thailand, Trinidad & Tobago, Turks & Caicos, Uganda, United Arab Emirates, Vanuatu, Zambia

Sources: Coopers & Lybrand, Price Waterhouse.

Those who perpetuate the capital-gains-tax stand are stubbornly rooted in doctrines of taxation established fifty and sixty years ago, when theoreticians like Robert Haig of Columbia University and H. C. Simons of the University of Chicago developed the expansive tax model for annual income used by the Internal Revenue Service ever since: Income equals existing wealth (at the start of a year) plus consumption minus wealth at the end of the year. In that mind-set, any differential between general income tax and a tax on capital gains constitutes a subsidy or "tax expenditure" by the federal government. Such underpinnings are not academic in any sense. Every year, bureaucrats validate the model by circulating catalogs of such "expenditures" granted to American investors, underscoring the perception by legions of policymakers that the only real issue with respect to capital-gains taxation is the size of the handout to those who hold capital assets (i.e., the differential between the capital-gains tax and the general income tax).

The reality, however, is that the capital-gains tax constitutes a huge monkey wrench dropped into the plumbing of global capital. It creates a vast clogging in the flow of our financial system, since, ironically, it doesn't meaningfully affect the wealth of the "rich" (i.e., the capital without its gain) but affects only *when* they realize gain. It is a tax on the most vital aspect of the new capital—*liquidity*. Its most direct impact is on those trying to become rich—those responsible for moving most capital, always the most important economic forces in any country. The effects of capital-gains taxes on entrepreneurs, the source of most innovation, growth, and new jobs, is stark. Between 1982 and 1986, when capital-gains taxes were 20 percent, new business incorporations rose 24 percent, about 4.4 percent a year. But from 1987 to 1993, after the tax was increased to 28 percent, new business incorporations rose a paltry 0.5 percent, a rate of 0.1 percent annually. Senator Connie Mack, chairman of the Joint Economic Committee, has estimated that at least $1.5 trillion in U.S. capital is locked up, unwilling to move because of Washington's capital-gains tax.[8]

Taxing those gains severely chills the reallocation of scores of billions in capital, meaning that when global capital flows across the United States, its vitality is weakened. Whenever those holding capital consider moving their money to investments made more attractive by new technology, new organizations, and new configurations of value, they find Washington squarely in their path, wielding a powerful and painful club. After the heavy tax increases of 1993, *Forbes* magazine published new advice on how to cope with Washington's latest measures: Don't sell any stock. In other words, *don't move capital*. The inflationary environment in America during the 1980s only increased the pain: Washington's failure to index capital gains for inflation meant that the government took nearly a 60 percent slice of profit on investments held for more than four years.

Global capital is acutely responsive to government claims on its returns. Because the United States imposes double taxation on returns to shareholders—taxed as income to the company and then again as income to the shareholder—U.S. investors are significantly disadvantaged. Gary Hufbauer of the Institute for International Economics has calculated that on the basis of federal taxes alone, a U.S. firm must earn $220 in gross income to pay net income of $100 to an individual shareholder. British, German, and French firms need earn only $165, $157, and $176, respectively, to provide the same return to shareholders.[9]

Clyde McAvoy, president of Avtek Pacific Inc., searched desperately for "American" capital to fund his firm's new Kevlar composite aircraft. His plane was 300 percent more efficient, flew faster and higher, weighed 30 percent less, was 15 percent stronger, and was cheaper than its metal-alloy counterparts. But those firms ready to put up the $20 million needed to start operations were all based outside the United States. McAvoy complains that $7 trillion in venture capital can be identified in the U.S. economy, "but most of it is locked up and unlikely to be unleashed with a capital-gains tax rate that acts as a disincentive to investment." Venture-capital investment has stagnated—in 1994 it was $2.7 billion, only $60 million more than the 1985 level and $500 million less than the 1986 level. McAvoy believes that America's sluggish capital pipelines have a lot to do with the fact that in 1992, America for the first time imported more planes that it exported.[10]

Avtek's plight highlights the aspect of capital-gains taxation that Washington consistently ignores: implications for global competitiveness. Far from being the perfect vehicle for funding social-welfare programs, as many in Washington have avowed, the tax strikes to the core of the country's competitiveness—because competitiveness is driven by innovators like Avtek. Firms with a high "competitiveness" content in the new economy also have a high capital content.

The impact of the capital-gains-tax increase in the Tax Reform Act of 1986 offered a sobering lesson that was conveniently ignored in Washington. The higher tax devastated U.S. venture-capital sources precisely when unprecedented opportunities were arising—in other words, when entrepreneurs needed them the most. The tax battered the price/earnings ratios of high-tech firms by denying them sources of growth. As traditional domestic capital sources dried up and Washington drove the dollar down to help commodity producers, a deluge of foreign investors was triggered in the high-tech sectors, investors who could not resist the bargains offered up to them by Washington. While U.S. investors "rationalized" their use of capital by locking it into less-productive but low-risk investments, investors from Europe and Asia picked up high-tech assets in the United States for 50 to 75 percent less than what they would have cost at home. Washington's response? It called for hearings to find ways to restrict the unfair invasion of foreigners in American's high-tech industries.

153

BANKING ON FAILURE

Washington has done little better in helping American financial institutions cope with the new realities of global capital. Its anachronistic concepts of how capital and financial systems work has become a huge burden on American banking. In 1991 the General Accounting Office examined the cross-border implications of the rules that govern America's financial institutions and concluded that they have resulted in "loss of international business and influence" for America. As an understatement, such a conclusion rivals the early reports that the Titanic had a minor encounter with an iceberg.

Of the thirty largest banks in the world, how many are based in the United States? Until 1995, only one—Citibank. It was ranked number one in the world in 1985. By 1990 it was number ten. In 1993 it was number twenty-seven. The merger of Chemical Bank and Chase Manhattan created the largest U.S. bank, but even that is only the twenty-first largest in the world. Of the thirty most creditworthy banks, how many are in the United States? Three. The list is dominated by banks from countries that nurture capital: Germany, Switzerland, and the Netherlands.[11] In the new economy, one would expect non–U.S. financial institutions to be somewhat involved in corporate lending. But according to the widely respected annual Greenwich Associates benchmark study of banking relationships in the United States, large American companies today are actually using *more* foreign banks than American banks for corporate lending. A recent Greenwich survey of 1,200 of the largest American firms showed that they used a mean of 8.4 non–U.S. banks and 8.2 U.S. banks for their overall banking needs. Even when looking at new lending for U.S. operations only, American banks are ahead by the slimmest of margins.[12] The explanation lies not with alleged differences in the cost of capital but with the international competitiveness of American banking generally.

The ever-weakening position of U.S. banks can be traced to the failure of Washington to adapt its financial regulatory policies to the new realities of global capital. "Second-tier banks in the first-tier market," is how one London banker based in New York describes the role of American banks in their own country. Congressman John J. LaFalce watched in frustration from his seat on the House Banking Committee as the competitive strength of American banks declined; he puts it in more statesmanlike terms: "No banking organization reflects the economic strength of our country as a whole."

At the root of the problem is the traditional protectionism erected not across geographic but across industry borders. The issue is a familiar one to the nation's financial press: Banking, securities, and insurance laws written sixty and seventy years ago restrict the scope of American banks more severely than the laws of any other nation. Elsewhere—especially in the countries that dominate the list of the world's strongest and largest banks—banks are widely permitted to engage in securities, insurance, and real-estate activities, as well as participate in cross-shareholding in industrial firms.[13] But such activities are strictly limited or absolutely prohibited in the United States. Banking executives are painfully aware of the irony that Washington's antitrust laws would otherwise prohibit what Washington's banking laws strictly require. They could not agree within their industry not to compete with insurance or securities firms, but they are compelled to refrain from such competition by their own government. They haven't had to worry about expanding outside the United States—they have had a big enough struggle simply finding a way to expand from Pennsylvania into Ohio.

Reform of the Depression-era Glass-Steagall Act that historically limited banks' participation in securities markets has been debated for years, but meaningful reform of that law and others restricting banks has yet to arrive. As a result, it is easier in some respects for U.S. banks to venture overseas. When they do so, the Federal Reserve Board's Regulation K imposes strict limits on their participation in equities trading and underwriting—which means they must do battle with one hand tied behind their backs since foreign competitors have no similar restrictions. It is no wonder that one of the primary offshore activities of most large U.S. banks during the first half of the 1990s was the dismantling of foreign operations established by a prior generation of managers who had more confidence in both the competitiveness of America's financial institutions and the competitiveness of American financial regulatory systems.[14]

The problem has only been aggravated by recent efforts to "modernize" the system. In the aftermath of the savings-and-loan disasters of the 1980s, Congress in 1991 handed down the Federal Deposit Insurance Corporation Improvement Act, a complex, poorly drafted set of rules that introduced hundreds of new provisions and imposed rigid new capital restrictions, burdensome new reporting requirements, regulation of bank-officer pay, and detailed management rules. Armed with the new measures, regulators were empowered to compel a merger or stock issue for banks they consider inadequately capitalized, remove managers, restrict increases in assets, and control payment of dividends. The share of banks in the total U.S. financial-service market has dropped from nearly 60 percent twenty years ago to a third today.

THE NON-BANK THAT WASHINGTON BUILT

No American financial institution has been more successful in capturing the advantages of the new capital than GE Capital. By navigating around the clutter of Washington's financial regulation—primarily by refraining from retail banking business —it has had a free hand to build new configurations of value, and in doing so has become the envy of banks everywhere. GE Capital has $150 billion in assets. It issues vastly more commercial credit than any other organization in America. Only one American bank, J.P. Morgan, has a higher credit rating. Its profits have exploded by over 20 percent annually for more than a decade. It provides M&A financing, life insurance, mortgage insurance, credit cards, consumer finance, leasing, and traditional corporate financing within its total of twenty-three separate financial businesses. Observers have called it America's "foreign, homegrown bank" because it functions with the competitive flexibility enjoyed by banks outside the United States.

More than a few American bankers have considered turning in their banking charter and selling their retail businesses—probably to one of the many foreign banks moving into America—so they can emulate GE Capital. While they can't be certain of matching the firm's management acumen, they can be certain of one point: GE Capital's lack of constraint from Washington is a primary reason America's most successful bank isn't a bank at all.

Despite their ever-increasing restraints, U.S. banks have been able to construct impressive new configurations of value with the new global capital, developing many popular market-leading products. But Washington has denied them the opportunity to reap many of the benefits. Precisely when rapid technological change was offering bold new opportunities to American banks, Washington denied them the flexibility to exploit those opportunities. In many cases, American banks are forced to confine their innovation to their own shrinking offshore markets due to product-line restrictions imposed by Washington, or license them to foreign competitors better situated to exploit them. Even Federal Reserve Board member David W. Mullins Jr. is frustrated by the system that his own body helps perpetuate. "We have financial institutions that aren't allowed to exploit their experience," Mullins complains. Washington's neglect of its financial institutions has grown so severe that John Reed, chairman of Citibank, has threatened on several occasions to shift the headquarters of America's most global bank from New York to London.

Given the weakness of American banks, the large role played by foreign banks in this country should be no surprise. As noted above, global capital has not ignored the world's largest market; commercial lending by foreign banks in America has sharply increased. Foreign banks' assets in America total over $800 billion; although that capital represents millions of jobs—many of them newly created in high-tech industries—Washington has decided to "protect" Americans from capital originating outside the United States by imposing extra layers of regulation.

Under the Foreign Bank Supervision Enhancement Act, the Federal Reserve has new authority—redundant, since the Comptroller of the Currency and state regulators also control foreign banks—to approve virtually every aspect of a foreign bank's activity in the country. Banks not based in the United States must obtain the Fed's approval to open a branch; denial can be based on a finding that the bank is not adequately supervised by governments outside the United States—no matter how severe its U.S. supervision—as the Fed did in blocking an application by Banco Nacional de Mexico in 1991. The Fed must also bless any foreign stake of more than 5 percent in an American bank. Flying in the face of the reality of global capital was another 1991 measure, which required that foreign banks' lending capacity in the United States be determined solely by reference to its U.S. activity rather than the capital of the whole bank as was previously the case—giving such banks the choice of keeping extra unproductive capital on hand to satisfy Washington or leaving the U.S. market. "Imperialistic" is how one French banker describes these rules—and "redundant." "Why," she asks, "if Washington is going to require me to keep a capital cushion in the United States for protection of customers, does it also need to interfere with the way I am regulated at home?"

THE SEC VERSUS THE WORLD

Global capital, of course, is not confined to the plumbing that flows through America's banks. In fact, the process by which it converts ideas into value is far better suited to direct investment relationships. As global capital markets expand at almost geometric rates, Washington has stubbornly manned barriers against investment by Americans in global operations, making only token concessions to new realities. Just as global companies based in America are able to avoid the disincentives of dealing with American banks by utilizing non–U.S. banks, so too can they tap global capital by reaching out to markets around the planet. But the same is not true for investors within the United States. Washington has effectively forbidden access by many American investors to global firms based outside America. With a few well-publicized exceptions, like the Wall Street listing of Daimler-Benz in the spring of 1993, most foreign firms have been foreclosed from full participation in U.S. equity markets.

Such protectionism for direct investment capital breeds weak markets. It inhibits innovation. It denies opportunity to American investors. It denies those investors the experience of capital diversity enjoyed by global investors elsewhere—leaving them less capable of addressing new opportunities as they arise. It pushes global industry leaders to nurture their roots outside the United States. It makes debt more attractive in many cases than international equity. It isolates the American financial sector precisely when it desperately needs to enjoy greater integration into world markets.

As in the banking sector, security regulators cling to concepts born sixty and seventy years ago to address the very different problems of today's very different world. The most fundamental—though certainly not the sole—problem is the Securities and Exchange Commission's (SEC) traditional requirement that every foreign company that is traded in the United States provide a mirror-image reflection of the books and records kept by domestic U.S. firms. In a new world where diversity is an asset, where looking at circumstances from multiple perspectives is a competitive advantage, the SEC has traditionally required every firm that opens the door of U.S. markets to fit the agency's Procrustean bed. When Daimler-Benz sought listing on the New York Stock Exchange, it was forced to totally reorganize its accounting systems just to satisfy the SEC. Adding to the complexity for such offshore issuers is the need to contend with a patchwork of confusing, usually redundant, state security laws that may impose completely separate registration requirements for equity sales within their borders.

Many in Washington, invoking the SEC's need for comparability of data, consider the requirement to amount to a simple accounting exercise. The concept of applying Generally Accepted Accounting Principles (GAAP) seems eminently fair on its face. This notion couldn't be more wrong. GAAP is not a global concept. As thousands of global enterprises have learned, "generally accepted" means "prevailing American" accounting principles. The tyranny of American GAAP has derailed many global investments—or at least American participation in them. Changing to U.S. accounting practices puts some firms in violation of home-country requirements. Even when such violations are not threatened, having two sets of books is simply not a viable exercise for many global operations. American accounting standards are unique in many respects, and compliance with U.S. standards is immensely complicated and costly for firms with a non–U.S. focus—another hidden but huge American tax on international capital. When Daimler-Benz listed its stock in New York, the firm was sharply criticized at home for confusing its traditional investors with a new dual set of accounting standards and implicitly inviting tax authorities to reexamine the treatment of losses, reserves, and profit—not only at Daimler but at all German companies. In the protest following Daimler's U.S. listing, many German firms declared that they would never float equity on the U.S. market under such onerous terms.

Most large global companies have steadfastly refused to submit themselves to restatement of their books demanded by the SEC. Swiss food giant Nestlé, for example, has steadfastly refused to expand its U.S. equity presence to a full exchange listing. "We do feel that as a service to shareholders and to increase liquidity it would be a good thing [to have a full listing]," notes Reto Domeniconi, Nestlé's executive vice president for finance, "but not at any price."[15] Many foreign executives ask a simple question: What we do is accepted in every other country on earth; we are committing no fraud—why should we change just to satisfy bureaucrats in Washington? While he served as SEC Commissioner, Philip R. Lochner Jr. began to sense that something was seriously wrong with the system: "Many SEC rules are arbitrary and were written in an era when U.S. securities markets could exist in splendid isolation."

Securities regulators protest that they are just trying to reduce financial reporting to a common denominator. Of course, seldom do they ask what denominator is best suited for the global economy; Washington is notorious around the planet for its insistence that common denominators always be American common denominators. Those American denominators, moreover, grow more complex and less useful every year; as former SEC Commissioner J. Carter Beese has written, "Our prospectuses have gone from consumer information documents to litigation tools, written by lawyers for lawyers."[16] In reality what the regulators seek is to *raise* reporting to a uniformly complex, costly basis that will snugly drop into security lawyers' pigeonholes but will not jibe with financial analysis—and therefore capital decision making—

elsewhere in the world. Liquidity is driven by simplicity, which is not a term that exists in the vocabulary of Washington's financial regulators.

Simplicity means commonality across borders, where comparability of data in a broad sense is an obvious necessity. But global capital already speaks a global language, and Washington doesn't have a prayer of substituting its own peculiar regulatory dialect. Managers with global perspective have learned an ironic lesson from such an exercise: Preparing two sets of books to satisfy different regulators often becomes confusing, even misleading, to investors; instead of building confidence in data—as the SEC assumes—it erodes investor confidence. Exchanges elsewhere in the world have worked through the problem, learning to respect home-country accounts. In November 1995 the European Union even proposed a new simplified format for financial reports to help European companies deal with their "American" problem. But the EU would not and should not adopt U.S. standards.

A common playing field is certainly available, but it is not the uneven, inefficient one Washington has created. A senior manager for a British financial house was too polite to raise the point during an international symposium on American capital markets held in Washington—but he opened up over a nightcap. "I keep returning to the same image when I listen to your SEC. I am on a rugby field, and the boy who owns the ball gets roughed up. He sulks, then leaves, saying no one is going to play 'cause it's his ball. Except today there are balls and playing fields all over the planet. We don't need Washington or New York."

Managers of America's stock exchanges have long recognized the need to keep their field open—and globally attractive. They have even wrung enough compromises from securities regulators to bless U.S. stock offerings in the form of American Depository Receipts for about 320 foreign firms[17] and other forms of listing for another 600 companies. But that's only a fraction of the number listed on the London Stock Exchange, where nearly half the turnover is accounted for by foreign companies. It's an even smaller fraction of the several thousand non–U.S. firms that William H. Donaldson, as head of the New York Stock Exchange, identified as meeting Big Board qualifications for listing. A large segment of those firms, consisting of hundreds of sophisticated international companies, have a median market capitalization of $4 billion, twenty times that of U.S. prospects for Big Board listing.[18] Richard Grasso, current chairman of the New York Stock Exchange, estimates that listing by only one third of the foreign companies eligible for listing would double the exchange's market capitalization.[19] But the SEC refuses to approve listings by such firms as long as they decline to construct their financial reporting structures according to SEC specifications.

Washington's posture rests on the assumption that foreign accounting systems are inadequate to protect investors. The intellectual arrogance of that perception has blinded many regulators to compelling evidence that their assumption is incorrect. Numerous studies conducted in recent years have demonstrated that new communication practices in offshore markets have made them just as efficient, meaning as transparent, as U.S. markets. One widely accepted test for market efficiency, long used in U.S. markets, is an analysis of the advantages that professional, sophisticated investors with access to detailed company information have over the average individual who buys on the basis of available public information. Professors Burton Malkiel of Princeton University and William Baumol of New York University, for example, exhaustively studied such elements in the primary Asian and European markets. They found that professionally managed portfolios did not outperform average returns for investors. Malkiel and Baumol concluded that:

> . . . the evidence supports the view that markets for the shares of non–U.S. companies appear to be as efficient as those for U.S. firms . . . . Thus informed investors can expect that the shares of non–U.S. companies are reasonably priced in relation to those of other firms . . . . There is good reason to doubt that investors would benefit at all from any additional disclosure.[20]

Washington's push to Americanize global financial disclosure is wrong not only because it is superfluous but also because it is so counterproductive for the management of capital. Many foreign companies don't provide less information to investors; they only provide *different* information, reflecting not just different financial practices but different management and organizational structures. Rewriting data as if those structures were U.S. structures is often deceptive and insulates investors from the very diversity they need to embrace. Such rewriting doesn't facilitate capital decision making, it only complicates it—and often totally frustrates it.

William C. Freund was chief economist of the New York Stock Exchange during the years when global capital emerged. He has fought a frustrating battle to educate Washington about its distortive rules. "If the

SEC continues to insist that foreign firms abide by America's anachronistic accounting standards," notes Freund, "it will strangle U.S. markets and do irreversible harm to the United States as the world's dominant financial center."[21]

The insensitivity to non–U.S. accounting systems seems endemic to Washington. A program at the Brookings Institution examined how well the Department of Commerce adapted to foreign accounting systems in conducting its investigations into pricing of imports. "There seems to be an implicit bias against a national GAAP that does not correspond to U.S. practices," it reported. The Department of Commerce "after the fact introduces an alien (i.e., U.S.) system of accounting standards and then finds firms and governments guilty of 'unfair,' 'pernicious' conduct for failure to meet the alien, after-the-fact standards."[22]

In some cases, the penalty posed by America's accounting differences extends far beyond a matter of disclosure. One of the great burdens of American telecommunications firms is that U.S. accounting practice requires them to keep the 65 million tons of copper wire currently strung across and under America on their books, depreciating it as a hit against capital every year. U.S. firms seeking to acquire offshore assets, moreover, have long been frustrated by rules that require them to load goodwill onto their books, then amortize it—resulting in an annual hit to earnings (and therefore available capital) for up to forty years.

Firms in many other countries have never faced a similar burden; typically, they are able to simply deduct goodwill from equity. Robert Willens, an analyst with Lehman Brothers, believes that the difference in rules frequently creates "an insurmountable advantage" for foreign firms in investment contests against U.S. companies. The gap between U.S. and foreign practice began to slowly shrink in 1995, when the International Accounting Standards Committee recommended rules for U.S.-style treatment in other countries—but thus far only a handful of countries have adopted the rules.[23] The real-world significance of the goodwill "differential" was dramatically demonstrated in the late 1980s, when British firms launched an unprecedented flurry of U.S. acquisitions—750 separate deals of a total $60 billion value— immediately after the British government announced its plans (later withdrawn) to adopt U.S. style goodwill rules.

Less obvious are many other rules that distort accounting treatments for capital. As a result, "profit" does not mean the same thing in America as it does in Germany, France, Japan, or Great Britain. When it had to recast its books to U.S. GAAP, Daimler-Benz had a $1 billion profit under home-country rules when it sought listing under SEC rules;

the SEC forced the firm to recast that profit into a $100 million loss. The International Accounting Standards Committee and the International Federation of Accountants has slowly been effecting change in such rules, but for many U.S. firms the damage has already been done, and many deeply entrenched accounting differences continue to burden those competing with foreign investors. By the accounting standards in vogue in the United States, many Asian and European firms would have shown chronically unattractive results in recent years, even as they have been securing leading positions in global automotive, chemical, and electronics industries—and all the while attracting satisfied investors who have not had the benefit of the SEC looking over their shoulders.

By forcing global companies to subscribe to an American version of comparability, Washington bureaucrats posture themselves as global regulators. That stance doesn't stop with the listing of securities. Britain's Guiness Plc., for example, wanted to offer stock bonuses to workers in a joint venture in the United States; without a costly process to obtain the SEC's blessing, it wasn't permitted to do so.

Foreign-investment advisers have frequently sought to establish operations in the United States—but of course their presence is inconsistent with the SEC's campaign against international investing by Americans. Vital to the functioning of global markets is access to the diverse views that drive innovation and inform risk-taking. The global economy offers up such information and views with unprecedented efficiency—except for Americans seeking the services of such non–U.S. investment advisers. For many years, under the SEC's so-called Ellis criteria, a non–U.S. investment adviser essentially was not permitted to operate in the United States unless it was capitalized at a level approved by the SEC, had a structure providing for a buffer between its U.S. subsidiary personnel and parent personnel—such as a board consisting of independent American directors—and had employees who were not engaged in giving advice for their offshore parent and who made independent (i.e., U.S.-based) decisions on investment advice. In effect, foreign advisers understood Washington to say that they could operate in the United States only so long as their personnel, structure, and advice had no foreign content—in other words, the SEC told them they could only be "foreign" by being American.

In 1992 the SEC announced that it had liberalized its position to be more internationally sensitive. New criteria were announced when a Brazilian adviser sought access to U.S. customers. Included in the new criteria: All personnel of the U.S. subsidiary and the foreign parent would have to be available at any time to respond to any SEC request for information—meaning any employee of the foreign firm would be subject to mandatory testimony at the arbitrary request of Washington. The SEC confirmed that it intended to reach even information that was not related to U.S. activities of a foreign parent firm. The SEC did not concern itself with the fact that its requirements were in direct conflict with rules in the home countries of many advisers, which often prohibit disclosure of customer information to anyone. The parent, moreover, had to agree that it would waive the right to use any home-country law to shield itself from an SEC request—meaning in essence that the SEC expects a waiver of the very customer confidentiality rights that within the United States it so assiduously protects.

In short, the SEC's global "opening" was the position that "you can open here so long as you put the interests of Americans over the rights of your customers elsewhere in the world." Another requirement imposed by Washington: The adviser would have to keep its books and records of transactions outside the United States in English.

American securities brokers obviously must have global underpinnings to succeed in global capital markets. But the SEC's "ready market" rules pose yet another disincentive to dealing in foreign securities. The "ready market" rules require that a broker dealer take 100 percent deduction in computing its own net capital for any foreign securities it holds for which is there is no "ready market." The SEC's definition of ready market—following its own peculiar notion of the global economy—excludes many foreign markets, meaning the SEC will not permit U.S. brokers to ascribe value to securities that by definition (having been underwritten and subscribed to by major brokerage houses) have already been ascribed value by the global market.

From many perspectives, mutual funds were the great investment success story of the past decade. As mutual funds grew from $135 billion in assets to over $1.8 trillion today, global investors began to develop a great appetite for them. While foreign direct investment in the United States shrank dramatically during the early 1990s, offshore investment in U.S. mutual funds offered a major new hope for American capital markets. There were welled-up rivers of capital ready to pour into the funds. But Washington preempted any flood of investment from abroad by imposing a withholding tax on the capital returns of foreign investors in U.S. mutual funds. The tax doesn't apply to those foreigners who buy U.S. securities directly—which for many outside the United States is much more difficult to accomplish than investment in mutual funds—nor does it apply to investment from Americans in funds based outside the United States. But if you're American, don't waste time seeking foreign-based funds. With inimitable Flat Earth flair, the SEC ruled in 1992 that although Americans may buy a foreign fund in America, foreign funds may not be *offered* in America.

Former Commissioner J. Carter Beese attacked the SEC's piecemeal, uninformed regulatory system in "Confessions of a Securities Regulator," an essay published in the *Wall Street Journal* (September 19, 1995). Beese has long fought for globally sensitive reform but is frequently frustrated by the inbred antiglobal prejudice in American policy. The SEC desperately needs to reconsider its role in the new economy. But, as Beese notes, what we are faced with is a:

> . . . system riddled with redundancy and inefficiency— overlapping state and federal registration requirements, futures, and cash markets overseen by different bodies, and a virtual alphabet soup of financial regulatory agencies . . . . For decades, our markets have simply absorbed these costs. Investors and issuers had little choice. After all, the U.S. markets were the only game in town. In recent years, however, issuers and investors have been able to conduct their business in virtually every corner of the globe with the stroke of a computer key . . . . With the explosive growth of international activity, we can no longer afford to regulate from our borders inward.

FIXING THE PLUMBING

The global economy has turned Washington's obsession with managing capital into a grand illusion. The control that it exercised in another age is today attainable neither by Washington nor any national regulator on the planet. The paradigm of control must be abandoned. It is the most hollow of premises today. The reserves held by central banks in the old world, for example, far exceeded daily trading, allowing them to manipulate rates when they deemed it necessary. Today if the Federal Reserve and the Treasury Department spent their entire reserves at their disposal, the amount would equal less than 4 percent of the total daily trade in global currency markets. The International Monetary Fund (IMF), under U.S. leadership, once exercised overwhelming clout to resolve any international financial crisis. The IMF's emergency financing mechanism—which was more than doubled in 1995—today equates to about *85 minutes* of global foreign-exchange trading.

But it is not the volume of global capital that is its defining characteristic. It is its liquidity. And what drives the phenomenon of liquidity is the phenomenon of choice. The power of global capital includes the power to choose not to venture where it cannot efficiently operate. Try as they might, government regulators and managers who cling to strategies relying on control can never hope to snare it. They can only hope to attract it, and then they must nurture it.

The stark reality Washington therefore must face is that the prosperity of the nation—and the revenue of government—is dependent on the share of global capital it is able to claim—or more precisely, the share that will accept Washington's jurisdiction. No matter how hard Washington insists on control, it will ultimately be powerless to reach that capital that chooses to ignore it. Capital *will* be reached by governments—and the revenue it generates shared with governments—but it will respect no decree from Washington that it must reside in or even pass through the United States.

The solutions begin with understanding that the key to the global economy lies not in the dynamics of trade but in the dynamics of this new global capital. If, as sometimes appears, new congressional aides and trade bureaucrats have been taught "manufacturing, manufacturing, manufacturing" as their guiding mantra, then that mantra must be changed to "capital, capital, capital." By attending to capital, they will attend to jobs, they will attend to nurturing high-tech industries, they will attend to building knowledge and new opportunity.

The dilemma is the familiar one of Washington's addiction to traditional tools and traditional fixes. Because for decades international financial problems were viewed as simply aspects of international trade problems, Washington's financial "fix" for poor international performance has been manipulation of exchange rates, which only pumps up exports of commodities like soybeans and timber. Because capital was perceived as carrying flags, pressures from non–U.S. capital was attributed to "unfairness" in foreign financial systems (it was unfair that Switzerland did not tax capital gains or that Britain permitted write-off of goodwill). Because non–U.S. companies applied different accounting systems, U.S. investors had to be protected from them.

In effect, what regulators have been saying is that because those controlling capital outside the United States do not apply identical criteria when offering and using capital, their capital must be denied Americans—or regulators must insert themselves between such foreigners and Americans. But as members of the global plebiscite, Americans already deal effectively with "foreign" content. Even more importantly, it is precisely the diversity of capital feared by regulators that keeps the global economy so dynamic and healthy.

Reform is already under way, argue many in Washington. They have sponsored conclaves of experts on the global economy. They have debated for days on end reform of certain banking and securities statutes. They have signed onto the 1988 Basel Accord, which imposes international capital adequacy standards on institutions in the most active financial centers.[24] Access to financial markets was agreed to with Canada and Mexico in the North American Free Trade Agreement. In May 1995, the United States signed the Windsor Declaration for international cooperation to address market disruptions caused by failure of derivative trading firms. Washington's authorization in 1994 for most interstate bank branching, allowing seamless national networks, was another step in the right direction. Lifting at least some of the nonbanking restrictions appears at long last within reach, but much effort is still needed to remove the burdens facing American banks in the new economy. The truly sweeping reforms to launch American banking into the twenty-first century seem as distant as ever, and reformers are chronically frustrated by old-world thinking. Efforts to eliminate redundant rules by consolidating banking regulators into one agency—one of the most obvious steps needed to rationalize America's capital control systems—were killed in 1994 by territorial warfare between the existing agencies.

Certainly some key regulators appreciate the implications of global capital. Secretary of Treasury Robert Rubin announced in June 1995 that "Our [financial regulation] institutions must be made as modern as the marketplace."[25] Rubin has even declared that "We have to help Americans understand that their economic well-being is directly related to this country's engagement with the global economy."[26]

But the deep-seated Flat Earth compulsion to treat capital issues as sovereign issues, bilateral issues, or zero-sum ("capital must be balanced") issues have undermined every reform effort to date. The European Union, in an effort led by Trade Minister Leon Brittan, labored for years during the Uruguay Round talks to build a global financial service accord that would for the first time provide common global standards and clear access by member nations to financial markets in more than 150 countries. Although the accord was in many respects more valuable to U.S. firms than the tariff reductions that preoccupied Washington during the Uruguay Round, the United States torpedoed the effort by withdrawing at the eleventh hour. The U.S. Trade Representative defended his action by declaring that Washington would not surrender its capital markets to non–U.S. firms merely on the terms agreed by seventy-six other nations and that it preferred to pursue bilateral concessions from key countries as a means of better balancing financial flows between the United States and those countries. In other words, the historic agreement was gutted because Washington asserted sovereignty over capital in pursuit of outdated zero-sum goals.

U.S.-led efforts to expand the Basel Accord have been mired in similar mentalities. Instead of working to expand coverage to those industrial nations not already in the accord and to include less developed nations (none belong), reform has focused on complex new risk models with burdensome requirements for three "tiers" of capital, models that resound with the official micromanagement that characterizes Washington's own regulations. The efforts have been sharply criticized by the international financial community as one more attempt to equate American traditions to global solutions.[27]

The challenge in fixing our financial system lies in not fixing it in the sense of Washington's traditional fixes. Only a deep-seated conceptual overhaul with an emphasis on deregulation and market efficiency will be enough to unclog the capital pipelines passing through America. It is not difficult for those closest to capital markets to identify what we need: new devices for valuation of markets and capital, new frameworks for accounting that are truly global—not clones of the inefficient ones molded sixty years ago—new flexibility to allow innovation to extend its reach to archaic financial structures, and elimination of protectionism in the flow of money. None of this will be possible within the current clutter of American financial regulation. In 1993 the chairman of Goldman Sachs reported that twenty different financial regulatory bodies oversee his operations.

The SEC has also made helpful gestures. By easing disclosure under its Rule 144A, it allowed foreigners to sell securities to large institutional investors based on their home-market data. In late 1993, the agency announced that it would seek ways to further modify existing standards to help international firms tap into U.S. investors. In April 1994, new rules to facilitate disclosure for foreign companies and extend the availability of shelf registrations to foreign firms were promulgated. Under Chairman Arthur Levitt Jr., the SEC has begun to make the American Depository Receipt program for foreign issuers more user-friendly.

Dedicated globalists like J. Carter Beese are helping to focus the effort. SEC Commissioner Steven M. H. Wallman took an important step forward in August 1995, when he called for securities and accounting regulators to recognize that the entire U.S. framework of corporate accounting and disclosure is obsolete.[28] Our accounting rules have subtle, largely unexplored implications for competitiveness and are in desperate need of updating. They preserve bricks and mortar as "capital" when in fact today such fixed assets are often the most significant liability a firm possesses. Regulators still require that the software that may constitute the most significant strategic assets of a firm be treated as an expense. Banks are unable to adequately address the value of innovation in allocating capital because accounting rules deemphasize intangibles; as a result, not only high-tech companies but every knowledge-intensive company—including most successful "industrial" companies[29]—are handicapped.

In looking at corporate disclosure, regulators must step back and consider how vastly different today's markets are from those that defined their roles six and seven decades ago. That regime was based on the premise that market forces do not generate the information needed for the rational, informed allocation of capital by investors. Everything the SEC does, from quarterly 10K reports to insider-trading suits, is in effect related to canons of disclosure chiseled out in the 1930s, reflecting the outdated philosophy that market forces fail to supply sufficient data for informed decision making and that therefore the government is the best institution to arbitrage economic information.

Today the rapidly expanding legions of private, independent professional advisers, not Washington's regime, are the drivers of information. Information in a format required by law in many industries is a garbled footnote compared to what these advisers—including analysts, stock arbitragers, brokers, industry specialists, and fund managers—offer to investors. Since they owe their jobs to global markets, their information is not skewed to outdated accounting and disclosure rules. Their information analysis and presentation, moreover, is supported by sophisticated pricing models and portfolio theories that did not exist when the SEC was created—and it is driven to accuracy and efficiency by the relentless global plebiscite for capital. They understand that the best standards for global capital are the simple ones. William Freund suggests that the dilemma caused by the SEC's disclosure rules could be solved by simply requiring foreign-company shares on American exchanges to be identified with an asterisk to indicate they are subject to different data reporting standards.

The private sector has far outpaced regulators in addressing global banking standards as well. Regulators could find no common voice when confronted with spectacular collapses like those at Barings Plc. or Kidder

Peabody—although they did strike some familiar Flat Earth chords. Outlaw derivatives, some said, while others clamored for strict new barriers at the U.S. borders so that such innovations enter the United States only through Washington's regulatory filters. But the markets understood that such products have become valuable risk-limiting devices. The Group of Thirty, an unofficial association of international banks, and the Derivatives Policy Group, a New York–based coalition of nonbank derivative dealers, have made great advances in dealing with new risk-management systems.

One of the most vital lessons for global capital markets has been that those markets themselves place huge costs on those who do not retain adequate capital and manage their risks voluntarily. Such private-sector entities, acting without the burden of official tradition, are addressing issues that national regulators have barely begun to identify—like how to deal with cross-shareholding in risk management. Such shareholdings are vital in the new economy, but traditional rules cause them to distort financial figures. Forty-five percent of the shares on the Tokyo Exchange, for example, are beneficially owned by other firms listed on the exchange—meaning that you could buy the whole market for only 45 percent of its stated capitalization.

The Bank for International Settlements has slowly and informally accepted the risk-modeling practices of global financial firms and, thus far, wisely deferred from pushing member governments into second-guessing the market with new regulatory programs. But the threat of such programs, invented unilaterally by uninformed regulators, remains and is itself among the biggest competitive risks firms face.

The calls for sharply increased restrictions on international capital following the high-profile failures at Daiwa Bank and Barings threaten to reverse the progress that is gradually being made. Those incidents involved nothing more than fraud, inevitably magnified by the new scale of global finance. Existing laws worked in those cases. Barings lost its independence after being acquired by a Dutch firm. The penalties to Daiwa, which was summarily ejected from the U.S. market and stiffly fined in Japan, could not have been more severe. Such incidents simply underscored the one traditional role that must be preserved for regulators: Entire volumes of securities and banking regulations should be scrapped and replaced by stripped-down government offices charged with enforcing simple laws against fraud.

In the fall of 1995, Representative Jack Fields of Texas introduced a reform package to recast much of America's capital control laws. Fields called for preemption of redundant state laws that burden firms issuing securities and establishment of new procedures for every new SEC rule:

The SEC would have to consider not only protection of investors as part of its mission but also the promotion of capital flow, increasing market efficiency, and effects on global competitiveness of U.S. firms. The proposal, the first serious effort to break capital regulators out of the boundaries of their anachronistic thinking, was quickly attacked by traditional regulators as a "giveaway" to Wall Street firms.

Erik Peterson, vice president and director of studies at the Center for Strategic and International Studies, examined the political challenges created by global capital in a 1995 article in *The Washington Quarterly*. Peterson cogently captured those challenges in his conclusion:

> If the United States is destined to lead in this new age of global finance, it must devise and enact a strategy that brings its economy into equilibrium, that recognizes the growing power of global market forces, that stresses international economic engagement as the key to domestic success, that adapts to the onset of the knowledge revolution in economic activity. . . . But if the economic and financial challenges confronting the country are allowed to fester, U.S. policymakers will effectively renounce their country's international leadership position and the welfare of future generations of Americans.[30]

Bold new policy initiatives will be required to nurture what should be America's most basic competitive resource, initiatives that recognize that the new capital has become the great equalizer, the common denominator that, when understood and applied adeptly, unlocks the formula for winning in global industries. If it fails to do so, Washington will instead learn that global capital is also becoming the great illuminator of Flat Earth behavior: The channels through which it moves will circumvent those countries, industries, and enterprises that do not embrace it, leaving them to a slow and conspicuous stagnation.

171

PUTTING THE CHILL ON INVESTMENT

The Battle for
Global
Presence

It is virtually impossible to be globally competitive without being globally present. Industry leadership in the new economy is never built from isolated fortresses, not even from those built within the largest market on earth. No matter how effective such fortresses may have been in the old economy, operating out of one location, one nation, even one continent is not enough for success in global industry. No enterprise becomes a leader without far-flung foreign investment in research, sales, and production. Firms lacking such investment are left unable to fully tap the diverse aspects of capital, labor, technology, distribution, and other factors that create competitive advantage.

For managers of successful global enterprise, such observations are axiomatic. But for many Washington policymakers, they seem to be anathema. Raising the topic of foreign investment along the Potomac is like jamming a stick into a hornet's nest. To many members of Congress, foreign investors are invaders. They are stealing our assets. They are looting our treasures. From the floor of the Congress we are told that in another generation, most Americans will be working in fast-food restaurants waiting on fat-cat foreigners. U.S. firms investing offshore, moreover, are unpatriotic. They are tax evaders. They are stealing jobs from America and, we are told, unjustly enriching foreign countries. Here more than in any other context, Flat Earth folklore runs amok.

In the context of public policymaking, foreign investment is both highly visible and without a strong direct constituency—making it an easy target for those pressed by the changes brought by the global economy. During the years following World War II, scores of governments on the planet yielded to that temptation, imposing foreign investment restrictions—and since the late 1980s, they have, without exception, sharply retreated from such practices. But Washington has steadily moved in the opposite direction—toward greater regulation of foreign investment. As the global economy has created vast movements of investment capital, countries like Indonesia, India, France, Sweden, Brazil, Spain, Colombia, Korea, Poland, and Russia have studied the lessons of that movement and reduced or eliminated their restrictions. At the same time, Washington has erected new barriers that have either directly or indirectly chilled the atmosphere for foreign investment.

Today it is impossible to be seriously interested in competitiveness without being interested in cross-border investment. No firm can successfully leverage the diversity and liquidity of the global economy by staying within its home-country borders. No American company becomes competitive in China, Brazil, or Hungary by staying at home. In many industries, no firm stays competitive *at home* by staying at home: The supply of components, materials, and innovation from abroad is a vital ingredient in the formulas for success found by many American firms—and the best leverage against foreign competition in the home market often is moving into their own home markets.

Investment by non–U.S. firms within the United States, moreover, has become a major engine for growth, accounting for more than 4 million direct jobs and hundred of billions in new capital during the past fifteen years. U.S. companies without international investment grow demonstrably slower than those with such investment—half as fast, according to a recent study by the Conference Board.[1] Firms with investment ties overseas—whether to parents or subsidiaries offshore—are also firms that export. In a typical year, for example, one fourth of American exports are to U.S.-owned affiliates overseas; U.S. multinationals overall account for more than 60 percent of shipments from the United States.[2]

Billions more are shipped by "foreign" companies operating within the United States; the second-largest U.S. auto exporter in 1993, for example, was Honda Motor Company. Businesses in the United States established by Japanese investors alone account for more than 10 percent of American exports every year. Foreign multinationals in the United States were responsible for 23 percent of U.S. exports in 1990—the last year for which data is available.[3] Operations within this network of international investment not only mean more jobs but better jobs. Firms that sell to customers outside the United States pay an average of 17 percent above their average industry wage and enjoy higher productivity growth and greater stability.[4]

For American competitiveness, foreign direct investment—both inward and outward—is not part of the problem but part of the solution. Jobs and exports, however, are only the most obvious benefits of that investment. The role of cross-border investment is even more pervasive and significant than such data imply. Foreign investors in the United States tend to build larger plants and engage in more capital-intensive businesses than the average American firm. Research and development expenditures by foreign affiliates in the United States are much higher than for U.S. firms overall. In 1991, for example, such affiliates spent $2,450 per worker on research in the United States; U.S. firms overall spent only $820 per worker.[5]

A direct correlation also exists between the productivity in local industry segments and the access of foreign investment to that sector. Denying a sector the liquidity and diversity brought by such investment breeds stagnation. For example, Japan has low relative productivity in food processing, and Germany has surprisingly low productivity in auto parts, electronics, beer, and steel. Economists were long confused by the disparities. But international managers experienced in those countries understand a vital point: The sectors where Japan and Germany lag have been traditionally closed to foreign investment. Protection from their governments insulates producers from significant competition from direct foreign investment.

The evidence is more than anecdotal. The Global Institute of McKinsey and Co. completed a comprehensive study of international productivity in 1993, examining the dramatic productivity disparities in national segments of industries such as auto parts, metalworking, soap and detergent, steel, and food processing. McKinsey confirmed the vital role of ownership diversity in improving productivity: "Foreign direct investment has been far more powerful than trade as a force for improving productivity."[6] Productivity improvements moved rapidly across borders in industries with widespread international investment; in fact, McKinsey concluded, "Foreign direct investment—transplant factories—play the pivotal role in moving them around the world." Such transplants were found to:

1. directly contribute to higher levels of domestic productivity

2. prove that leading-edge productivity can be achieved with local labor and many local inputs

3. put competitive pressure on other domestic producers

4. transfer knowledge of the best practices to other domestic producers through the natural movement of personnel

As McKinsey partner William Lewis emphasized in announcing the study, "Eventually the battle is won by the most productive."

That battle is being waged by global investors on a huge scale. In each year since 1987, the value of cross-border movement of ownership shares has exceeded $1 trillion. In 1960 foreign investment in the United States was approximately $4 billion; by 1985 it was $185 billion, and by 1992 it was $426 billion. Foreign affiliates in the United States had a 5.3 percent share of U.S. manufacturing value-added in 1980; that figure rose to 15 percent by 1992.[7] Current trade data is almost meaningless in large part because of this investment flow. Forty thousand international "parent" enterprises produce over $10 trillion annually in sales, and over half of that is from 250,000 affiliates selling within their host countries.[8] While policymakers lamented chronic trade deficits during the 1980s, the U.S. share of goods and services made or performed and sold from other countries (i.e., goods and services from foreign subsidiaries) steadily increased.

While manufacturing jobs have decreased within America, American enterprises have kept their share on a global basis. The U.S.-controlled share of total manufacturing jobs in the combined United States, Europe, Japan and the newly industrializing countries has been a steady 30 percent for many years. In most years, the value of goods and services sold by American subsidiaries within Japan is greater than the amount of the U.S. trade deficit with Japan.

Some of those offshore operations were driven by logistical concerns many years ago. Kellogg makes cereal at seventeen plants overseas. "Cornflakes don't travel very well," explains Charles Elliott, chief financial officer of the company. Non–U.S. units of Philip Morris make over $13 billion in sales, mostly of products that couldn't travel well or were required to be produced locally by local rules—meaning if the sales hadn't been conducted through foreign subsidiaries, they would not have been made. Other investments are being made to take advantage of extraordinary opportunities represented by overseas privatizations— like the huge investments in 1994 and 1995 by U.S. telecommunications firms in South America, Eastern Europe, Australia, and New Zealand.[9] But most of today's investment is about building global legs— establishing local presence in every major market to create a global network.

Cross-border investment is ingrained in the American way of life. In another century, it built cattle ranches and railroads. Today it is tightly woven into our economic and social fabric. Even many of foreign investment's biggest detractors are surprised to learn that foreign investment is behind such American fixtures as Saks Fifth Avenue, Burger King, Pillsbury, Ball Park Franks, National Steel, Firestone, Carvel Ice Cream, Howard Johnson, Ex-Lax, Columbia Pictures, Doubleday Publishing, 7-Eleven, Hardees, Keebler, A & P, Smith & Wesson, and Carnation. Attacking such enterprises because their owners don't carry U.S. passports makes as much sense as it would for host governments to attack firms like Godiva Chocolate, Jaguar, Opel, and the largest television cable operator in Britain because their owners are American.

KEEPING AMERICAN ENTERPRISE OFF THE MAP

"American companies must act like American companies again," the 1992 Democratic candidate for president announced to his party's convention, "exporting products, not jobs." Bill Clinton vowed to raise $45 billion in new taxes by making international corporations behave "fairly" and made good on his promises with an aggressive series of tax-reform proposals. Among other things, the reforms called for U.S. firms to pay tax on earnings from foreign investment that were not brought back to the United States. This meant, among other things, that a U.S. firm with a German factory would effectively have to return earnings to America rather than maintain its global competitiveness by applying those earnings in its European operations or face a substantial tax penalty. The plan expanded Flat Earth innovation disincentives by limiting the ability of international firms to utilize credits to offset foreign royalty income. Managers in such companies were more than a little confused when they heard a concurrent campaign theme: the need to push U.S. companies back into the position of industry leadership many had lost to competitors from Europe and Asia.

Such proposals, each of which was to some degree adopted by new laws or regulatory action, only increased an already heavy burden on

U.S.-based international firms. Taxation has long been a weapon of choice in confronting foreign investors. The National Chamber Foundation commissioned Price Waterhouse to examine that tax burden in 1991. The conclusion: U.S. firms face a "significantly higher effective tax rate on foreign income than would a similarly situated multinational" headquartered in Great Britain, the Netherlands, Canada, France, Germany, or Japan.[10] Compared to major non–U.S. competitors, American firms with international investment have a 4 to 10 percent tax disadvantage. Dow Chemical has calculated, for example, that it pays 4 percent more in taxes for its international operations than a competitor in Holland as a result of the international prejudice in the U.S. system.[11]

Washington's rules for taxing international operations are a confused patchwork developed over seventy years. They are based on the view that global, not national, income should be taxed by Washington—a view not taken by a number of other industrial nations, giving their companies a fundamental advantage in international investment. U.S. firms thus pay minimum tax at U.S. rates wherever they locate around the planet—even though many competing firms pay only local rates. Tax credits are allowed for local taxes but only under strict limitations. Where taxes in excess of U.S. rates are paid by the U.S. affiliates, the "excess" credit can be used only in highly restricted carryback and carryforward scenarios—meaning that U.S. investors are pushed by the U.S. tax rules not to invest in countries with higher tax rates.[12] The most important country in this category: Japan, targeted by Washington for having "too low" a presence by U.S. firms.

U.S. firms with offshore operations invariably provide some form of headquarters services to those operations, since many aspects of financial, legal, environmental, personnel, and logistical services are most effectively provided on a global basis. In most global firms, such services are provided on a relatively seamless basis: Financing arranged by headquarters often benefits the entire company, for example, without differentiation across borders. But Washington insists on such differentiation. Under current law, headquarters expenses must be divided between U.S. and foreign-source income. The portion allocated against foreign-source income does not benefit from a uniform deduction overseas, however, primarily because the services take place in the United States. Headquarters activities carried on by U.S. firms on behalf of their foreign units thus trigger a tax penalty not borne by foreign competitors.

Washington's most pervasive device for tampering with international investment is Section 482 of the Internal Revenue Code, which authorizes Washington to "adjust" international income from foreign affiliates when it considers it to be unrealistic. The original goal of Section 482 was the reasonable one of assuring that commercial realities, not tax evasion, drove the international movement of funds between related parties. Washington has driven that standard into the realm of the unreal by using it to tax not income actually earned by the affected international parties but that which it considers *should have been* earned.

A computer firm based in Texas, for example, may decide to simultaneously answer its need for a competitive global source for a disk component and its need to serve Asian customers as an "insider" in their markets by building a factory in Singapore, where skilled labor is highly cost-effective and a critical mass of computer expertise already exists. The Singapore unit may then sell the components to the United States at an 18 percent return—a return necessary to sustain the ongoing investment needed to keep the plant within competitive product cycles. Using Section 482, however, Washington may declare that the return "leaves" too much with the local unit on the basis of data it has for what it considers to be normal "like" businesses and increase the tax on the U.S. firm to make it conform to the IRS template—even though in some sectors, the "normal" firm may not be particularly profitable. Singapore has already taxed the local income and may not declare a refund for a U.S. tax based on a scheme it does accept—so Washington has asked the company to accept double taxation, an added burden its non–U.S. competitors do not face.

THE ADVANCE PRICING AGREEMENT PROGRAM

The Internal Revenue Service responded in 1991 to complaints about the uncertainty created by its transfer price regulations with a new Advance Pricing Agreement (APA) program, by which international companies are able to obtain advance approval for their international pricing. For policymakers, the program was a perfect answer to the complaints, since it allowed them to assert that they had offered pre-clearance for prices. For global managers, however, the program created a still greater dilemma by moving further from the realities of their businesses. The program required them to negotiate with foreign tax authorities (an aspect viewed by more than a few governments as an extraterritorial intrusion by Washington), required a vast documentation effort costing as much as $2 million per case for some firms, and exposed companies to added scrutiny of past policy practices (and therefore retroactive penalties). Washington's lackluster response to the program? It imposed stiffer penalties for pricing "misvaluation."

Global firms based in the United States complained that the more complex regime singled them out unfairly, since foreign firms with U.S. operations typically had only to address transactions with one U.S. subsidiary, while they had to deal with transactions involving multiple foreign subsidiaries. Firms with large global operations, moreover, pointed out how unrealistic it would be to invest in an APA for one or a few product lines involving sales to stipulated countries since such an approach contravened the realities of competition: Shifting production among global sources, shifting product design and specifications, and shifting cost structures to meet rapidly changing competitive conditions are vital in many industries—but totally inconsistent with Washington's push for advance clearance of prices.

Michael E. Granfield is a professor of business economics at UCLA, where he has studied the effects of such taxes on American competitiveness. Washington's use of Section 482, Granfield concludes:

> . . . demonstrates a belief that multinationals exist only to move profits around the world to avoid the IRS's grasp. This belief is contrary to virtually all the academic literature on this issue. It also ignores the commercial success of these organizations.[13]

An additional penalty arises in the form of double taxation of foreign-source dividends: Unlike most of their foreign competitors, American firms must pay taxes on income in their local country of operations, then pay Washington another tax when the net foreign income arrives in the United States as dividends, a tax only partially offset by foreign tax credits. Another disparity of treatment that represents an increasing burden is the inability of American firms to apply the tax benefits of the long-standing Foreign Sales Corporation exemption program to their export of business services. Additional tax penalties that serve to keep American firms off the global map: regulation of pension plans of foreign subsidiaries maintained under foreign laws for foreign workers and rules for "controlled foreign corporations" that require certain foreign income to be taxed in the United States as it is earned, not when it is sent back to the United States.

The cross-border technology disincentives discussed in Chapter Four are all inherently cross-border investment disincentives. Failure to take the international prejudice out of deductions for research, taxation of royalty income and deductions for royalty expense hurts every American firm trying to become competitive through foreign investment.

Gary Hufbauer, former director of the Treasury Department's international tax office and currently a fellow at the Institute for International Economics, puzzles over the continued push for such penalizing measures. The policy behind such provisions, observes Hufbauer, seems to be "that you can produce in America and then export abroad. I don't know if that vision was correct in the 1960s, but it's sure not correct in the 1990s." Yet the campaign for punishing global outreach by U.S. firms continues. The Secretary Treasurer of the AFL-CIO recently expressed alarm to the Congress that American firms are able to deduct as "ordinary" expenses the cost of building plants overseas. He pointed with dismay to another provision of tax law that permits U.S. firms to deduct operating costs of foreign plants as costs of doing business.[14]

Proposals to penalize foreign operations have become popular grist for Washington's policy mills. Every initiative may not ultimately be adopted, but the fact that such proposals have increased in number, with strong support from leading members of Congress, is itself significant. Among recent initiatives and perennial favorites of Congressional leaders:

- authority to allow U.S. stockholders to sue any American company with foreign investment that fails to comply with foreign laws governing its investment (without regard to the enforcement policies of the host government)

- removal of federal funding for a company that moves an operation to a country where the wages are more than 50 percent below U.S. wages

- retroactive changes in U.S. treatment of foreign pension plans

- revocation of the charter for the Overseas Private Investment Corporation on the grounds that it supports competition with U.S. manufacturing

- authority to allow U.S. citizens to sue American firms for "negligence" by foreign subsidiaries in their local operations (effectively changing standards of conduct overseas from that of a "reasonable" person to that of a "reasonable American" acting overseas)

- registration in Washington of offshore investments by American firms

- approval by Washington for offshore investments by American firms

The clear trend of such proposals defies both the increasing support for foreign investment in other capitals and the surging competitive need for American firms to meet competition on a global stage.

American firms attempting to make international investment also face myriad indirect barriers. Virtually every trade-protection measure, by distorting the efficiency of global investment, distorts investment decisions. Arco Chemical made the globally astute move of investing in a joint-venture factory in Japan to establish a global relationship with its customer Toyota; the move was hailed by strategically minded managers as an example of how American automotive firms and their suppliers could regain leadership in the global auto industry. Then Washington negotiated "voluntary" import quotas to push Japanese carmakers into buying U.S.-sourced goods. The quotas effectively forced Arco to ship material from the United States to its Japanese customers, severely undermining its new Japanese investment.

Firms trying to build global production and sourcing networks often find themselves running afoul of their own country's local preference rules for government purchases. Many of those Buy America regulations have long ago outlived the national security purposes they were drafted to meet and simply interfere with the sourcing networks that create leadership in many industries. In the interest of national security, for example, the Navy may not, with narrow exceptions, purchase anchors and chains from overseas sources.[15] Any firm supplying the Department of Defense under a contract worth over $10 million must tell the department if it intends to perform any of the work overseas.[16] Even in national emergencies, the Federal Emergency Management Administration is not allowed to give a contract to an entity organized overseas unless the firm bids more than 6 percent below the closest domestic bid.[17] The Department of Defense similarly requires U.S. sources for pliers, hammers, and stainless flatware.[18]

Over thirty-five states have rules that restrict the procurement of goods or services from non–U.S. sources; many of these are absolute prohibitions on foreign-made products. Although the Delaware legislature passed a similar law precluding the use of foreign steel in state construction projects, it was vetoed by the governor on the basis that "a healthy American economy requires aggressive competition in the international marketplace rather than withdrawal behind . . . barriers."[19]

Infrared Research, a small firm making remote-control devices for consumer electronics, buys all its components from U.S. suppliers and makes its own products in Illinois. But federal rules prohibited the company from labeling its product "Made in the United States" because the firm's suppliers had overseas units that sourced some of the parts. Washington forbade the label due to that indirect foreign-investment connection—but when Infrared's products go to overseas markets, local authorities require them to conspicuously display another label: "Made in the United States." In the words of Robert Moore, president of Infrared: "We are recognized in every nation as an American manufacturer—every nation except the U.S."[20]

BATTLING DIVERSITY: THE CAMPAIGN AGAINST INVESTMENT IN THE UNITED STATES

One of the greatest ironies of all Flat Earth policymaking lies in its treatment of foreign investment within U.S. borders. In the name of saving U.S. jobs, preserving U.S. technology, and protecting U.S. security, Washington maintains an expanding regime of control over foreign investment within American borders. The record of such investment over the past two decades, however, demonstrates that such investment provides more and better jobs, upgraded technology, and consequently more economic security for America. It also shows that foreign owners are much more tolerant of poorly performing operations and more apt to reinvest capital in their operations than U.S. investors. Past allegations that foreign investors leave high-value, high-compensation jobs at "home" also have been proved to be myths.[21]

The "invasion" of foreign investment, moreover, is more like a minor trickle: Foreigners own only 3 percent of American assets, less than half the average foreign investment share in most European countries. Slightly over .5 percent of American land belongs to foreigners. Until the late 1980s, when the global economy emerged, American investment overseas vastly surpassed in value foreign investment in the United States.

Historically, the United States provided an open door for foreign investment. For much of its history, no country on earth was more permissive toward offshore investment. But that position has changed in recent years as a result of three significant developments. Around the planet during the past ten years, governments began to recognize the benefits of such investment and scrambled to eliminate foreign-investment restrictions. Today, foreign investors receive a warm welcome in scores of countries that once scorned them. The second development is inextricably related to the first: the rise of the global economy, which has vastly underscored the importance of capital moving across borders. Long-standing sectorial restrictions in the United States that once seemed of minor consequence have become more conspicuous and burdensome as global industries have emerged. Finally, Washington has erected new impediments to such investment, defying the trend everywhere else on the planet.

"We're more welcome in Kazakhstan than in the United States," groused a senior manager for a French company after a flurry of protest from Congress caused his company to back out of the acquisition of a large U.S. electronics firm. Such rebuffs are becoming common, just when the United States needs such investors more than ever to build its base of global industry.

Sectorial restrictions against foreign investment have been common for over a century in the United States, based on traditional concepts of national security. Washington still maintains large bureaucracies to strictly enforce restrictions, such as:

- Under the Federal Aviation Act of 1958,[22] a non-U.S company may not form a U.S. airline subsidiary or acquire control of an existing U.S. airline.

- Federal licensing (certification) of a company for airline operations within the United States is permitted only if 75 percent of its voting shares are owned or controlled by U.S. citizens and two thirds of its directors and managing officers are U.S. citizens.

- Under the Foreign Bank Supervision Enhancement Act of 1991,[23] foreign banks may not establish a subsidiary, branch, agency, or commercial lending unit in the United States unless the Federal Reserve Board finds that it is subject to comprehensive supervision or regulation in its home country.

- Foreign banks are prohibited from owning state-chartered banks in a number of states.

- No foreign bank may merge with another foreign bank that has a U.S. branch without approval of the Federal Reserve Board.

- Under the Communications Act of 1934,[24] no radio or television license may be granted to a non–U.S. individual or corporation or to any U.S. company in which an officer or director is an alien or more than one fifth of the capital stock is owned or voted by aliens.

- Under the Mineral Leasing Act of 1920, mineral deposits on public lands may not be leased to foreign citizens or corporations.

Public-policy rationales may still exist for some of these restrictions—preventing foreign investors from controlling militarily strategic resources, for example—but the scope of those rationales has vastly diminished. Washington passed mining restrictions in another century in part to avoid foreign control of certain coal resources; it wanted to assure a steady supply for its steam-powered naval fleet. Today, were there a shortage of uranium used for the American submarine fleet, such a rationale for restriction may still exist—but there is no such shortage, nor will there be, due to stockpile programs. Many other rationales are similarly outdated, undermining global industry without any commensurate benefit to the country. Still, Washington zealously prosecutes such restrictions—and with an ever-expansive interpretation of its powers. The Communications Act restrictions, for example, were expressly designed to prevent "alien activities during the time of war" within the communications sector; modern technology offers many alternatives to controlling such a remote threat that fall short of the pervasive capital controls applied by Washington. The Federal Communications Commission, for example, spends millions of taxpayer dollars to scrutinize terms of international financings to determine, for example, if an offshore loan creates alien "control" of a potential broadcast operator.

When a Canadian trucking firm sought to acquire a failing U.S. freight operation, the deal was temporarily blocked by the federal aviation authorities on the grounds that the U.S. firm had an indirect air-carrier operation in the form of a freight forwarder that handled air cargo. The Secretary of Transportation invoked national security to block an expanded alliance between an ailing midsize American air carrier and a European operation ready to infuse $400 million of capital desperately needed to save American jobs and equipment. Defending the move, the U.S. trade representative explained: "We are basically for as much open investment as possible so long as it does not create a problem for our national security or our strategic interests."[25] Those words were small comfort to the individuals who lost their jobs and the cities that lost their air service when the deal collapsed.

INCOMMUNICADO

The outdated framework for regulating the communications business according to nationality has created one of Washington's most confusing regulatory quagmires:

- A license for the Mormon Church was denied because a member of the church's Joint Council was an "alien," thereby not falling within the spirit of the requirement that a company's directors be U.S. citizens.

- Licenses held by Capital Cities Communications, one of the largest American media companies, were challenged on the grounds that the company could not demonstrate the nationality of its public shareholders, none of whom owned controlling blocks of stock. On the basis of a company questionnaire to shareholders, the firm concluded that less than 3 percent of its shareholders had non–U.S. passports. The FCC rejected the evidence on the grounds that the firm did not prove that virtually every one of its thousands of shareholders had responded.

- A federal court of appeals had to intervene to direct the Federal Communications Commission (FCC) to preserve a license for Loyola University, whose license was challenged on the grounds that the ex officio president of the university was the Superior General of the Society of Jesus, then a Belgian residing in Rome.

- The FCC's traditional concepts of ownership and control are grossly inadequate for dealing with the advent of new equity derivatives and other vehicles for global capital. The Commission interprets its authority to include the right to examine and regulate indirect stock interests, subordinated lending arrangements, and limited partnership interests. Thus, for example, under the FCC rules, if a U.S.-based limited partnership holds a 22 percent interest in a station and a non–U.S. citizen holds a 25 percent uninsulated limited partnership interest in the limited partnership while all other interests in the station are held by U.S. citizens, the license will be denied due to the small indirect interest held by the non–U.S. citizen. This second-tier restriction has blocked several telecom investments by partnerships controlled and managed by Americans.

When policymakers speak of national security and strategic interest, they conjure up red-white-and-blue images of past wars and valiant defenders of freedom. International managers have seen a very different image: They remember how the same "national security" has been invoked to prevent them from selling memory chips that could otherwise be found in talking dolls in Hong Kong or off-road diesel trucks available in a dozen other countries around the world. "National security has taken on surreal dimensions in Washington," notes a computer-company manager who lost half his sales in one year due to such restrictions. "It's the last bastion for America's xenophobes."

Such outdated notions of national security became the impetus for America's broadest regime of foreign investment control. After more than a century without any systematic direct-investment controls, at a time when the chill was quickly being removed from the Cold War, Washington empowered the Committee on Foreign Investment in the United States to screen foreign investment for national-security implications. Under the authority of the Exon-Florio Act of 1988, the president has the authority, without judicial review, to prohibit or suspend foreign investment projects in the United States. The committee may investigate any proposed transaction for national-security implications.

To obtain clearance, firms must submit detailed information regarding their U.S. and foreign operations, including plans with respect to their plans for research and "changes" in product quality. By deliberately not providing any precise definition of "national security" or guidance on the quality or weight of evidence to be used in such assessments, the regime provides vast discretion for regulators to include their own notions of economic security in their review. In theory, their focus is on national-security transactions that involve control of the subject U.S. entity; control is so equivocally defined that it includes even the power to decide whether to lease an asset of the business. Managers who have repeatedly seen foreign investors transfer technology to the United States are confused by one of the many "security" criteria used in the law: Government bureaucrats are required to assess whether an investment will jeopardize "U.S. technological leadership."

Defenders of the act point out that it was a necessary supplement to existing law and that only one transaction has been officially blocked since its enactment. International managers understand differently. Existing export-control laws already provided broad authority to stop the flow of sensitive U.S. technology to foreign investors—even between U.S and non–U.S. managers meeting within the United States—and the chilling effects of the act have forced hundreds of investors to scale back plans. Several planned investments have been cancelled altogether, including intended investments by Japan's Fanuc in Moore Corporation, a machine-tool maker; by Britain's BTR in the Norton Company, an abrasives maker; by India's Lalbhai Group in Tachonics; and by Japan's Tokoyama Soda in General Ceramics.

The preempted plans were not dark conspiracies to steal the nation's missile-targeting systems. They were legitimate commercial investments in the computer, electronic equipment, aviation, communications, publishing, semiconductor, and other industries, which quickly lose attractiveness when overlaid with the long delays, massive legal fees, voluminous disclosures (including required disclosures of strategic investment plans), and often brutal publicity that are entailed in an Exon-Florio review.

By virtue of its oversweeping language, the Exon-Florio Act also places a huge burden on international banks. Any financing that includes an asset-foreclosure clause represents a potential "control" over the borrower. A foreign-based bank involved in financing an entity that may somehow fall within the "national security" umbrella of Exon-Florio runs the risk of being unable to exercise such a clause, since theoretically it could be blocked from "control" under the law. The Exon-Florio rules provide no means by which a bank can "clear" such a loan; international bankers thus must bear the risk—or stay out of U.S. investments or foreign deals involving parents of U.S. subsidiaries that may fall within the shadow of Exon-Florio.

Approximately 800 foreign investments have been submitted for review by the Committee on Foreign Investment in the United States. Included among those closely investigated by the committee: investments in biotechnology, electrical transmission equipment, aircraft parts, and the takeover by Minorco, a Luxembourg firm, of Consolidated Gold Fields, a British company that owned an interest in an American mining company. In 1991, unhappy with President Bush's record of permitting reviewed transactions, the Congress attacked the Bush administration for not, in the words of the senior senator from West Virginia, preventing foreign firms from "raiding the U.S. economy." Congress amended the law to require the president to explain his reasons to Congress each time he decides *not* to block an investment. Soon afterward, the House Banking Subcommittee on Economic Stabilization began considering amendments to add U.S. "economic competitiveness" as a criteria for blocking investments.[26]

Policymakers seem able to constantly find new red flags to wave at foreign investors in the United States. While Washington presses against foreign investment, state governors compete for hundreds of millions in new investment by non–U.S. companies. Over forty states have offices in Tokyo alone for the purpose of luring large investments to their hometowns. But Flat Earth thinkers found one state ally: California. Sacramento yielded to the temptation of taxing nonconstituents, imposing a "worldwide unitary" tax on international companies with affiliate operations in the state based on the global earnings of their foreign parents. Although the uniform practice in other jurisdictions has been to treat each domestic corporation (whether parents or subsidiaries of foreign firms) as a separate taxable entity, taxing only the income of that unit, California issued tax bills totaling billions to international firms based on their income outside the United States.

The California system required submission of worldwide accounting information for companies maintaining even minimal operations in the state. Foreign-based firms faced a huge penalty for complying: They were compelled to keep a second set of records in English, based on U.S. financial and tax principles that did not otherwise apply to their internal systems. Huge costs have been incurred in compiling and reporting global data required by California regulators. Such firms have been subjected to double taxation in many instances, since local profits from operations around the planet are taxed locally but included in California's taxation of global profit. Even if—as was true in some sectors—the high operating costs in the state meant an enterprise had low or no profits in the state, California still reached beyond its borders to participate in higher profits earned in Singapore, Brazil, or France.

International corporations from the United States and overseas fought the tax due to the huge burden it placed on them and the still greater threat it posed should other jurisdictions choose to adopt such an antiglobal bias. Barclays Bank, which led a judicial attack on the tax, had only three out of 220 affiliates with operations in the United States; 98 percent of its revenues came from outside the United States. But to comply with the California tax, the bank was required to spend over $5 million to establish a reporting system and $2 million annually to maintain it. British tax authorities insisted that they would levy equally punitive taxes on U.S. companies in England if the tax were maintained.

Over thirty-five diplomatic protests were filed, including complaints from the governments of Germany, Japan, France, Denmark, Italy, Canada, Finland, and Australia. They correctly pointed out that the unitary tax method had been expressly examined by the League of Nations decades earlier and rejected as detrimental to global growth. The State Department, which complained that the California system presented an almost irresistible temptation for revenue-hungry regulators in developing countries to adopt look-alike laws, reported that it had been repeatedly asked by foreign allies if the United States had one foreign policy or fifty-one.[27] Although California eventually modified a few of the more egregious features of its system, it was only after billions in additional taxes had been paid and at least six other states had adopted tax laws with similar features. The unitary tax remains on California books, upheld in a judicial challenge in the U.S. Supreme Court in which the White House filed a brief to support the argument that the tax was a valid exercise of the state's power.[28]

Earnings-stripping rules have long worked against international firms with U.S. operations; for many firms these rules effectively eliminate the deduction for interest paid or accrued on intercompany debt owed by U.S. subsidiaries to foreign parents. Under Section 163 of the

Internal Revenue Code, a U.S. corporation with a debt-to-equity ratio of greater than 1.5 to 1 is not permitted a deduction for interest due a related foreign party if the U.S. firm's interest expense exceeds 50 percent of its income. Despite long-voiced complaints that the rules discriminate against foreign firms trying to put capital in the United States, which they obviously do, the rules were tightened in 1993 to cover not only direct loans but also debt guaranteed by a corporate parent. Alexander Spitzer, chief U.S. tax manager for Switzerland's Nestlé S.A. voiced the sentiment of many international investors when he stated to the *Wall Street Journal* that "It isn't a big revenue-raiser. It was done for political reasons. It's just bad law all around."[29]

The manipulation of antidumping laws against cross-border movements of their products have soured many foreign investors. After its imported typewriters were repeatedly attacked under the U.S. antidumping laws, Brother International Corporation of Japan invested in a large electronic-typewriter facility in the United States; its primary U.S.-based competitor then began competing with Brother's U.S. production by importing its own machines from Asian sources. But when Brother's U.S. plant tried to use the antidumping laws in the same fashion in which they had been used against it, the Department of Commerce ruled that it was not a U.S. producer. Brother had to go to court to compel the agency to recognize its rights under U.S. law.[30]

The flurry of new steel antidumping cases filed in 1992 produced a sea change for many global owners that funded recovery in the U.S. steel industry. Japanese producers alone had invested over $7 billion during the 1980s to upgrade U.S. steel production through joint ventures with U.S. firms. After the dumping cases were filed, Yoshitaka Fujitani, president of NKK America, was ready to call off more investment. "Japanese companies feel they've put in enough money," Fujitani complained. The Japan Iron and Steel Federation warned that the cases raised "serious questions about the wisdom of continued partnerships" with U.S. firms.[31]

Nissan Motor Corporation wanted to expand investment at its Tennessee plant to build cars of nearly 100 percent U.S. content; it was prevented from doing so by Environmental Protection Agency (EPA) fuel-consumption rules that were written with a severe antiglobal bias. The rules artificially separated "U.S." and "import" model fleets for fuel-economy standards. Under a uniform standard, Nissan could have met the EPA criteria and built its extra capacity in Tennessee. But the EPA rules forced Nissan and others, including producers based in Detroit, to allocate production of some highly fuel-efficient models to foreign countries—just when market forces were pressing for them to invest in U.S. capacity.

DEPRESSING THE ENVIRONMENT FOR INVESTMENT

From their inception, the EPA's "corporate average fuel economy" (CAFE) rules have required producers to separate their products into "import" and "domestic" fleets. Each fleet must separately meet the CAFE standard for miles per gallon. The purpose of the separation was to discourage producers from importing large volumes of high-mileage cars to "subsidize" the production of gas guzzlers. The rules have created bizarre distortions in international investment. Detroit has converted many of its low-mileage vehicles to "imports" by moving production of key components offshore. Honda's strategy has been to move to the United States production of all its Accord models sold in the United States; but the EPA standards cause it to keep importing enough Accords from Japan to classify the model as an import, allowing its mileage to be averaged with high-mileage compacts.

Ford prefers to make its top-end products—sold for many years as Crown Victoria and Mercury Grand Marquis—in the United States, but the CAFE rules forced the firm to reduce their domestic content from 94 to 73 percent to be classified as "imports." The rules cause similar manipulation of investment in "domestic" cars; the Mercury Tracer gets high mileage, needed to balance out lower-mileage cars in Ford's "domestic" fleet. The company ships parts to Mexico for assembly so that the Mexican-produced car can be called "domestic." General Motors equipped a special 747 to ferry body parts for its Cadillac Allante from Italy. The company could make the car in the United States, but then it would trigger EPA fines by lowering the mileage of its "domestic" fleet. Toyota plans to invest in new U.S. capacity so that all its U.S. cars have 75 percent U.S. content, but the CAFE rules may change that. Notes James Olson, the company's U.S. vice president of external affairs, "If we ended with severe enough CAFE problems, we would have to reassess our drive toward 75 percent local content" in the United States.

The same Section 482 of the tax code that hits America's global firms also penalizes foreign investors in the United States. On the grounds that foreign firms set high transfer prices for materials brought to the United States from affiliates to return added profit to their "home," Washington adjusts the income of such firms to reflect what "normal" firms would have paid. When the Clinton administration in 1992 promised to wring $45 billion out of foreign firms, Section 482 was its intended weapon. The "objective" standard used to benchmark such international transfers is typically the rate of return in the U.S. domestic industry. It does not take into account the much longer time frame in which most non–U.S. companies make investment decisions—meaning the investment mentality that has saved hundreds of U.S. firms whose U.S. owners were too impatient to nurture them is punished by the IRS.

Foreign managers are seldom obsessed with cash-flow multiples, as many American managers seem to be. They make strategic investments for the long term. Siemens, the German electronics firm, has made over thirty acquisitions in the United States and, due to its program of pumping in capital for research and improvements, at last report had yet to show a profit on any of them.

Such foreign firms frequently make lower returns due to higher investment in research, redesign of production, worker retraining, even different marketing strategies. The IRS demands, however, that all such firms be reduced to one common Flat Earth denominator. The House Ways and Means Committee has repeatedly considered measures to require foreign investors to pay taxes on "constructive" profits that "should have been earned" by such operations if they had been run by "American" managers. A 1993 proposal that, although not enacted, gained approval from many senior members of Congress provided that for tax purposes, foreign firms would be deemed to earn at least 75 percent of the income of American-owned firms in the same industry.

In 1990, 200 members of Congress intervened with letters calling for "Americanization" of assets when one British investor simply sought to buy the interests of another British firm in the United States. Local politicians in several regions have dusted off century-old laws to try to block "aliens" from buying local real estate.[32] The acquisition of a Silicon Valley firm by an Asian company was unofficially blocked on national-security grounds—even though the California unit was already owned by a French company.

Net foreign investment in the United States plummeted to $11.5 billion in 1991 from over $67 billion in 1989. In 1992, for the first time since World War II, foreigners took more money out of the United States than they put into it. By traditional measures, total investment everywhere slumped in that year of recession. But the reports of that slump ignored an important piece of information: Investment by U.S. firms overseas during that period rose by a dramatic 30 percent—despite the erosion of the dollar's value—reflecting both the inexorable demand for international investment and the relative attractiveness of foreign locations versus the adversarial climate created by presidential and congressional campaigns filled with threats against international enterprise. Investment has climbed back since then, but the message of 1992 remains. Veteran international investment counselor Martin F. Klingenberg has seen a new breed of investors emerge recently. "Prominent on their due diligence lists are questions about whether Congress has new foreign-investment measures pending. And high on my own lists of tasks is a regulatory comparison of the potential investment venues." Every investment by global enterprise involves a verdict on regulatory systems.

THE NEW AMERICAN CHALLENGE

For American policymakers, the only problem with foreign investment is that it's foreign. Every measure Washington applies to it is based on negative perceptions, on a pejorative connotation of "foreign" that is so deeply embedded in policy and perspectives as to be instinctive. A look at our international-investment laws and policy statements reveals a conspicuous use of terms like *alien, tax evasion*, and *threats to security*. Investment figures are never presented in terms of competitive advantage to an industry, a firm, or a work force. We always hear about investment "balances," about "net" positions based on weighing "our" investment versus "theirs."

When new data revealed that foreign investment in the United States exceeded that of U.S. firms overseas, the chairman of the Senate Subcommittee on International Trade quickly reacted with a public statement that "the figures confirm that the United States has become a major international debtor."[33] Our measurement systems do indeed show foreign direct investment as "debt"—even though only a small part of the investment in the data is in the form of loans or direct debt. The "debt" figure, the figure bemoaned as a defeat for the United States, represented the hundreds of billions of dollars invested—not loaned but invested for the long term—in U.S. factories, jobs, and research. It defies reason and economic sense to consider that money as a liability to America.

But the prejudice runs deep. On a regular basis over the past five years, proposals have surfaced in Congress to punish non–U.S. firms that have invested in U.S. auto and truck plants by treating their output as imports, subject to tariffs and quotas. It is ironic that the automotive sector continues to be the target for some of the most conspicuous—and often the most virulent—anti-foreign-investment rhetoric. There are few better examples of how cross-border investment invigorates an industry than the auto sector. Detroit grew stagnant under the protective schemes of the 1980s. But that very protection had a result that galled the Flat Earth policymakers who sponsored it: Foreign automakers poured billions into new factories within the United States, driving new liquidity and diversity—of ideas, workers, capital, and management styles—into the industry. Quality control, inventory systems, product-design cycles, worker management, and supplier relationships were revolutionized. By 1993 Detroit was enjoying an unexpected renaissance. That year, America regained the title of the top car producer on the planet in terms of production volume.

Flat Earth cynics complained that it was because foreign firms were producing so many cars in the United States. But the flag of the producers—if one could be found—was irrelevant; the quality, productivity, value, and assets that created that leadership were all based in America. Flat Earth policymakers have had a difficult time accepting that reality: Their response has been to propose rules that will require all cars built in "foreign" plants within the United States to be counted as imports, then impose strict "import" limits on such production.

A best-selling American book in 1988 was a diatribe against foreign investment entitled *Buying into America: How Foreign Money is Changing the Face of Our Nation*.[34] The book was in effect an American version of the 1968 European best-seller by Jean Jacques Servan-Schreiber, *The American Challenge*. Servan-Schreiber's book spread alarm about U.S. investment in Europe that was zealously embraced by EC politicians. It was the point of embarkation for two decades of misguided industrial policy and intervention from which the European Union is only now recovering. The titles of both books inadvertently captured a vital message for policymakers: Foreign investment *does* represent a challenge and *is* changing our society. But by every objective standard, that change is for the better. Foreign investment does not hold us prisoner. It does not restrain our economy. It is a vital catalyst for growth and innovation. It is how enterprise captures the global capital that drives the new economy. Policymakers have to ask what is more important: that owners of American business eat only sirloin—and no sushi or pickled herring—or that owners of American business create jobs, innovation, and growth?

The political process at least allows globally aware American enterprises to inject their views. Foreign firms investing in America don't vote and have the weakest of voices in Washington, but firms like Boeing, AT&T, IBM, Motorola, and 3M are heard much more clearly. In the context of investment and other Flat Earth policymaking, such enterprises whose fate is inextricably linked to the global economy are often the primary voices for change. When Washington proposed trade restrictions on a ceramic chip mount made in Japan, it wasn't lobbyists from Kyocera, the Japanese producer, that protested but representatives of IBM, the American Semiconductor Industry Association, and the Aerospace Industries Association, who explained how vital the component was to their global sourcing investments. When Honda's Ohio plant was challenged over compliance with domestic-content rules, those who registered the loudest protests were U.S. suppliers and the Canadian government, concerned over the implications for Honda's Canadian plant. When KLM's bailout investment in Northwest Airlines was blocked by the Secretary of Transportation, a storm of protest from U.S. interests eventually caused reconsideration of the decision. The department relented and permitted KLM to fill one third of Northwest's board seats—the amount already authorized under the Federal Aviation Act.

Despite some policymakers' efforts, "foreign" simply doesn't work as a paradigm for economic policy. Among British Petroleum, Exxon, Shell, and Mobil, who are the foreigners, and who are the natives? Each of the companies has massive investments in Europe and North America, each of the companies employs thousands of Americans, and each pays vast sums to the U.S. Treasury Department. Why should the Department of Commerce classify Du Pont as a foreign (Canadian) company simply because Canada's Seagrams owns 23 percent of Du Pont?[35] If regulators cannot totally abandon their traditional mind-sets, then perhaps as a first step they can start thinking about international investors as immigrants, not as foreigners. They share many attributes of the immigrants of another century that made this country strong: confidence in America, new skills, new perspectives, ambition, creativity, long-term commitment, and dogged determination.

Regulators must accept the reality that enterprises can and do move billions of dollars around the planet in reaction to government policy. It is the height of folly to consider, for example, that international investment can be taxed, with impunity, more heavily than "domestic" investment or that international capital can be manipulated for blatantly political reasons without economic consequences. It is no coincidence that following the emergence of global capital and high-volume movement of investment, there has been a global trend (not consistently matched in the United States) toward lower tax rates, relaxation of trade and service restrictions, industry deregulation, simplified tax systems, and privatization of government services.

Washington has the same choice available to other world capitals who have lost their traditional captive markets for investment as a result of the global economy: It can maintain its entrenched regimes for control and protection or it can proceed with a fresh perspective in tune with the new global realities. International investment is the primary conduit for the benefits of the new economy, but those benefits are never forced into a country's borders. They must be attracted.

GOVERNMENT FROM A GLOBAL CORE

Building the
Innovation
Infrastructure

In February 1995 policy leaders in the White House unveiled what they characterized as proof of their global engagement. With great hoopla, they released their report on an initiative for a Global Information Infrastructure, built around state-of-the-art technology intended "to capture the promise of the Information Revolution."[1] The report, replete with new-age technical jargon and calls for reform of foreign laws to support global communications, attracted considerable international press attention and promises of resources for the national initiative from which it was extrapolated, the information superhighway.

Global managers who studied the plan were skeptical. "Very pretty," was their basic reaction, "but where's the meat?" The meat that was missing, of course, was any meaningful reform to the U.S. policies that restrict the global efforts of the Americans who would be using the infrastructure. To the extent that policy obstacles existed, the report essentially said, they were primarily outside the United States.

The global information initiative has become the perfect global solution for those who have been waiting for robots in their kitchens to announce the future. It is rife with cybernetics and talk of the coming millennium. It is so heavily draped with the rhetoric of change that many of its well-intentioned supporters have equated it with change. But in itself, it represents no shift in policy paradigms, no transition to globally attuned policy. It has merely draped old concepts with new high-tech garb.

Distracted by what he perceives to be dazzling new clothes, the emperor manages to ignore the real challenges of the new economy. There is nothing wrong with the information superhighway, except that it has diverted many policymakers from much more important work. The global plebiscite will assure that the superhighway will be built and that it will span the planet—with or without government help. But only public policymakers can move government away from the Flat Earth.

So far there has been little movement. Washington's aged policy machines sputter blissfully along. Notwithstanding the global lip service occasionally offered by those at their controls, they churn along the paths chiseled out to support the American manufacturing base that existed forty and fifty years ago.

That world might as well be in the Cretaceous period. It is gone forever. Like a tectonic plate, the global economy has moved, irrevocably changing our landscape. Yet most regulators refuse to accept that reality; many refuse to even consider it. They keep pulling old creatures from worn-out policy hats, pretending their fossilized remains are alive and well. Such intransigence is not only a vast disappointment for those who believe in the American system of governing. It also belies the most basic premise of that system: its ability to evolve and grow with its people and their economy.

ECLIPSE OF SOVEREIGNTY

The nation-state is not in danger of extinction. It retains many vital functions related to the security and health of its people. But the new economy has brought the end of economic sovereignty. Government has lost control of every element that defines competitiveness and will not regain it, short of measures that would amount to economic mass destruction. Policymakers may ignore that reality, but they cannot change it. The problem for global enterprise, however, is that the complex machinery erected in another age to exercise such control continues to operate. It may have lost its power to determine economic outcomes, but it retains ample power to hinder the economic process and to inflict inefficiency and handicap American firms. Those machines will continue to hurt America until their operators listen to the global plebiscite.

Above all, what the plebiscite is telling them is that the movement of capital and ideas, which is the basic process of global enterprise, is focused on where they realize the most value, and that such enterprise is well aware of the capacity of regulation to detract from that value. Cynics view this process as a form of irresponsible regulatory arbitrage, a worldwide contest for laxity in regulation. But they are wrong. Global enterprise in this context is not about a crusade for laissez-faire; it is about pushing government to provide value. Regulatory arbitrage is inevitable the moment any enterprise or entrepreneur has the ability to cross a political border; it occurs constantly within the United States, as witnessed most dramatically by the flight of companies out of California and New York over the past fifteen years. It is a healthy process, one that helps policymakers and voters understand the context of their decisions. There is, moreover, a vast spectrum between the complex, redundant, and costly rules imposed as part of Washington's communications, trade, competition, technology, and capital policies and no rules at all.

Global enterprise does not seek anarchy, but ultimately it will refuse to pay for regulation that adds no value—meaning that unstable regulation, complex regulation, and anachronistic regulation drives away enterprise. Whether Boeing builds its next generation of aircraft in the United States or whether there will be a Silicon Valley in the United States ten years from now will be determined by the extent to which Washington interferes with the global process.

The innovation that has devalued traditional corporate structures has also sharply devalued the contribution of traditional government. But the new forces of liquidity and diversity that are vitalizing enterprise can also work in government. The knowledge derived from those forces presents vast opportunities for meaningful reform. The new economy, moreover, offers an unprecedented vehicle for policymakers; for those who learn how to listen to it, the global plebiscite offers instant verdicts on public-policy initiatives.

Those ready to accept the challenge of introducing globally driven innovation to government must start with the wholesale abandonment of the anachronistic concepts discussed in these pages, as global firms began to do years ago. Global winners—among both enterprises and governments—can only be built by leaving the old world behind. There is no turning back in the new economy. And there is no place to hide.

LISTENING TO THE GLOBE

One important reason the leaders of institutions are so readily able to ignore changed realities is that the information decision makers receive about their world is screened by the institutions themselves. Good policy is impossible to wring out of bad data. If Washington policymakers ask for data on the new economy, they are given printouts from statistical bases designed to monitor exports, imports, and manufacturing jobs. When they are asked to react to new patterns of imports, they are presented with data on those whose jobs are directly threatened by imports—which is like determining welfare policy by asking welfare recipients if payments should be continued. If they want to understand the effect of foreign investment, they confer with tax or labor officials, whose databases will tell them of lost tax revenues and lost jobs. Consider a sampling of the most recent proposals from such policymakers when they were asked how to improve government for the new economy: Shorten the time period for antidumping cases to expedite new duty barriers, push companies to confer with the government in advance before setting international prices to preserve tax revenue, more strictly enforce country-of-origin marking programs to discourage international sourcing networks, authorize American unions to expand membership by organizing overseas plants owned by U.S. investors to penalize foreign investment, compel Japan to balance its shipments of cars to the United States with purchases of U.S. auto parts, and treat output of U.S. plants owned by foreign investors as "imports" to be manipulated by tariffs and quotas. Every such proposal is driven by outdated views of the world, entrenched by obsolete data. Like administrative and control systems anywhere, they are driven to control what they can measure and to ignore what they cannot or do not measure.

What is needed is an abandonment of the systems that reduce our complex global flows to simplistic columns of imports and exports, that wave red flags of deficits before officialdom's eyes. What is needed are better measures for the integration of global capital, productivity, sources of growth, the flow of intangibles, and the indirect costs of economic regulation. Measuring devices must be found to meaningfully explain value-added activity within webs of enterprise.

Discarding balance-of-trade statistics as the centerpiece of international economic policy is the first step. Such statistics obscure the most important transactions in the new economy, such as those between units of global enterprise. The systems that reduce the complex dynamics of such enterprises to one word—*deficit*—have long been criticized as misleading,[2] but today they have become destructive of rational policymaking. Much more important than knowing the net balance of transactions at one particular point—the U.S. border—along a long chain of value-added activity involving multiple countries is knowing that one third of all U.S. exports and one third of all imports are made by U.S.

firms shipping to foreign affiliates, both parents and subsidiaries. Such figures tell policymakers that these intrafirm transactions must be supported in *both* directions—outbound and inbound—in order to support U.S. involvement in vitally important networks in which American knowledge and other value-addeds are integrated into products and services for the global plebiscite.

Casting U.S. transactions on the basis of global ownership instead of geographic venue would go far to underscore this point for the policy process. Doing so shows that U.S. firms are earning more abroad than non–U.S. investors in the United States ($62 billion versus $56 billion in 1993) and that in most years, American enterprises sell more in international markets than all non–U.S. enterprises together sell to the United States. In October 1995 two analysts in the Department of Commerce, Obie Whichard and Jeffrey Lowe, demonstrated that data already exist to allow the government to switch to such global aggregate statistics for policymaking.[3]

Listening to the global plebiscite also tells us that *much more emphasis is needed in policy information systems on the role of human capital and innovative structures that are improving capital efficiency.* Outsourcing relationships, for example, fall through the cracks of government figures. By traditionally measuring productivity on the basis of sales and employees, the Commerce Department has ignored outsourcing, thereby distorting productivity figures and grossly underemphasizing the importance of such new relationships. Firms founded on outsourcing, like Nike or Benetton, do not compute in such traditional machinery—and therefore the significance of their structures is lost on the policy process. Government analysts readily admit, moreover, that traditional devices provide no reliable way to measure the productivity of service enterprises—meaning they have no way to gauge the productivity of 80 percent of America's workers.

Growth in the new economy depends on growth in knowledge and transfers of knowledge. Without being able to gauge the effects of expanded knowledge—meaning more productive human capital— policymakers will not be able to fully understand the new process of growth. Rather than focus on loss of "American" technology through such clumsy devices as comparing royalty payments, government policymakers should be asking for data that show the *global connections*—or lack thereof—*of American innovation.* Efforts already under way to obtain *international comparisons of knowledge concentrations*[4]—based on criteria like education and knowledge content in jobs—also merit closer attention by policymakers.

Perhaps the fundamental challenge in identifying updated policy inputs is *finding meaningful ways to illuminate the hidden constituency of the new economy.* Flat Earth structures are attributable in no small part to the phenomenon described by the late Tip O'Neill, former Speaker of the House: "All politics is local." Policymakers are regularly reminded of the negative aspects of the adjustments under way as a result of the new global economic process in the form of complaints about lost jobs. Information machines need to convey the message of the less vocal, less conspicuous, but vastly more numerous beneficiaries of the new economy. The challenge is not unlike that of the military base-closing process, in which Washington eventually found a way to preempt traditional politics in order to allow sound economic information and judgments to prevail over local complaints. The creation of a new Global Economic Policy Commission with powers to challenge traditional policy inputs and structures could serve the same purpose fulfilled by the Base Closing Commission in adjusting the U.S. military to new realities.

The facts of the new economy are there for all to see, available to anyone ready to lend them an objective analysis. But too many regulators, puffed up with the tradition that government can and should arbitrage economic information, deny themselves the knowledge needed for meaningful reform. Inviting meaningful reform into the process will be a worthless exercise until Washington completes a crash course on the new economy. To assure their matriculation, every economic policymaker should carry a crib sheet of the new realities—which they should quickly consult whenever they feel the temptation to protect another inefficient job, block a foreign investment, or bludgeon the dollar to ease a trade deficit. They should inscribe prominently on their policy notebooks:

- The global economy does not separate itself into "U.S." and "foreign" segments. The United States is a region of the global economy. "Domestic" and "international" economic policymaking can no longer be separated.

- Success in the global economy is not obtained by depriving others of their participation.

- We do not lose jobs or ideas by competing across borders.

- Nations do not have a sovereign right to competitiveness. It cannot be compelled, decreed, or enacted by law.

- American competitiveness derives from the value of American content in the global economy—not the number of products bearing a "Made in the USA" label.

- Every job kept alive as a result of protection from Washington is a blow to American productivity and therefore to the competitiveness of American enterprise.

- Foreign investment, both inbound and outbound, plays a vital role in boosting competitiveness.

- American competitiveness is not a function of trade balances. Trade deficits have absolutely no significance for competitiveness.

- Governments cannot stake exclusive national claims to ideas—and therefore cannot control the process of creating value in the new economy.

It is only by paying attention to these basic realities that the Flat Earth can be left behind.

SHIFTING TO GLOBAL

Emigrating from the Flat Earth is not merely a process of updating old laws. Breaking away from its boundaries is only possible through what, in the context of traditional politics, entails a virtual revolution. Mere incremental improvements will not be enough, nor will acceleration of existing government processes. As has been shown by conspicuous failures in every recent effort by government to intervene in technology-intensive sectors—witness its efforts in the export control, computer, and communications arenas—keeping up with global realities cannot be accomplished by simply shortening cycles of regulation or updating technical criteria.

Striking at the heart of Flat Earth policy means striking at the basic assumptions of government. Fundamental shifts in existing paradigms of policy are required. For decades those paradigms have been the foundation of all international economic policy and much economic policy generally. But they have been overwhelmed by the global tide. Policymakers who continue to cling to them look increasingly like Canute bidding the waters to recede.

Their implications are profound and complex, but the paradigm shifts required for Washington to catch up with planet's economic transformation can be simply expressed:

Bilateralism ➔ Multilateralism
Manufacturing ➔ Innovation
Exports ➔ Integration
Protection ➔ Diversity

Control → Interdependence
Competition → Liquidity

In total, the concepts in the left column comprise the anachronistic paradigms that have led American policy to where it is today. In one permutation or another, they entirely account for Washington's powerful antiglobal bias. On the right appear the new paradigms needed to address the counterpart set of issues in today's economy. With these six fundamental shifts, Washington can emigrate from the Flat Earth.

Such a revolution will not be achieved overnight. But global reform will never be achieved without a goal in sight. For each of these shifts, moreover, short-term steps are available that would provide real, immediate boosts for America's global enterprise as a transition to the more compelling task of fundamental reform.

Bilateralism → Multilateralism

Bilateralism has always meant unilateralism: International relations are posited in terms of "us" versus Japan or Europe, China, or another "them." Bilateral policy is not global policy. It is the beggar-thy-neighbor attitude that drives policymakers to zero-sum protestations that computer chips or autos are not "balanced" and calls for retaliation against every deficit in trade with a major partner. It compels officials to posture every international challenge as a struggle between geographic entities and to even consider that the U.S. solution to any problem is necessarily the global solution. But unilateral solutions don't work anymore, and zero-sum mentalities obscure the dynamics of the new economy in which value is created and flows through multiple countries. Not even the largest economy on earth has the power to impose its economic judgments on others today. The United States has to join the rest of the world; like every nation, it must consider events in other countries in fashioning its economic policy. Setting policy, if it cannot be a multilateral exercise, must at least apply multilateral criteria.

The Multilateral Solution: Washington has not begun to tap the real potential for global consensus on economic issues. It is not only in the United States that global enterprise is showing government how outdated traditional policy has become. The transformation of the economic environment is conspicuous everywhere; the ground is set for an era of unprecedented economic consensus across borders. Washington, moreover, is the natural candidate for taking the lead in building that consensus. But its reputation is so tarnished that other countries enter talks with Washington on the defensive, ready for tirades and threats of unilateral retaliation if Washington is not satisfied. Such approaches do not achieve constructive results in cross-border negotiations between enterprise, and they do not achieve results in the context of government negotiation—witness the meager results of the Uruguay Round. Washington's bullying is already causing other nations to leave it behind in some global initiatives, the most important being the World Trade Organization's agreement on financial services.

In the short term, the multilateral shift means creating a new negotiation dynamic. It means building a new reputation for American negotiators by no longer paying lip service to multilateral solutions while still reacting with retaliatory, unilateral crowbars to every issue that arises with a trading partner. It means favoring multilateral remedies to cross-border issues rather than resorting to Section 301, Washington's most notorious legal weapon against foreign governments. Another move, helpful not only for its symbolic value, would be to convert the annual trade-barrier inventory compiled to define targets for Washington's trade warriors into lists of priority actions for multilateral harmonization efforts to address the same problems.

In the long term, political forces need to be mobilized to obtain meaningful global accords in support of global enterprise. It means allocating resources to such efforts commensurate with their vital importance. It means moving aggressively forward with open-market agreements with other countries but with an inclusive, not an exclusive, approach: A North Atlantic open-market agreement between the European Union and the United States, for example, should be built not around special privileges for American firms but as a vehicle for attracting other nations to join—the countries of Eastern Europe and others in North and South America being natural candidates.

Bilateralism is always tempting because it is the arena for macho trade politics. It was no coincidence that while the White House was preparing its reelection campaign plans in early 1996, the Office of the U.S. Trade Representative concurrently announced that it would redouble its efforts to use crowbars to punish wayward trading partners. But the global plebiscite has cast its own verdict on the bilateral deals obtained with American crowbars: They defy global markets, so global markets will defy them.

Manufacturing ➜ Innovation

American government matured with the assumption that manufacturing was the centerpiece of all sound economic policy. International business was conducted with factories, and the spoils belonged to those who reaped economies of scale. This preoccupation with manufacturing always skewed economic policymaking toward the hard assets and natural resources that drove comparative advantage in the old economy. But manufacturing is not where strategic value is added in the new economy.

By aiming policy engines and diplomatic energy at trade in manufactured goods, Washington ignores the most important opportunities to add American value in the new economy. By making big export factories the symbol of American machismo, political and business leaders are trying to fight the competitive battles of the '90s with the weapons of the '60s. It is the dynamic process of innovation that must be supported. Innovation has evolved away from production; instead of following manufacturing as it once did, innovation leads it. At even the largest industrial firms today, knowledge assets far exceed the value of hard production assets. It is innovation that builds productivity, it is innovation that builds American competitiveness, it is innovation that accounts for the success of those U.S. firms that lead their global industries.

The Innovation Solution: In the short term, Washington should refrain from further interventions in commercial technology and otherwise second-guessing the global plebiscite in determining the best new ideas for global markets. It should bring to a halt the destructive campaign begun at the Federal Trade Commission and the Department of Justice to manage "innovation markets," as well as the campaign to sharply limit the immigration of foreign experts to the United States.

In the long term, the bias toward hard assets and production lines must be filtered out of American tax laws, as must the disincentives for innovation across borders. It should update intellectual property regimes, then push them onto a global platform to eliminate differentials in the treatment of the "property" of ideas. Most importantly, America's participation in global innovation must be liberated by building the innovation infrastructure discussed below.

Exports → Integration

Imports are no longer inherently bad. Exports are no longer inherently good. If policymakers listened to the globe, they would find that many of their vaunted exports bear an American label only because their point of final assembly happened to be in the United States—and their reviled imports often contain knowledge content vital to U.S. competitiveness.

An export of purely American commodities like soybeans or timber is not nearly so important for American well-being as an import of motherboards for the American firms that lead the computer industry. Washington's enslavement to trade accounts has become a huge burden on American productivity. Merchandise trade deficits are not only worthless as indicators of economic prosperity or decline—the United States ran deficits during many of its boom years and surpluses during the Great Depression—they are counterproductive. They are mere political lightning rods that blind policymakers to the new realities.

In many ways, this shift is another means of expressing the shift from manufacturing to innovation: Growth today isn't a simple matter of pushing manufacturing to push exports but rather a matter of pushing innovation to support America's share of global enterprise. The transition from manufacturing by "national" industries as the foundation of all international business to dynamic interchange of value-added within global networks of firms and industries means "country of origin" (as traditionally used to signify manufacturing origin) is meaningless— meaning, in turn, that "export" itself has lost meaning as a crux for policy. America desperately needs to end its enslavement to the one-dimensional paradigm of international business as export business. Instead of focusing on exports, policymakers must focus on the dynamics of the integration that makes cross-border exchange of value possible, improving the efficiency of those dynamics *in the United States*—and thereby upgrading the value added by U.S. enterprise.

The Integration Solution: In the export-control arena, detailed reform hammered out by industry and quasi-official groups over the past five years is drafted and ready for formal passage by Congress. Export controls inhibit the integration of American ideas into the new economy, including not only external shipments but use of American venues in global networks. The existing law, dating back to the Cold War years of the 1970s, has been operating by administrative extension for years and is begging for reform to eliminate unilateral controls that have no reference to markets (i.e., controls on U.S. sales even though the subject goods are readily available overseas).

Over the long term, the barriers to both incoming and outgoing value-added must be reduced to terms that reflect the realities of global markets. Export clearances from domestic agencies like the Environmental Protection Agency, for example, either impede the sharing of U.S. knowledge across the border—restricting both the value received by U.S. firms for their knowledge and the cross-fertilization that drives innovation—or drive production offshore. When Washington forces a firm to choose between serving 250 million at home or 5 billion outside the United States, it has inflicted injury on the American people—no matter what the firm's decision may be.

Protectionism ➙ Diversity

Washington's love affair with factories has built a protection machine that America can no longer afford. By pretending that the country is enriched by walls to protect old factories, Washington deceives itself and its citizens into thinking those factories are integral to economic vitality. Every low-skill job that is put on life support by Washington hurts us all. Protectionism is not only a choke point in the economic process, it breeds unhealthy, uncompetitive enterprises whose inefficiencies are infectious, contaminating every industry they touch. The global economy has an answer to such inefficiencies: diversity, meaning access to new ideas, new capital, new products, and new services. Extending protection to any industry or company is extending weakness. Just as destructive are the capital controls implicit in every effort to manage "deficits" caused by "too many" imports. Every deficit means more offshore capital for American enterprise, capital often used much more effectively than the short-term profits generated by the increased exports pumped up by Washington's deficit-management tools like driving down the dollar— which is not to say that imports should be a policy goal but only that they need not be feared. Supporting diversity is supporting strength, and the wider the spectrum of diversity (meaning increased flows from nontraditional sources), the greater the potential opportunity.

The Diversity Solution: Policymakers can support diversity immediately by applying their administrative discretion to eliminate arbitrary interference by Washington in market-based pricing decisions by foreign companies, thereby improving their ability to present new products to American consumers. Foreign firms should not be penalized for "dumping" caused by *any* foreign-exchange fluctuations or by the artificial cost constructions created by trade bureaucrats. Washington's push for its trading partners to adopt look-alike trade laws should be halted. By proselytizing for clones of the U.S. law around the planet, Washington is arming its trading partners with neutron bombs for border protection in every trade war to come. Damage to U.S. interests will be profound in coming years if foreign countries begin to pay back American firms with the treatment their own firms have received in Washington.

In the long term, Washington must divorce itself from its protectionist traditions. Disruptive border controls must be replaced with expanded measures designed to ease the pain of individuals hurt by job adjustment, which primarily means educational efforts. In the new economy, the most important investment of taxpayer money for economic growth is always that of education; it is hard to envision how America can be a world economic leader while 20 percent of its high school students drop out before graduation and the majority of Americans cannot identify ten countries on a map.

GETTING GLOBAL, NOW

The revolutionary shifts in the economic role of government required to integrate new global realities involve profound—and time-consuming— challenges to existing structures. But many initial elements of global reform are available virtually overnight:

- New *export control* legislation to replace Cold War frameworks with one reflecting global realities is drafted and ready. Unilateral-policy foreign-policy controls, long proven ineffective, must be eliminated and replaced with streamlined national security controls and multilateral regimes.

- The authority of trade bureaucrats under the *import-relief* laws to interfere with market-driven pricing decisions could and should be eliminated by administrative fiat. Penalties for "dumping" as a result of foreign-exchange shifts should be entirely removed, and the use of artificial cost constructions sharply curtailed.

- One of the biggest clouds over *foreign investment* could be removed by providing the Committee on Foreign Investment in the United States with a precise, narrow definition of "national security" to apply in reviewing proposed foreign investment.

- Officials reviewing *mergers, acquisitions, and joint ventures* should abandon the use of outdated antitrust devices such as the HHI Index, cease making assumptions that business combinations are harmful to innovation, and solicit private-sector help in teaching government the new dynamics of competition.

- Capital and innovation levels in the *telecommunications* sector could be greatly enhanced by an administrative decree that international investment in U.S. telecom firms is in the public interest, ending the FCC's lockgrip on the capital and growth plans of those firms. Further liberation of U.S. telecom firms needs to be achieved by halting the current micromanagement of the industry conducted by the Justice Department.

- Global firms could be attracted to U.S. *equity markets* by further easing of the SEC's standards for listing, allowing such firms to participate on U.S. exchanges by using simplified global-denominator reporting instead of U.S. GAAP.
- Competition officials should call off new efforts to manage *innovation markets* in the context of reviewing mergers and acquisitions.
- Trade officials should submit to *multilateral dispute resolution* established by the World Trade Organization instead of continuing to resort to unilateral retaliation as the answer to every issue arising with a trading partner.

Control → Interdependence

International flows—of goods, capital, people, and technology—always had to be controlled in the old economy. Anything out of balance had to be "fixed"—by tariffs, currency manipulation, export licenses, investment controls, taxes, or naked political clout (witness Washington's foray into the international flows of semiconductor chips, autos, and machine tools). The assumption of sovereign economic control has become a delusion. Washington pretends to control exchange rates, for example, but in reality it is almost powerless to fight currency markets. It inserts itself into the flow of autos in the United States on the assumption that there is a national industry that can be controlled. Government must abandon the illusions that it obtains global value only by seizing control of it from others and that growth for others on the planet means stagnation for us. Interdependence brings more to everyone and must be supported by government.

The Interdependent Solution: America's role in the interdependent networks of global industry must be supported by liberating flows of global investment. Capital for the telecommunications sector could be sharply expanded by simple acknowledgements that modern technology makes it impossible for foreign governments to seize American airwaves—the reason foreigners are restricted from making large-stake investments in U.S. telecommunications firms—and that such new capital is always in the public interest. Such recognition of reality would open the door for new capital and new knowledge. Much of the cloud over foreign investment could be removed by publishing a precise and realistically narrow definition of the "national security" assets, which, if in play, could trigger federal restrictions on investment.

Over the long term, Washington's institutionalized bias against foreign investment—inbound and outbound—must be eliminated. In the name of controlling foreign investment, Washington pretends that competitiveness is served by raising barriers against firms that offer greater innovation and productivity and, despite its dangerous obsession with manufacturing jobs, ignores the fact that half of the new American manufacturing investment in recent years has come from foreign investors. Similar barriers around the world must be addressed in the same fashion. Washington needs to commit itself in earnest and with urgency to the efforts already underway at the OECD to develop a global treaty for protection of investment, replacing the disruptive patchwork of bilateral investment treaties in place today.

Competition → Liquidity

Traditional competition policy is bankrupt. To fulfill their existing policy mandates, competition bureaucrats must second-guess markets, second-guess capital, and second-guess technology. They can't. But they try, and in the process they have sent industry after industry into turmoil—or at least the U.S. participation in global industries. Infatuated with the idea that big is bad and that larger market shares and larger companies are unhealthy for growth, they have misread some of the most important dynamics of the new economy. Why is liquidity the new analog? Because what is important is the competition of ideas, not entities. It is global liquidity—the competition for knowledge empowered by the flow of capital—that is the critical ingredient for healthy markets.

Antitrust regulators must learn to live with what by their standards is the great paradox of innovation today: In many sectors, knowledge will only be obtained by or flow to large concentrations of capital. The power of market concentrations has become a vital foundation for innovation; the first product out of an innovation cycle at many software, pharmaceutical, and other knowledge-intensive industries may cost $500 million while the second unit costs $50; without monopoly power over the product—and patents are increasingly ineffective as a vehicle for protection—no one will make such huge research investments. What traditionalists see as insidious monopolies are in many instances the product specializations that permit global industries to exist—and the global plebiscite invariably sees that such product-power is short-lived. The new liquidity, moreover, does not respect the traditional lines of industry and enterprise that were the focus of traditional competition regulators, whose policies are rapidly becoming antigrowth. The traditional paradigm forced regulators to look at companies as occupying competitive boxes, keeping industry structure "rational" along lines of horizontal and vertical relationships that have blurred everywhere but in the minds of regulators.

The Liquidity Solution: Antitrust enforcement is largely a function of policy discretion. Today, enforcement is arbitrary and, when global markets are in question, based on inadequate data, miscued definitions of industry, and speculation about competitiveness and innovation. Informed consideration for global industry dynamics should be directed in reviews of mergers, acquisitions, and joint ventures; for any industry in which products move across borders, global market analysis should be used. When American parties are involved, emphatic attention should be paid to implications for American competitiveness.

■

The long-term liquidity solution involves a convergence to common policy denominators. Ultimately, all of the shifts described above converge on the basic goals of liquidity, diversity, and interdependence. But those goals cannot be obtained unless policy itself converges across long-standing conceptual boundaries. The long-term remedy to Washington's outdated competition and protection paradigms lies in breaking the boundaries between trade and competition law. Washington's import-relief and antitrust institutions work at counterpurposes today.

America's first statutory antitrust and import-relief laws date to 1890 and 1898, respectively. It is time to end Washington's enslavement to that century of tradition. The import-relief laws subject companies to separate restrictions on their competitiveness for the sole reason that they are foreign. American firms, for example, engage in dumping all the time; in the domestic context, the phenomenon is called "discounting" or "sales." The competition laws effectively subject companies to separate standards on their competitiveness for the sole reason that they are American. The distinctions in both instances defy the realities of the market and restrain liquidity and diversity.

Ironically, the original purpose of U.S. import-relief law was pro-competitive in the sense that it sought to keep domestic firms alive in the face of predatory behavior by foreign firms.[5] But decades ago, enforcement of the antidumping laws drifted away from that predatory scope; in most cases today, foreign firms are not even aware that they are dumping until long after the sales are consummated. As enforced today, the laws disrupt international value-added networks and grant immunity from competition to complaining firms.

The shift to liquidity and diversity from the old paradigms of competition and trade policy would mean the century-old laws would have to be scrapped. The same slimmed-down set of rules against predatory behavior, conspiracy, and fraud based on actual effects of actual transactions—not speculation about long-term effects of proposed transactions—that are the solution to the nation's antitrust quagmire are also the solutions to our outdated trade laws.

Such a process has already begun in the European Union, where antidumping actions between EU members are no longer permitted, replaced by a generally applicable unfair-trade law. In September 1995, Canadian Minister of Industry John Manley made the same proposal for North America.[6] Noting that "in this instance, business is light years ahead of legislation," Manley said, "It's time for government to recognize a continuing need to revamp legislation to deal with the changing economy." Such a globally oriented set of rules would be the platform for taking competition law itself global, with streamlined rules against unfair competitive conduct that would replace antitrust and import-relief laws.

Enlightened policymakers like Minister Manley have begun to understand that the most effective economic role for government is supporting the global economic process as conducted by those within its borders. What matters is not the specific hard assets, the specific companies, or the specific products that have so often preoccupied Washington, claiming a right to protection at the expense of the American people. What counts is the process of adding value.

American competitiveness as a concept is meaningful only if understood to derive from the value of American content in the global economy. Others have said the same thing by stating that what counts is American productivity. But speaking to traditionalists about productivity has become ineffective: Bound to systems incapable of meaningfully measuring activity outside the manufacturing arena, they compulsively think of productivity in terms of American factory output, economies of scale, and industrial technology. They have difficulty grasping, for example, the many ways in which Nike's offshore sourcing network, IBM's research in England, and Motorola's production of cellular telephones in Malaysia help American productivity. American content is not the same as American assets in the traditional sense. It may be far easier—certainly more politically expedient—to pretend that the fight for America's competitiveness is a government-led assault for shiny new factories. But what is at stake is not the trophies of yesterday. What is at stake is the context for innovation, for it is this *context*—not any specific technology—that determines the trophies of tomorrow.

BUILDING THE INNOVATION INFRASTRUCTURE

Government institutions have failed to meaningfully respond to the connection between innovation and growth. The new process of innovation is too dynamic, too untraditional—and too international—for traditional structures. For many policymakers, the problem is still more basic: They have difficulty even identifying innovation. Confusing innovation with technology, regulators pretend to preside over the future by doling out subsidies for high-definition television, display panels, or other research-of-the-month. Confusing it with science, they ignore the awesome power and awesome importance of innovation in capital markets—and the role of capital in *all* innovation.

The paradigm shifts described above define one overriding role for government in supporting growth, that of building a policy infrastructure for innovation. What is needed is infrastructure in the purest sense, a framework only, without the clutter of micromanagement that has plagued old-world policy. The purpose of that infrastructure must be to support the liquidity and diversity—and through them the interdependence—that drive all innovation.

In practical terms, the basic demand of this new infrastructure is *interoperability*. Those linked in computer networks understand interoperability in the narrow context of interface between computer operating systems. But for global enterprise, interoperability has a vastly broader context. Interoperability is not only the basic need of global enterprise, it is one of the few needs that public policymakers can readily address.

The purposes of interoperability are the purposes of the new infrastructure for innovation: simplifying, fostering, and expediting the exchange of information, expertise, and value in all its forms across the boundaries of function, enterprise, nations, and industry. Interoperability has a thousand measures and dimensions, from ease of joint-venture formation and access to optimal telecommunications to the ability of foreign experts to immigrate, the ease of conducting research in foreign locations, and the regulatory cost of bringing new products to market. The barriers to cross-border investment, international research, and transfers of components discussed in these pages are barriers to interoperability. Every barrier to the liquidity and diversity of owners and managers, ideas and technology, and contracts and relationships is a barrier to interoperability. So, too, are the many tax and securities laws provisions that hinder communication and capital movements across borders.

Interoperability requires global common denominators for the administration of enterprise and claims by government on shares of its revenue. A Tower of Babel confronts any firm that tries to coordinate or reconcile regulatory filings and standards across borders—underscoring findings by the OECD that international firms are at a disadvantage to purely domestic operations. The burden of inconsistent tax and accounting standards causes firms not only to stumble over treatments for pensions, profits, losses, debt, hyperinflation, equity, fixed assets, hedging, dividends, tax credits, depreciation, and reserves but also to reach investment decisions based on financial distortions. The $1 billion loss imposed on Daimler-Benz by the SEC in 1993 when the firm floated stock in the United States was only one of the more dramatic examples of the problem.

The slow progress made by bodies like the International Accounting Standards Committee (IASC) or the Bank for International Settlements in conforming accounting and capital treatments is not the answer. Treating such issues as mere technical details only exacerbates the problem. What is at stake is not merely common formats for reports to governments. Far more important for many firms is the need for consistent ways to speak to banks, investors, and partners. Cross-border joint ventures, shared research, mergers, acquisitions, venture-capital funding, sourcing contracts, and licensing agreements all suffer from the lack of a common financial and administrative language.

Building the innovation infrastructure, moreover, is not just a matter for multilateral action. It begins at home with the reforms discussed in earlier chapters. By upgrading its treatment of knowledge transfers, for example, Washington could create a *de facto* common infrastructure for such vitally important elements—where U.S. practices differ sharply from that overseas. This means changing policy to provide that cross-border royalties, technology fees, and cost-sharing charges are uniformly allowed as business expense deductions to establish prohibitions on subnational (state and local) taxation of foreign income and to guarantee that all headquarters expense can be deducted in the headquarters country. Uniform treatment of foreign-source income— meaning income for U.S. value-added overseas—is essential. U.S. firms face a debilitating handicap in the form of Washington's tax penalties on foreign operations, a burden typically not shared by enterprises from other countries.

But ultimately, the innovation infrastructure cannot be completed without global action. Washington should make common administrative and financial denominators a urgent priority, beginning with a fast-track international accord for defining basic principles for global balance sheets to be accepted in each country where an enterprise operates. The task may appear daunting—the European Union has been unable to even agree on "European" accounting standards—but the international political task may be overestimated by many: Once a core group of industrial nations—the Group of Seven, for example—committed to common denominators, scores of other nations would have little choice but to sign on, for fear of losing their appeal to the global firms that are pumping up their economies. A broad accord establishing common standards for both financial reporting and taxation would be far more important for future American competitiveness than further GATT-style agreements for merchandise trade. Built correctly, such a framework would provide for the seamless movement of enterprise across every border and would liberate American innovators to assume greater leadership in global industry.

Private bodies that are close to markets—not the bureaucrats who have made careers of administering arcane capital controls—should be empowered to play a leading role in constructing such global accords. The London-based International Accounting Standards Committee (IASC) currently is coordinating private efforts, but the IASC has four full-time staff members and an annual budget of less than $2 million, compared with the forty-five staff members and $16 million budget of its U.S. domestic counterpart, the Financial Accounting Standards Board. Left to its own resources, the IASC does not expect to achieve meaningful harmonization for years. The SEC needs to push the International Organization of Securities Commissioners (IOSCO) to sharply accelerate the heretofore glacial pace of current IOSCO/IASC cooperation.[7] Progress has been mixed at best. Recent efforts by separate U.S. and foreign bodies to deal with emerging issues like derivatives and other hedging devices have been widely divergent. The derivatives efforts have been particularly disappointing, due not only to the new found importance of derivative products to many global firms—85 percent of Fortune 500 companies use derivatives—but also because the lack of any preexisting treatment created a prime opportunity for moving directly to a global standard, an opportunity not even seriously considered by any of the government bodies charged with financial regulation.

INTEROPERATING KNOWLEDGE

The global significance of setting technical standards for products, information systems, and testing procedures in the global economy has been widely underestimated in policy circles. Washington declared victory in the standards arena after negotiating an agreement on technical standards during the Uruguay Round. But that agreement took only the first small step of confirming that countries would not use their technical standards to discriminate against foreign goods. In many knowledge-intensive sectors, standards *are* the infrastructure—and addressing that infrastructure vitalizes enterprise. As policymakers in Tokyo and Washington squabbled in 1995 over access of U.S. firms to Japanese software markets, for example, two private bodies, the American National Standards Institute and the Japan Accreditation Board, met and quietly agreed to harmonized procedures to bridge conflicting product standards, defusing what otherwise threatened to escalate into another high-level trade war.

Infrastructure to more fully address such knowledge-transfer issues—in addition to the administrative, financial, and operating issues described above—should be a priority for policymakers. Most basic is the need to establish clear *procedures for establishing standards* as needs arise; government can play a key growth role by shepherding frameworks by which industries can efficiently reach agreement on standards. To date, much effort has been wasted on what might be called the "furniture" issues, epitomized by the months' delay in several international negotiations caused by bickering over the shape and size of the table to be used by negotiators—but also including such points as antitrust laws, which intrude whenever industry groups sit down together.

Despite the awesome advances made in electronic communication, disparate telecommunication standards across borders continue to handicap the process of innovation. Without standards, the electronic liquidity of the new economy is frustrated. Fax-machine technology existed in the 1960s but did not enter the mainstream until standards were introduced that allowed machines from different producers to speak to one another. Transactions worth over $600 billion—greater than the annual value of all shipments from the United States today—are expected to be completed electronically by the end of the century; such efficiency will be frustrated if government agencies cannot agree on standards to protect payment authorization and customer information. Electronic commerce will not be trusted by the global plebiscite until such standards are reached. Progress on the issue has been painfully slow, hampered by such archaic features as the State Department's role in setting subscriber identities for international mobile-phone networks and the Federal Communications Commission, which stubbornly carves out a government role in every new telecommunications technology.

ACHIEVING INTEROPERABILITY OF ENTERPRISE

Constructing the innovation infrastructure means liberating entrepreneurs across borders through domestic reform and multilateral accords that:

- Eliminate all differential treatment of investment, capital transfers, and equity listing on the basis of nationality.

- Create common eligibility across borders for all publicly funded research other than for exclusively military applications.

- Provide for mutual recognition of product safety and performance approvals by which approval in any country that applies shared criteria will be valid in other countries.

- Establish common technical standards for global products, with priority given to common standards for large knowledge-intensive sectors like motor vehicles, telecommunications, computers, and consumer electronics.

- Establish basic standard-setting parameters that provide that all technical regulation will be based on functional criteria, not origin, design, or process.

- Provide certification procedures by which government testing for standards compliance will be replaced by manufacturer certifications, bound with strict penalties for false certification.

- Eliminate all government restraints that prevent telecommunications firms from competing across borders.

- Eliminate U.S. tax penalties on internal research done overseas and headquarter services provided in the United States for such affiliates.

- Eliminate all market access barriers for information systems technology.

- Harmonize all documentation required for customs clearances.

- Provide for international administration of patents and trademarks, starting with protocols to share patent search and examination tasks between the European Patent Office and the U.S. Patent and Trademark Office.

- Convert the annual trade-barrier listing currently used to focus trade retaliation against specific countries into priority lists for harmonization and convergence in commerce with those countries.

- Eliminate all barriers to relocation of the personnel of global enterprise and their families across borders.

- Eliminate tariffs on high-technology products such as computers, semiconductors, and telecommunications equipment.

A sizable portion of the foreign value being added in the pharmaceutical, medical device, and specialty chemical sectors could be captured by American firms as a result of harmonization of health and safety standards. Pharmaceutical experts believe that mutual recognition of testing procedures between Washington, Brussels, and Tokyo alone could cut in half the cost of launching a new drug. The stakes extend far beyond added convenience for lab technicians: Increased intergovernment cooperation would greatly expedite the delivery of innovation to the marketplace, allow researchers to test more new drugs, and improve the health of global consumers. Just as importantly, it would permit American value-added in testing to be globally leveraged by allowing U.S. research to substitute for value previously added overseas. The minimal effort to date in this context has been discouraging. The head of the EU's pharmaceutical unit predicts global standards are at least twenty years away. At one recent meeting on the topic, U.S. and EU regulators could not even agree on how to define the ingredients of talcum powder.

Effective standards add value because they are simple and shared. Regulatory reform for the innovation infrastructure must meet the same measure. Both private standards and government regulation are in essence organizational and informational systems; global competition has proven that the most effective systems invariably are the streamlined ones that rely on a few core common denominators. The more complex the inputs and applications, the more simple organizational and informational systems need to be. It is impossible to build America's innovation infrastructure without forcing simplicity into the process— first at home, then in new global structures.

In 1994, when the Canadian government prepared a list of the problems its firms encounter in the United States, prominent on the list was the complaint that the United States has a total of 44,000 standards "jurisdictions"—including federal, state, local, and quasi-official bodies—that enforce 89,000 separate standards.[8] The price paid by American enterprise for a Byzantine regulatory system have been well documented elsewhere. Since 1965, there has been a 3,000-fold increase in federal regulations. The U.S. Chamber of Commerce estimates that American business pays $600 billion annually to comply with regulations. Each year, Washington publishes 70,000 pages of new rules and policy statements in the *Federal Register*. The OMB estimates that American managers spend *5 billion* hours a year in filling out papers for government offices.[9]

The regulatory arbitrage of global enterprise is casting harsh judgments on the dimensions of U.S. regulatory systems. Just as intimidating to international firms as the volume of American regulation is its unpredictability. Scores of Europe's large companies, cognizant that 18 million new lawsuits are filed every year in America, expressly direct their contract negotiators to avoid any provision that would expose them to U.S. jurisdiction. More than a few have sold American assets held for decades for this sole reason. "Like a roulette wheel" is how one Swiss purchasing director characterizes the U.S. legal system. "Or maybe Russian roulette. It's impossible to estimate liability exposure from one year to the next."[10]

The mind-numbing, ever-changing complexity of U.S. tax laws has become a significant obstruction in the flow of capital to American innovation—but Washington compulsively tinkers with tax laws. In the five years following the passage of the 1986 tax "simplification" act, Congress enacted 5,400 changes to the tax laws. The tax director at Hewlett-Packard made a shocking discovery during a recent visit to Japan: In the offices of a firm of equal size to HP, he found a finance staff of five people who reported that they typically completed their corporate tax filings with two weeks of work each year. At home, he had a staff of fifty working full time all year long to accommodate U.S. tax requirements.

PRISONERS TO A CENTURY

On February 8, 1994, an armistice was declared in one of the longest and most bitter trade wars ever fought in Washington. Smith Corona, headquartered in Connecticut, and Brother Industries, headquartered in Nagoya, Japan, had spent millions in legal fees and lost even more in missed opportunities invoking U.S. laws to enlist Washington in their battle over the U.S. market for typewriters and word processors. Smith Corona had fired the first round fourteen years earlier by charging dumping by Brother. As global competition evolved, pushing the firms to be close to key markets and efficient production sources, Brother moved production to Tennessee and Smith Corona moved production to Singapore. Brother then claimed it was an injured U.S. producer and charged dumping of imports by Smith Corona. While the companies carried on a slugfest in federal courts over arcane issues of antidumping law, officials became embroiled in a metaphysical debate: Could a Japanese company be an American producer to complain about an American firm operating as a Singapore producer? After Hanson Plc. bought Smith Corona, the issues reached the level of complete regulatory conundrum: Could American managers working for British owners be penalized for sourcing product sold to Americans from a plant in Asia?

What was significant about the end of the feud was that its resolution did not come from government. The two companies issued a joint statement to proclaim that they were ending the war. Mark Thompson, general counsel for Brother, observed: "It was crazy; we were chasing tails. . . . The two parties had been using litigation to compete. . . . At the end we decided to use the marketplace to compete."[11]

The two firms understood at last that they could not rely on the institutions of government for competitiveness, but en route to that conclusion they discovered how hopelessly outdated and contradictory the premises of America's economic laws have become. The same lesson is being learned in every global industry. In the steel sector, for example, applying traditional competition policy tells officials that the problems of the American steel sector are caused by an unhealthy concentration. No, say trade officials who have handled scores of import-relief petitions for American steel giants over the past decade, the problem is obviously foreign competition. In combination, the result has been a patchwork of internal competition restraints and external protection, imposed against the interests of nearly every steel firm that is integrated across borders—meaning those who are leading growth in the U.S. sector. More blatant still has been the schizophrenic intervention in the aluminum industry, where trade agencies worked with U.S. producers to develop quotas on foreign production; those same producers were then attacked by the Department of Justice for conspiring to limit foreign production.

But instead of acting upon the global shifts that have created such convolutions, policymakers press on with enforcement of century-old laws. One of the greatest disappointments to globalists has been Washington's dogged campaigns, carried on with missionary zeal, for other nations to adopt clones of U.S. trade and antitrust laws. Such campaigns are greatly handicapping prospects for improving the innovation infrastructure. They are simply expanding the Flat Earth infrastructure in ways that are virtually guaranteed to haunt America's global enterprise—and every other global enterprise—for many years to come.

"Everything has changed but our ways of thinking," Albert Einstein observed after the atom was unlocked, "and if these do not change, we drift toward unparalleled catastrophe." While the catastrophes we face by failing to embrace the global economy may not be as physically devastating as those contemplated by Einstein, in the economic context they may prove nearly as destructive. Industries are in turmoil. Competitive advantage has lost its traditional anchors. Institutions that were once vitally important to economic growth have been rendered powerless—or even destructive of growth.

American enterprise has had no choice but to accept the challenge of global engagement. Some firms have quickly left behind the traditions of the trading economy and surged to leadership of their industries. Others continue to struggle with the legacies of the past—but the transition of enterprise is at least underway.

It would be comforting to say that Washington is also on a steady course away from the Flat Earth. But it would be wrong. Obsolete policy continues to devalue government—and change is nowhere in sight. Each new call for quotas, every cry for balancing trade accounts, every manipulation of exchange rates for short-term gains, and every demand for new regulation of national technology and capital defies the realities of the new economy. Every such proposal is based on the assumption that government can force enterprise to add value within its borders, the most basic and most damaging of Flat Earth delusions. Ultimately government's claim upon that value—represented by tax revenues—depends on choices by enterprise. Left undisturbed by anachronistic regulation, a disproportionate number will choose to take advantage of the glittering potential of American innovation. Otherwise they will look to America merely as a market, forcing Americans to spend a decreasing share of global wealth on an ever-increasing portion of value added in other countries.

This conflict between traditional government and the global economic process will be the defining force in determining the course of the global economy for the foreseeable future. Washington has the opportunity and the ability to assume the leadership role in eliminating that conflict, to the great benefit of every American and, eventually, everyone on the planet. Whether it will remains to be seen—because, so far, everything has changed but our ways of thinking.

NOTES

CHAPTER ONE

1. See, e.g., R. Grant, M. Papadakis, and D. Richardson, "Global Trade Flows: Old Structures, New Issues, Empirical Evidence," in Bergsten and Noland, ed., *Pacific Dynamism and the International Economic System* 45 (Institute for International Economics, 1993); M. Papadakis, "Changing International Relations and U.S. Japanese Competitiveness," in Lambright and Rahm, ed., *Technology and U.S. Competitiveness* (Greenwood Press, 1992).

2. The National Science Foundation reports that ratios of advanced-technology product shipments to all shipments have dropped sharply in the recent years, from nearly 40 percent of all shipments in 1991 to less than 25 percent in 1994, the last year for which data is available. Since the mid–1980s the United States has been losing world market share in electronic products at a rate of 3 percent a year.

3. See, e.g., Competitiveness Policy Council, *Report on Savings and Investing*, released September 14, 1995. The adjusted earnings of the top 10 percent of American workers showed no real growth from 1979 to 1993, the last year for which data is available. In Britain, by contrast, the earnings of the top 10 percent increased by over 60 percent. The reason for the stagnation of wages is the near stagnation in American productivity: Productivity grew less than 1 percent annually from 1974 to 1989, a trend that has slowly improved in recent years. Since 1990, productivity has risen by 1.2 percent annually. See, e.g., "In New Figures on Productivity, U.S. Reports Less Growth in '90's," *The New York Times*, 9 February 1996.

4. In his 1995 study "Closing the R&D Gap: Evaluating the Sources of R&D Spending" prepared for the Levy Economics Institute of Bard College, Dr. Thomas Karier revealed that U.S. firms have chronically spent less on commercial R&D than their major foreign competitors and that the gap is expanding. In 1994, U.S. firms spent 1.9 percent of GRP on nondefense research and development, compared to 3 percent for Japan and 2.7 percent for Germany. The only U.S. firms that led the world in R&D expenditures were those in the aerospace industry. See "Closing the R&D Gap," *International Business*, October 1995.

5. Other countries with more multinational firms than the United States are Japan (with half the U.S. population), Sweden (with 8.7 million population), and Switzerland (with 7 million population). *World Investment Report 1995* (United Nations, 1995).

6. The Center reported in 1994 that the share of employment, both inside and outside the United States, by U.S. international firms declined since 1977, as well as the share of U.S. GDP provided by such firms. *World Investment Report 1994* (United Nations, 1994). Other studies also show that transnational activity by enterprises from other nations has sharply increased in the past fifteen years, while such activity by U.S. enterprises reached a plateau in 1977 or in some respects has declined since then. See R. Grant, M. Papadakis, and D. Richardson, "Global Trade Flows: Old Structures, New Issues, Empirical Evidence," in Bergsten and Noland, ed., *Pacific Dynamism and the*

International Economic System (Institute for International Economics, 1993); R. Lipsey, "The Internationalization of Production," Working Paper 29 (National Bureau of Economic Research, April 1989); "The Discreet Charm of the Multicultural Multinational," *The Economist*, 30 July 1994.

7. See "From Multilocal to Multicultural," *The Economist*, 24 June 1995; "Global—Or Just Globaloney?" *Fortune*, 27 June 1994; "More U.S. Companies Venture Overseas for Directors," *Wall Street Journal*, 22 January 1992. The *Directorship* survey revealed, moreover, that most of the foreigners on U.S. boards were Canadians.

8. "U.S. Firms Are Letting Saudi Market Slip," *Wall Street Journal*, 30 November 1989.

9. Sources for the data in this paragraph are the United Nations Conference on Trade and Development, *World Investment Report 1995* (United Nations, 1995); the OECD; the IMF; and the Bank for International Settlements.

10. G. C. Hufbauer, assisted by J. V. Rooij, *U.S. Reform of International Taxation: Blueprint for Reform* (Institute for International Economics, 1992), 47.

11. In his insightful book *American Trade Politics* (Institute for International Economics, 1992), I. M. Destler charts the vacillations in the positions of the two major parties on trade protection issues over the course of recent decades. Destler notes that the shift primarily reflected shifts in the geographic bases of the parties, particularly political shifts in the industrial concentrations of the Northeast.

12. Negotiators emphasized, for example, that as a result of the Uruguay Round, 98 percent of the import tariffs of developed countries would be bound, meaning they would be capped at an obligatory level. But prior to the Round, 94 percent of such tariffs were already bound. Going into the Round, tariffs in the United States and the European Union were already low, at 3.9 and 4.3 percent respectively—levels at which tariffs had little competitive effect in many sectors.

13. Studies conducted by the World Bank, the GATT Secretariat, and the OECD agree that the increase in world GDP will be between $213 and $274 billion in less than ten years (i.e., 2005), representing approximately a 1 to 1.2 percent gain. Many knowledgeable observers, in fact, favored the conclusion of a private study that estimated that a realistic gain ten years out was a mere $118 billion, or slightly more than .5 percent of global GDP. (T. Nguyen, C. Perroni, and R. Wright, "The Value of Uruguay Round Success" in *The World Economy*, 1991). The vast majority of that gain derives from liberalization in agricultural trade. A joint World Bank/OECD study concluded that of its projected $213 billion gain, $190 billion would be in the worldwide agricultural sector, while only $23 billion would be realized in other trade. See Evans and Walsh, *The EIU Guide to the New GATT* (Economist Intelligence Unit, 1994).

14. Although no empirical study has been conducted of the precise combination of reforms proposed herein, many studies have quantified the economic gains to be achieved by certain elements of that reform. The Institute for International Economics, for example, has estimated that quotas and other managed trade measures alone impose a cost equal to 1.3 percent of American GDP. Elimination of textile and apparel import restrictions would provide an additional $24 billion gain to the U.S. economy; elimination of agricultural and maritime quotas would provide an additional $4.4 billion gain. See G. C. Hufbauer and K. A. Elliott, *Measuring the Cost of Protection in the United States* (Institute for International Economics, 1994). It has been estimated that injecting new competition into American industries by updating the competition rules discussed in Chapter Three, including those applied by the agencies regulating high-tech

joint ventures, could add billions directly to the U.S. economy; some have estimated this gain to be as high as $50 billion. See, e.g., Hahn, "Regulatory Reform: The Whole Story," *Wall Street Journal*, 27 February 1995. Lifting overexpansive export controls that have no connection to national security could add several billion dollars more; one study pegged the growth available from such reform to be approximately $9 billion annually. More difficult to quantify with existing analytical tools but potentially vast in scope are the gains to be obtained by the reforms of technology, monetary, banking, and foreign investment policies discussed herein.

CHAPTER TWO

1. One of the more comprehensive articles discussing this distorted deficit/jobs connection was "Best Selling Fiction 3 Million Jobs Lost," *Wall Street Journal*, 29 July 1985.

2. The National Association of Purchasing Managers reports, for example, that 88 percent of American manufacturers utilize imported components or materials in their production operations.

3. Source: Organization for Economic Cooperation and Development. See also Robert J. Samuelson, "The Useless Jobs Summit," *Newsweek*, 24 March 1994.

4. A number of studies have explained why developing countries with low wages do not dominate global commerce, by confirming this link between low wages and low productivity. One of the most recent was a 1995 study by economist Stephen Golub of Swarthmore College, which reviewed the dynamics of wages and productivity in Korea, Thailand, Malaysia, and the Philippines. "Comparative Advantage and Absolute Advantage in the Asia Pacific Region," Federal Reserve Bank of San Francisco Working Paper (1995). See also "Not So Absolutely Fabulous," *The Economist*, 4 November 1995.

5. Rules of origin are not only anachronistic in the hands of the U.S. government, but they are also confusing and contradictory. Washington applies over twenty different rules of origin, administered by different agencies for different purposes. The rules are not consistent, sometimes resulting in pitched battles between agencies over origin issues. The Department of Commerce has stated repeatedly that it is not bound by the country-of-origin rulings of the Customs Service, although most firms rely on Customs Services rulings for guidance on such issues. When Commerce levied antidumping duties on semiconductors from Japan, for example, it included semiconductors assembled in third countries using materials made in Taiwan because they had been shipped from Japan, despite the fact that the Customs Service had expressly ruled that the assembly operations had conferred origin elsewhere. Global firms are chronically frustrated in their planning—and frequently placed in double jeopardy—as a result of such inconsistent rulings. For a more comprehensive discussion of this point, see N. David Palmeter, "The U.S. Rules of Origin Proposal to GATT: Monotheism or Polytheism?" *Journal of World Trade*, April 1990.

6. "In Debate Over NAFTA, Many See Global Trade as Symbol of Hardship," *Wall Street Journal*, 20 October 1993.

7. See, e.g., "Selling of America to Japanese Touches Some Very Raw Nerves," *Wall Street Journal*, 19 June 1990.

8. A survey of 1,250 American manufacturers by the Conference Board, "U.S. Manufacturers in the Global Marketplace" (The Conference Board, 1994), showed that firms with no operations abroad had average sales growth of 8 percent versus 16 percent for firms with international operations. The Conference Board study also demonstrated that profitability rises for firms with an international scope. Firms with international operations have also been shown to pay higher wages and benefits and offer higher productivity. See, e.g., David J. Richardson, "Why Exports Really Matter!" (Institute of International Economics, 1995).

9. "America's Little Fellows Surge Ahead," *The Economist*, 3 July 1993.

10. "Smaller Firms in U.S. Avoid Business Abroad," *Wall Street Journal*, 24 August 1993. David Richardson of the Institute for International Economics has reported that approximately 10 percent of U.S. firms with 100 or fewer employees make international shipments. See "New Lift for the U.S. Export Boom," *Fortune*, 13 November 1995.

11. Conference Board, 1994, supra, footnote 8.

12. Mira Wilkins's in-depth early history of international enterprise, *The Emergence of Multinational Enterprise* (Harvard University, 1970), details the activities of early international pioneers like Singer.

CHAPTER THREE

1. This correlation between low-skilled imports and growth in high-skilled production was noted as early was 1941 by economists Paul Samuelson and Wolfgang Stolper, who captioned it the "factor-price equalization theorem." When low-skilled imports arrive, Samuelson and Stolper explained, corresponding domestic factors of production will inevitably be reduced in value, and those responsible for allocating capital will turn it to more productive use in higher-value (high-skilled) applications. In their 1994 study, "Trade and Jobs in Manufacturing," (Brookings Papers on Economic Activity, Brookings Institution, 1994), economists Jeffrey Sachs and Howard Shatz of Harvard University extended this research to demonstrate a correlation between reductions in production of low-skilled products and *exports* of high-skilled products.

2. Although many experts agree on this range of figures, it is difficult to precisely judge the full economic impact since it is a function of assumptions on how customers will react to changes in prices and supply. The most recent comprehensive analysis was a 1994 study by Gary C. Hufbauer and Kimberly Ann Elliott, *Measuring the Costs of Protection in the United States* (Institute for International Economics, 1994), in which the cost of all protection, including tariffs, was calculated at $70 billion annually; the annual cost in just twenty-one selected sectors with high incidence of protection and markets of $1 billion or more was pegged at $32 billion. A 1993 report by the OECD estimated the cost of American protection for agricultural commodities alone to be more than $33 billion. Organization of Economic Cooperation and Development, *Agricultural Policies, Markets and Trade: Monitoring and Outlook* (OECD, 1993). See also U.S. International Trade Commission, *The Economic Effects of Significant U.S. Import Restraints*, USITC Pub. 2699 (USITC, 1993); "The High Costs of Protectionism," *The New York Times*, 12 November 1993 ($32 billion cost from tariffs alone).

3. The first textile-protection arrangement was negotiated in 1961 and known by the misnomer "Short Term Arrangement." The existing MFA was extended in December 1993 until 2005, at which time it is not to be eliminated but incorporated into the General Agreement on Tariffs and Trade.

4. Hufbauer and Elliott, 1994 ($24 billion estimate); William R. Cline, *Future of World Trade in Textiles* (Institute for International Economics, 1990), 193 ($40 billion estimate).

5. W. B. Estell, "Shoddy Tariff Reform," Reform Club of New York, Vol. 5, No. 16, October 30, 1892.

6. Cline, 1990, 195-196.

7. Cline, 1990, 195.

8. L. Hunter, "U.S. Trade Protection: Effects on the Industrial and Regional Composition of Employment," *Economic Review* (Federal Reserve Bank of Dallas, January 1990).

9. William R. Cline, "Car Crash: Clinton Ignores Trade Facts," *Wall Street Journal*, 15 May 1995. See also Bill Bradley, "Why the President Is Wrong on Japan," *Wall Street Journal*, 27 June 1995.

10. See, e.g., "Dear Mickey," *The Economist*, 24 June 1995.

11. See "Toyota Loves GM," *Forbes*, 18 December 1995; "U.S. Auto Makers Revamp Lineups, Strategies to Expand in Japanese Market," *Wall Street Journal*, 25 October 1995.

12. In 1994, the latest year for which figures are available, the most productive auto plant in America was the Nissan plant in Smyrna, Tennessee (an average of 2.23 worker days for each car), followed by two Toyota facilities. The fourth most productive plant was Ford's facility in Atlanta (2.63 days). "U.S. Big Three Trail Japan in Productivity," *The New York Times*, 18 May 1995.

13. This record sharply contrasts with that of thirty years ago: of 371 investigations commenced between 1955 and 1968, only 12 resulted in imposition of antidumping duties. See I. M. Destler, *American Trade Politics* (Institute for International Economics, 1992), 141.

14. Tim W. Ferguson, "Trade Policy's 'Chokepoint,' " *Wall Street Journal*, 11 April 1995. James Bovard's book *The Fair Trade Fraud* (St. Martin's Press, 1991) provides a much more detailed look at the costly effects of the steel restraints and other managed-trade programs.

15. "A Split Over Machine Tool Imports," *The New York Times,* 7 October 1991.

16. A number of small U.S. computer makers and their suppliers were reported to have been forced to close as a result of the pact. See, e.g., "Chalk One Up for Protectionists," *Wall Street Journal*, 22 November 1995; "The Semiconductor Pact's Bad Example," *Wall Street Journal,* 27 April 1993.

17. Several studies show that the pact promoted much closer coordination of production and sales by the Japanese producers than existed earlier. Policy analyst Kenneth Flamm reported to an industry conference: "The irony of [the semiconductor pact] was that, after a decade of complaints by American producers over the role of MITI [the Japanese government's Ministry of International Trade and Industry] in issuing 'administrative guidance' to Japanese industry, U.S. trade policy helped create a regime that considerably reinforced MITI's power and influence over the Japanese semiconductor industry and encouraged Japanese producers to limit competition with each other." K. Flamm, "Policy and Politics in the International Semiconductor Industry"

(paper presented to the SEMI ISS Seminar, Newport Beach, Calif., January 1989). See also K. Flamm, "Making New Rules: High Tech Trade Friction and the Semiconductor Industry," *The Brookings Review*, spring 1991.

18. George Gilder, *Microcosm* (Touchstone, 1989), 330.

19. See Hertel, Thompson, and Marinos, "Economy Side Effects of Unilateral Trade and Policy Liberalization in U.S. Agriculture," and A. Feltenstein, "Agriculture Policy and U.S. Federal Budget and Trade Deficit" (papers submitted to the Global Agricultural Trade Study of the Center for International Economics, May 1988).

20. R. D. Boltuck and S. Kaplan, "Conflicting Entitlements: Can Antidumping and Antitrust Regulation be Reconciled?" 61 *U of Cin Law Rev* 903, 914 (1993).

21. See, e.g., "Don't Call It a Cartel, But World Aluminum Has Forged New Order," *Wall Street Journal*, 9 June 1995; "Aluminum Tasks Clinton's Mettle," *Wall Street Journal*, 12 January 1994.

22. The comprehensive 1992 study by Michael Podgursky, "The Industrial Structure of Job Displacement," *Monthly Labor Review* (September 1992), reported that approximately 1.8 million workers are dislocated annually, for all reasons. In their 1994 study (Hufbauer and Elliott, 1994), Gary Hufbauer and Kimberly Elliott of the Institute for International Economics estimated that 70,000 workers would be displaced annually for a period of adjustment estimated at five years (for a total of 320,000 jobs affected) if trade protection were lifted in the 21 sectors subject to the heaviest protection.

23. "An Industry That Doesn't Need Saving from Japan," *Wall Street Journal*, 2 January 1992.

24. *Congressional Record*, S12462, 14 September 1988.

25. "The Family with the Sweet Tooth," *Forbes*, 14 May 1990.

26. Paul Craig Roberts, "Tariffs Protect Bad Economic Policy," *Wall Street Journal*, 12 September 1995.

27. "Trade Warriors: Baby Boomers Toy with Matches," *Wall Street Journal*, 17 March 1993.

CHAPTER FOUR

1. James F. Moore, "Predators and Prey: A New Ecology of Competition," *Harvard Business Review*, May/June 1993.

2. The 1994 federal budget provided $62 billion in funding for research programs, a figure that was increased to $71 billion in the 1995 budget. See, e.g., "Economics Scene: Frugality That Could Backfire, Cutting U.S. Research Subsidies," *Wall Street Journal*, 9 November 1995; "Ridden with Debt, U.S. Companies Cut Funds for Research," *The New York Times*, 30 June 1992.

3. In 1995, the top ten corporate recipients of U.S. patents, in order from one to ten, were IBM, Canon, Motorola, NEC (Nippon Electric Corporation), Toshiba, Mitsubishi, Hitachi, Matsushita, Eastman Kodak, and Sony. In 1990, the top ten recipients were Hitachi, Toshiba, Canon, Mitsubishi, General Electric, Fuji Photo, Eastman Kodak, Philips, IBM, and Siemens. Source: U.S. Patent and Trademark Office.

4. General Accounting Office, *High Technology Competitiveness: Trends in U.S. and Foreign Performance*, GAO/NSIAD-92-236.

5. Of the G-7 leading industrial countries, which include the United States, Japan, Germany, France, Great Britain, Canada, and Italy, only Canada had a lower rate of productivity growth from 1984 to 1994. The U.S. growth rate was 9.9 percent for the period, compared with first-ranked Germany at 26.5 percent. In its report *Competitiveness Index 1995* (issued in August 1995), the Council on Competitiveness reported that U.S. industry-financed research and development dropped 0.7 percent in 1993 and 0.2 percent in 1994 and declined an average of almost 1 percent a year between 1985 and 1993.

6. The Missile Technology Control Regime seeks to avoid proliferation of such technology. MTCR members include Russia, the United States, Great Britain, Germany, Sweden, Japan, South Africa, Australia, Belgium, Argentina, Switzerland, Spain, the Netherlands, Italy, Austria, Canada, Denmark, Finland, Greece, Hungary, Iceland, Ireland, Luxembourg, New Zealand, and Portugal. A parallel group, the Nuclear Suppliers Group, includes most members of the MTCR and controls nuclear-related equipment.

7. "These Restrictions Do Not Compute," *Wall Street Journal*, 16 June 1993.

8. See, e.g., *R&D*, April 1993.

9. See, e.g., "Belgian Maker of Wire and Steel Cord Is Bringing Japanese Knowhow to U.S.," *Wall Street Journal*, 19 January 1990.

10. See, e.g., "Toyota Building Arizona Test Center," *The New York Times*, 13 March 1990.

11. "Japanese Knowhow Now Easier for U.S. to Acquire," *R&D*, April 1993.

12. See, e.g., "Two Foreign Firms Plan Investment in Biotech Concerns," *Wall Street Journal*, 16 September 1993; "Genentech-Roche Deal May Spur Similar Ties," *The New York Times*, 5 February 1990.

13. This standard was introduced in the Omnibus Budget Reconciliation Act of 1993, replacing a 64 percent standard introduced in 1989.

14. Statement of U.S. Council for International Business on Proposed Amendments to Reg. Sec. 1.861-8(e)(3), released 22 August 1995. See also K. Brown, 60 *Tax Notes* 233, 12 July 1993; "Reform of Taxation of U.S. Multinationals," 93 *Tax Notes Today* 225-228, 2 November 1993.

15. "Inside Intel," *Business Week*, 1 June 1992.

16. "U.S. Manufacturers Gird for Competition," *Wall Street Journal*, 2 May 1989.

17. "Motorola Loses Edge in Microprocessors," *Wall Street Journal*, 3 March 1991.

18. "These Restrictions Do Not Compute," supra, footnote 7.

19. International Trade Commission, *Global Competitiveness of U.S. Advanced Technology Manufacturing Industries* (October 1991).

20. "Block That Innovation!" *Forbes*, 18 January 1993.

21. See "How to Smother Innovation," *Wall Street Journal*, 9 June 1993.

22. In 1994, Richard Beason of the University of Alberta and David Weinstein of Harvard University conducted an empirical study of the record of Japanese industrial policy. Choosing thirteen sectors with a long history of support by MITI and other agencies, they charted correlations between growth in those sectors and the support provided by Tokyo and found a *negative* correlation in every instance. Industrial targeting did not enhance growth in any of the sectors. "Growth, Economies of Scale, and Targeting in Japan (1955-90)" Harvard Institute of Economic Research, Discussion Paper 1644 (1994). See also "MIT's Identity Crisis," *The Economist*, 22 January 1994.

23. See, e.g., "3 Companies in Chip Venture," *Wall Street Journal*, 26 May 1994; "IBM Joins with Siemens AG to Develop Advanced Chips, Hoping to Share Risk," *Wall Street Journal*, 25 January 1990.

24. Bureau of National Affairs, *International Trade Daily*, 21 July 1992.

25. "Technology Policy: Is America on the Right Track?" *Harvard Business Review*, May-June 1992.

26. See, e.g., 163 *Congressional Record* E2972, 20 November 1993.

27. L. M. Branscomb, "Does America Need a Technology Policy?" *Harvard Business Review*, March-April 1992.

28. "Technology Policy: Is America on the Right Track?" supra, footnote 25.

29. Ralph Waldo Emerson, *The Conduct of Life* (Houghton Mifflin, 1888), 85.

CHAPTER FIVE

1. By 1901, the American Tobacco Company held a two-thirds interest in British American Tobacco, which dominated the trade in most countries of the world outside the United States. In the 1911 case, U.S. v. American Tobacco, the company was ordered to sell its interest in BAT—today a thriving $25 billion company—and extinguish its marketing agreements for other overseas markets. In her *The Emergence of Multinational Enterprise* (Harvard University Press, 1970, pp. 91–93), historian Mira Wilkins chronicles how American Tobacco was pried apart by regulators, eventually evolving into four smaller domestic firms without international business.

2. U.S. v. Aluminum Company of America, 148 F.2d 430-431 (1945).

3. The breakup of AT&T as a regulated monopoly was a pro-competitive action, but such a breakup could have been accomplished with a simple and relatively short proceeding. Instead, the AT&T proceeding became a vehicle for serving much broader policy goals. The evidence in the case was focused on those broader goals and not on the specific legal standards being invoked for the breakup. The stated rationale for the breakup of AT&T was the traditional premise of consumer welfare: By introducing new competition in the market for long-distance service and equipment, consumers would benefit. But those who have scrutinized the records of the case have discovered a conspicuous absence of evidence for comparison of existing efficiencies versus those that would be created by a breakup. In their review of the evidence, economists Robert W. Crandall and Bruce M. Owen, for example, found no significant evidence of AT&T's prebreakup efficiencies—making it "very difficult to prove the divestiture is necessarily welfare enhancing." R. W. Crandall and B. M. Owen, "The Marketplace: Economic Implications of Divestiture," in H. Shooshan, ed., *Disconnecting Bell: The Impact of the AT&T Divestiture* (Pergamon Press, 1984), 57. An earlier important work that examined how antitrust laws have been employed as broader industrial policy tools was Robert Bork's *The Antitrust Paradox* (Basic Books, 1974).

4. "FTC Challenges of Mergers at the Highest Since 1980," *Wall Street Journal*, 15 November 1995; "More and More Firms Enter Joint Ventures with Big Competitors," *Wall Street Journal*, 1 November 1995.

5. Federal Trade Commission, Notice of Hearing on FTC Policy in Relation to the Changing Nature of Competition, 60 *Federal Register* 37449 (1995).

6. U.S. Department of Justice and Federal Trade Commission Horizontal Merger Guidelines (1992).

7. "Gillette Reacts to U.S. Move," *The New York Times*, 11 January 1990.

8. See, e.g., "Takeover of Parker Pen to be Contested in U.S." *Financial Times*, 23 March 1993; "U.S. Loses Bid to Prevent Gillette-Parker Pen Merger," *Antitrust and Trade Regulation Reporter* (BNA), 13 May 1993.

9. See, e.g., "The Siege of Intel," *Economist*, 12 February 1994; "Computer Makers Face Hidden Vulnerability: Supplier Concentration," *Wall Street Journal*, 27 August 1993; "Too Hard on Microsoft," *The Economist*, 31 July 1993.

10. Emerson Electric, 55 *Federal Register* 28824 (1990).

11. Institut Merieux, 55 *Federal Register* 1614 (1990).

12. "FTC Opens Hearings on Enforcement Policy Forged by Globalized Markets, Innovation," *Antitrust and Trade Regulation Reporter* (BNA), 12 October 1995.

13. "FTC Hearings on Enforcement Policy Delve Into Dynamics of Global Rivalry," *Antitrust and Trade Regulation Reporter* (BNA), 26 October 1995.

14. Numerous policymakers have claimed that antitrust policy enforcement has been the cause of the telecommunications revolution. In a December 1995 interview, U.S. Vice President Albert Gore, for example, stated that the "great growth spurt" in telecommunications resulted from a commitment for the enforcement of antitrust laws. "ASAP Interview: Vice-President Albert Gore," *Forbes ASAP*, 4 December 1995.

15. G. D. Hutcheson and J. D. Hutcheson, "Technology and Economics in the Semiconductor Industry," *Scientific American*, January 1996.

16. D. T. Armentano, *Antitrust Policy: The Case for Repeal* (Cato Institute, 1991), 32.

17. "Some Big Mergers May Be Justified in Certain Cases, Antitrust Officials Say," *Wall Street Journal*, 11 January 1994.

18. Sensormatic Electric Corporation, 60 *Federal Register* 5428 (1995); Montedison SPA, FTC File No. 941-0043 (11 January 1995); American Home Products Corporation, 60 *Federal Register* 60,807 (1994); Boston Scientific Corporation, 60 *Federal Register* 12,948 (1995); Glaxo Plc., 60 *Federal Register* 16,139 (1995); Wright Medical Technology Inc., 60 *Federal Register* 460 (1995).

19. Economist Joseph Schumpeter, in fact, stated that monopolistic firms tended to be leaders in innovation. F. M. Scherer, in a comprehensive empirical review of Schumpeter's theory and data on technological change and economic growth published in 1992, searched for evidence of linkage between innovation and concentration in markets and found none. F. M. Scherer, "Schumpeter and Plausible Capitalism," *J. Econ. Lit.* 30:1416 (1992). Scherer's findings have been supported by several other studies, including P. A. Geroski, "Innovation, Technological Opportunity, and Market Structure, *Oxford Econ. Papers* 42:586 (1990); W. M. Cohen et al. "Firm Size and R&D Intensity: A Re-Examination," *J. Indus. Econ.* 35:543 (1987); Z. J. Acs and D. B. Audretsch, "Innovation in Large and Small Firms: An Empirical Analysis", *Am. Econ. Rev.* 78:678 (1988).

20. "Drug Industry Still Has Room to Merge," *Wall Street Journal* 25 June 1991.

21. Pharmaceutical Research and Manufacturers of America, *New Medicines in Development for Cancer, 1995 Survey* (May 1995).

22. Jordan D. Lewis, "Western Companies Improve Upon the Japanese Keiretsu," *Wall Street Journal*, 12 December 1995.

23. "U.S. Firms Adopting Enterprise Model, Borrowing from Japan's Keiretsu, GAO Says," *International Trade Reporter*, Bureau of National Affairs, 25 August 1993.

24. See, e.g., "Cummins to Sell 27 Percent Stake to Ford, Kubota, and Tenneco for $250 Million," *Wall Street Journal*, 16 July 1990.

25. "Why Japan Keeps on Winning," *Fortune*, 15 July 1991.

26. "U.S. Uses Antitrust Charge as Message on Defense Jobs," *Wall Street Journal*, 20 January 1994.

27. See "House Rules Committee Removes Statement on Antitrust from Bill," *Antitrust and Trade Regulation Reporter*, Bureau of National Affairs, 6 May 1993.

CHAPTER SIX

1. In his provocative article "Reengineering Regulation: Maintaining the Competitiveness of the U.S. Capital Markets," (*The Washington Quarterly*, 18:133, autumn 1995), former SEC Commissioner J. Carter Beese examined the volume of foreign trading in U.S. securities compared to the growth of trading volume overall from 1984 to 1994. Foreign trading grew at a rate of 18.95 percent annually while overall volume grew at 12.34 percent.

2. "Exchanges Sprout in Developing Nations," *Wall Street Journal*, 15 November 1995.

3. C. Chesler, "Where the Investors Are Anywhere but Close to Home," *Investment Dealers Digest* 61 (supplement), 22 May 1995. It is estimated that the foreign holdings of U.S. pension funds will increase to $630 billion by 1998.

4. "U.S. Treasuries Are Luring Foreign Buyers," *Wall Street Journal*, 31 October 1995.

5. Except as otherwise noted, sources for the data in the preceding three paragraphs are the Bank for International Settlements, the International Finance Corporation, Barings Securities, the International Monetary Fund, and R. Herring & R. Litan, *Financial Regulation in the Global Economy* (Brookings Institution, 1995); and "The Global Capital Market: Supply, Demand, Pricing and Allocation," (McKinsey Global Institute, November 1994). See also "Back to the Future," *The Economist*, 7 October 1995; "The Cash Cache," *Wall Street Journal*, 2 October 1995; "Americans Pour Money into Foreign Markets," *Wall Street Journal*, 14 April 1994; "International Monetary Fund, World Economy and Finance," *Financial Times*, 24 September 1993.

6. In October 1995, the Bank for International Settlements, the organization of the world's major central banks, reported average daily foreign exchange trading to be $1.23 trillion. "Foreign Exchange Trade Grew 50 Percent in Past 3 Years," *Wall Street Journal*, 24 October 1995. Data from national banks indicates the figure is closer to $1.3 trillion. See "Back to the Future," *The Economist*, 7 October 1995. In 1973, when the United States walked out of the Bretton Woods Agreement for fixed exchange rates, $10 billion to $20 billion were traded daily on world foreign exchange markets. Ten years later that figure had grown to roughly $60 billion daily.

7. "Basel's Drug Giants Are Placing Huge Bets on U.S. Biotech Firms," *Wall Street Journal*, 29 November 1995.

8. "Capital Gains Taxes—A $1.5 Trillion Opportunity," *Wall Street Journal*, 29 August 1995. The U.S. tax burden generally has been set far higher. A 1996 study by economist Gerald W. Scully for the National Center for Policy Analysis concluded that if taxation had remained at the 21 to 23 percent in effect at mid-century, GDP would have been twice as high by 1989 than it actually was. "It's the Taxes, Stupid!" *Forbes*, 12 February 1996.

9. Those calculations were made prior to the 1993 tax increase, which only increased the differential. G. C. Hufbauer, assisted by J. M. Van Rooij, *U.S. Taxation of International Income: Blueprint for Reform* (Institute for International Economics, 1992), 39.

10. "How U.S. Taxes Ground U.S. Aviation," *Wall Street Journal*, 26 August 1993.

11. A September 1995 survey by *Global Finance* placed J. P. Morgan as ninth-most creditworthy bank, with Republic New York and Wachovia at twenty-ninth and thirtieth, respectively. Of the top ten banks, Morgan was the only one not from Germany, Switzerland, or the Netherlands. "How the Banks Stack Up," *Global Finance*, September 1995.

12. The Comptroller of the Currency has reported that during 1992, for example, foreign banks made 47 percent of all business loans in the United States. See, e.g., "Study Shows Foreign Banks Behind in Profit," *Wall Street Journal*, 13 June 1994; *Wall Street Journal*, 29 September 1992.

13. Only Japan, whose financial laws were heavily influenced by the United States during the post-war years, imposes a similar range of restrictions on its banks. All the other primary financial centers, including Germany, Canada, France, England, Switzerland, the Netherlands, Sweden, and Belgium, provide substantially more latitude for bank operations. R. Herring and R. Littan provided a detailed review of such differentials in *Financial Regulation in the Global Economy* (Brookings Institution, 1995), Appendix.

14. Chase Manhattan, for example, sold operations in twenty-two nations and closed 100 branches in ten other nations in recent years. Prior to their mergers into Chase, Chemical Bank and Manufacturers Hanover substantially scaled back their European and Latin American operations. See, e.g., "The New Chase Offshore," *Global Finance*, September 1995.

15. R. House, "A Question of Control," *Institutional Investor*, April 1995.

16. J. Carter Beese, "Confessions of a Securities Regulator," *Wall Street Journal*, 19 September 1995.

17. Although American Depository Receipts (ADR) were first devised by Morgan Guaranty Trust in 1927 so that Americans could buy interests in London's Selfridges department store, they have only attracted significant attention in the past decade. Filing of an ADR registration must be done under a complex set of SEC rules involving three levels of regulation: level one for unlisted securities, level two for restricted listings of ADR's, and level three for listing and issuance of new equity in the United States, the most meaningful vehicle for global companies. See S. Davis, "The Allure of ADR's," *Institutional Investor*, September 1994; D. Waroff, "Coming to America," *Institutional Investor*, May 1995.

18. Bureau of National Affairs, *Securities Law Daily*, 24 May 1993.

19. "Only in America Are Resources This Deep," *Financial Times*, 1 February 1996.

20. "That Trade Obstacle, the SEC," *Wall Street Journal*, 27 August 1993.

21. Id.

22. Francois, Palmeter, and Anspacher, "Conceptual and Procedural Biases in the Administration of the Countervailing Duty Law" (paper presented at the Brookings Institution Conference on Adminstration of the Trade Remedy Laws, Washington D.C., 27 November 1990), 39.

23. Under new IASC standards that became effective January 1, 1995, goodwill is deducted from profits over five to twenty years. The standards are mandatory, however, only when adopted by national authorities. Only a handful of nations, including Switzerland and Italy, have done so. See, e.g., "Foreign Firms ·Rush to Acquire U.S. Companies," *Wall Street Journal*, 1 July 1994.

24. The Basel Accord, backed by the Bank for International Settlements, was an agreement by the member nations of the European Union, Switzerland, Japan, and the United States to observe a common standard for the maximum capital adequacy of banks. Banks in participating countries must assess credit risk of all holdings (on and off balance-sheet holdings) and provide sufficient coverage from two designated categories of capital to back those holdings. Banks falling short of the standards are restricted from certain activities. Nonbanking institutions such as securities firms and insurers are not subject to the standards.

25. Robert Rubin, speech at the Center for Strategic and International Studies, Washington, D.C., 6 June 1995.

26. "A Wall Streeter Makes His Debut on the World Stage," *Business Week*, 19 June 1995.

27. See, e.g., the Institute of International Finance Report of the Working Group on Capital Adequacy: A Response to The Basel Committee on Banking Supervision (IIF Consultative Papers, October 1993).

28. "SEC Commissioner Wallman Supports Review of Accounting Disclosure System," *Daily Report for Executives* (BNA), 2 August 1995.

29. Economist Margaret Blair of the Brookings Institution has calculated the relationship between tangible assets and total market value for American *manufacturing* companies over a ten-year period beginning in 1982. At the start of the period, traditional "hard" assets accounted for 62 percent of such companies' market value. By 1992 such assets comprised only 38 percent of their value. A number of private organizations—most notably NCI Research of Evanston, Illinois, an affiliate of the Kellogg Business School at Northwestern University—have made important advances in developing models to more realistically account for intangible assets.

30. E. R. Peterson, "Surrendering to Markets," *Washington Quarterly*, autumn 1995.

CHAPTER SEVEN

1. The Conference Board, "U.S. Manufacturers in the Global Marketplace," Report No. 1058-94-RR (1994).

2. "An Ownership-Based Disaggregation of the U.S. Current Account 1982-1993," *Survey of Current Business*, (Bureau of Economic Analysis, October 1995); "U.S. Exporters on a Global Roll," *Fortune*, 29 June 1992; G. C. Hufbauer, assisted by J. M. Van Rooij, *U.S. Taxation of International Income: Blueprint for Reform* (Institute for International Economics, 1992), 5.

3. Edward M. Graham and Paul R. Krugman, *Foreign Direct Investment in the United States, Third Edition* (Institute for International Economics, 1995), 58.

4. Many broader studies have demonstrated the benefits to U.S. companies of participation in the global economy. The most recent comprehensive work was by David

J. Richardson, entitled "Why Exports Really Matter!" (Institute for International Economics, 1995). See also the September 1995 report by the Competitiveness Council, "Saving More and Investing Better: A Strategy for Securing Prosperity," (transmitted to the president on 14 September 1995); Jeffrey E. Garten, "Is American Abandoning Multilateral Trade?" 74 *Foreign Affairs* 6 (November-December 1995); "Reform of the Taxation of U.S. Multinationals," 93 *Tax Notes Today* 225 (2 November 1993).

5. Graham and Krugman, 1995, 74. Graham and Krugman also analyzed, and dispelled, the popular notion that Japanese firms withhold important research and higher-value-added jobs from the United States. They examined research and performance measures on the basis of country of origin and found no evidence that Japanese investors behaved differently than other investors in transfering technology, research, and the creation of high-value jobs in the United States. Graham and Krugman also noted that the fact that foreign investors build larger, more productive plants—while statistically correct—may be explained by the fact that foreign investment tends to concentrate in capital-intensive sectors.

6. "The Secret to Competitiveness," *Wall Street Journal* (22 October 1993.

7. Graham and Krugman 1995; R. McKenzie, *The Global Economy and Government Power* (Center for the Study of American Business, March 1989).

8. United Nations Conference on Trade and Development, *World Investment Report* (United Nations, 1995).

9. See, e.g., "2 U.S. Utilities Seek Counterparts Abroad," *New York Times*, 7 November 1995; "The Foreign Invasion," *Wall Street Journal* 2 October 1995.

10. "Clinton Tax Plan for Foreign Operations Draws Complaints from U.S. Companies," *Wall Street Journal*, 25 March 1993.

11. "Reform of the Taxation of U.S. Multinationals," 93 *Tax Notes Today* 225-228 (2 November 1993).

12. Hufbauer 1992, 52.

13. "The IRS Takes Up Protectionism," *Wall Street Journal*, 3 April 1992.

14. See Bureau of National Affairs, *International Trade Daily*, 3 June 1992.

15. Pub.L. No. 101-511, Section 8041, 104 Stat. 1856, 1883 (1990).

16. Pub. L. No. 102-484, 106 Stat. 2315, 2466 (1991).

17. Pub. L. No. 101-614, Section 13, 104 Stat. 3231, 3241 (1990).

18. Department of Defense, FAR Supplement Section 25.7003 et seq.

19. National Conference of State Legislatures, Memorandum on Buy American Laws, 5 January 1983.

20. "Mr. Clinton Please Check the Label," *Wall Street Journal,* 22 March 1993.

21. See, e.g., Graham and Krugman, 1995.

22. 49 U.S.C. Section 1301 et seq.

23. Pub. L. 102-242, Sections 201-215, 105 Stat. 2236 (1991).

24. 47 U.S.C. Section 152 et seq.

25. "Foreign Buyers Help, And Not Hurt the U.S.," *Wall Street Journal,* 9 October 1989.

26. See, e.g., Bureau of National Affairs, *Securities Law Daily*, 14 April 1992.

27. See, e.g., Petitioners Brief in Barclays Bank v. Franchise Tax Board, Sup. Ct. Docket No 93-13022.

28. See, e.g., "California Multinational Tax is Upheld," *Wall Street Journal*, 21 June 1994; "California Tax Policy on Multinationals is Backed by Clinton in High Court Case, *Wall Street Journal,* 20 January 1994. The judicial challenge involved a claim that

the tax was so onerous as to be unconstitutional. In upholding the tax the Supreme Court noted that the proper forum for addressing such issues is the Congress.

29. "Foreign Firms Fume, Seek Loopholes As U.S. Attempts to Collect More Taxes," *Wall Street Journal,* 14 June 1994.

30. See, e.g., "Typewriter Case Ruling," *The New York Times,* 21 September 1993.

31. "U.S. Steel Industry's New Strength May Soon Weaken," *Wall Street Journal,* 3 June 1993.

32. See, e.g., "Selling Off of America to Japanese Touches Some Very Raw Nerves," *Wall Street Journal,* 19 June 1990.

33. See, e.g., "Two Measures Still Show U.S. Investment Gap," *The New York Times,* 10 June 1991.

34. M. Tolchin and S. Tolchin, *Buying Into America: How Foreign Money Is Changing the Face of Our Nation* (Times Books, 1988).

35. The Department's treatment of such firms is one more example of the anachronistic methodologies applied to foreign investment. The Department's Bureau of Economic Analysis classifies Du Pont as "foreign" under its foreign investment criteria—which treats as "foreign" any firm in which a non-U.S. owner holds at least 10 percent—but under the same criteria treats it as a U.S. parent when preparing reports of U.S. overseas subsidiaries. Many other firms are treated in this same inconsistent fashion. See Graham and Krugman, 1995, 10.

CHAPTER EIGHT

1. "The Global Information Infrastructure: Agenda for Cooperation," issued 15 February 1995 by the Information Infrastructure Task Force.

2. The inflammatory, distracting nature of "deficit" accounting was raised as early as 1965, when an interagency committee of economic experts in the federal government was asked to evaluate the numeric methods used to explain the U.S. international economic posture. "No single number number can adequately describe the international position of the United States," the panel concluded. Eleven years later, a second group of experts was asked by policymakers for such a device. After careful deliberation, it instead endorsed the conclusion of the 1965 group, then warned that for policy purposes the "words 'surplus' and 'deficit' should be avoided insofar as possible," since "those words are frequently taken to mean that the developments are 'good' or 'bad' respectively though this interpretation is often incorrect." The 1976 panel strongly recommended that the merchandise trade balance figures be eliminated since they were an inaccurate reflection of U.S. economic performance. Policymakers rejected the advice, claiming that the figures were already commonly used and the concepts underlying them were "clear and not liable to be seriously misinterpreted by the public."

3. O. Whichard and J. Lowe, "An Ownership-Based Disaggregation of the U.S. Current Account, 1982-1993," *Survey of Current Business,* October 1995.

4. See, e.g., Robert J. Barro and Lee Jong-Wha, "International Comparisons of Educational Attainment," *Journal of Monetary Economics,* 32 (1993).

5. In explaining the antidumping law to Senate colleagues, the floor manager of the original 1921 law explained that a foreign company would not be found guilty of

dumping "unless it is sought by the foreign competitor to sell goods . . . for the purpose of destroying an industry in this country and, when the industry is destroyed, of then raising the price to an excessive amount." Remarks of Senator Porter McCumber, *Congressional Record*, 4 May 1921, 1021.

6. "Canadian Minister Tracks Growing Impetus to Replace Antidumping with Antitrust Law," *Antitrust and Trade Regulation Reporter* (BNA), 5 October 1995.

7. In 1995, the IOSCO announced a three-year program of cooperation with IASC for the purpose of further exploring global standards. In 1994 and 1995, the SEC got harmonization off to a slow, but not insignificant, start with the adoption of three standards intended to ease to burden of foreign firms listing in the United States—but the measures were postured as exceptions to U.S. rules, not true harmonized standards. See, e.g., "Bean Counters Unite!" *The Economist*, 10 June 1995.

8. "Register of United States Barriers to Trade," published by the Department of Foreign Affairs and International Trade (Ottawa, 1994).

9. The Center for the Study of American Business at Washington University has calculated that by the end of the 1980's compliance costs for U.S. companies represented nearly 5 percent of GDP. See, e.g., "The Papers that Ate America," *The Economist,* 10 October 1992.

10. America's uniquely severe product liability laws have been estimated to cost American firms an amount equal to 2 percent of GDP, a sum that equates to 60 percent of what is spent on public education and 250 percent of what is spent on police and fire protection nationwide. See, e.g., Robert Sturgis, *Tort Cost Trends: An International Perspective* (Tillinghost, 1989); Robert E. Litan, "The Liability Explosion and American Trade Performance: Myths and Realities," *Tort Law and the Public Interest* (Norton, 1991).

11. "Smith Corona, Brother Industries End Years of Litigation Over Dumping," *Wall Street Journal*, 8 February 1994.

INDEX

A

ABB, 44, 123
Abudawood, Hussain, 9
Accounting, American and global standards, 158–59, 161–63, 168–69, 214
Acquisitions and mergers, 6–7, 113–22, 123. See also Antitrust policy
Advanced Micro Devices, 104
Advanced Photo System, 16
Advanced Pricing Agreement program, 178–79
Advanced Technology Program, 105
Aerojet General, 138
Agriculture, 65–68
Agriculture Department, 66
Aircraft industry, 123
Airline industry, 183, 184, 194
Alcoa, 108–109, 110
Allen, Robert, 75
Alliant Techsystems, 138
Allison Transmission Division of General Motors, 132
Aluminum sales from Russia, 70
American Apparel Manufacturers Association, 58
The American Challenge, 193
American government. See United States Government
American Institute for International Steel, 62
Ameritech, 126
Antidumping laws, 68–70, 87, 189
Antitrust policy, 6–7, 18, 108–19
  computer industry and, 117, 118, 129–30
  failure of, 155
  innovation and, 132–34
  revising, 210
Apparel industry, 55–58, 71
Apple Computer, 45, 46, 47, 83, 88, 129
Arco Chemical, 181
Armco, 61
Armentano, Dominick, 131
Armstrong, 115–16

Asea Brown Boveri, 44, 123
Asia
  computer industry in, 49
  telecommunications in, 15
ATS Medical, 98
AT&T, 10, 118, 125, 128
  antitrust regulation and restructuring, 108, 111, 125, 128
  interaction with Japanese companies, 92, 104, 138
  in Russia and China, 84, 85
Automotive industry
  Environmental Protection Agency and, 190
  government involvement, 39, 58–60, 136–37, 189, 192
  interaction with Japanese companies, 38, 39
  in Japan, 135
  technology joint ventures, 92–93, 135–37, 189, 192
Aviation industry, 38
Avtek Pacific, 153

B

Baker Hughes, 120
Balance of trade statistics, 198
Banco Nacional de Mexico, 157
Bangladesh, 70–71
Bank for International Settlements, 170
Banking
  central bank reserves, 13
  deterrents to foreign companies, 183
  Exon-Florio Act and, 186–87
  global capital and, 154–57
  regulations, 167
Barclays Bank, 188
Barings Plc., 169, 170
Barriers to entry, diminished, 128–29, 130
Bartley, Robert L., 75
Basel Accord, 167, 168
Baumol, William, 161
Beazer Plc., 121
Beese, J. Carter, 159, 165, 168

Bell Atlantic, 126
Bell Canada, 127
Benetton, 199
Bergsten, C. Fred, 70
Biden, Joseph, 111
Bilateralism, shift to multilateralism from, 202–203
Biotechnology industry, 99–100
Blakeman, Ray, 62
Board members, foreign directors, 8
Boltuck, Richard, 69
Bovard, James, 61–62
Brach Candy, 67
Branscomb, Lewis M., 106
British Telecom, 124
Brittan, Leon, 167
Brother International Corp., 189, 218–19
Buchanan, Patrick, 73
Bush, George, 187
Business. See also Antitrust policy; International trade
  burden of managed trade, 51–75
  changing concept of industry, 122–24
  current industrial policy, 19
  decline of industry, 4–5
  international mistakes, 10–11
  response to global economy, 2–4, 8–10
  shift to global economy, 201–11
  U.S. failure to adapt to global economy, 1–25
Buying into America, 193

C

Cable and Wireless, 16–17
CAFE rules, 190
California tax on international firms, 187–88
Canon, 16, 29–30
Capital, global flow, 7, 142–71
Capital Cities Communications, 185
Capital-gains tax, 151–53
Carruba, Frank, 89
Caterpillar, 70
Center for Transnational Corporations, 8
Central bank reserves, 13
Chaparral Steel, 43
Chase Manhattan, 154
Chemical Bank, 154
Chemical industry, 92, 107
China, 15, 51–52
Chrysler, 59, 60, 136
Ciba-Geigy, 150
Cisco Systems, 130

Citibank, 48, 154
Clayton Act, 112
Clinton, Bill, 102, 176
Clinton Administration, 95, 190
Clothing industry, 55–58, 70–71
Coelho, Tony, 22
Colombo, Umberto, 104
Commerce Department, 56, 68–69
Communication, electronic, 215
Communications Act, 183, 184
Communications industry, 184–85. See also Telecommunications industry
Communism, 22
Compaq, 45, 83, 88
Comparative advantage, 27, 48–49
Competition/competitiveness, 108–41
  American industry and, 4–6
  antitrust policy and, 113–22
  interdependent, 16–17
  rediscovering, 21–23
  shift to liquidity from competition, 209–11
  sovereign framework, 38–40
Computer industry, 14, 45. See also Semiconductors; Software
  antitrust policy and, 117, 118, 129–30
  DRAM production, 142–43
  early development, 1–2
  export controls and, 84
  global economy and, 16
  government involvement, 103–104, 193
  laptops and screen production, 44–47
  motherboards, 83
  production facility shifts, 49
  rapid change in, 129–30
  technology sharing in, 83–84
Consumer demand, 10–11
Control, shift to interdependence from, 208–209
Corporate average fuel economy rules, 190
Corporate structure, 44–49
Country-of-origin, 35
Cox Cable, 126
Cray Research, 86
Cummins, 137
Cygnus Support, 100

D

Daimler-Benz, 158, 159, 162
Dai Nippon Printing, 117
Dairy trade, 66
Daiwa Bank, 170

DEC, 10, 84, 130
Defense Department, 181
Democrats, 21–22
Destler, I. M., 22
Digital Equipment Corp., 10, 84, 130
Diversity, 15
  in innovation, 89, 90–94
  shift from protectionism to, 206–207
Domeniconi, Reto, 159
Donaldson, William H., 160
Dow Chemical, 177
DRAM production, 142–43
Drug Price Competition and Patent Term
  Restoration Act, 98
Dry milk, 66
Dumping, laws against, 68–70, 87, 189
Du Pont, 80, 108–109, 134, 194

E

Earnings-stripping rules, 188
Economies of scale, 32
Economy
  change in, 14–17, 22, 196–97
  global
    failure of America to adapt to, 1–25
    shifting to, 201–11
    protectionism and, 53
Education, foreign students, 78, 90
Einstein, Albert, 219
Electronics industry, 95, 127
Elliott, Charles, 175
Ellis criteria, 163
Emerson, Ralph Waldo, 107
Emerson Electric, 119
Employment. See Jobs
England. See Great Britain
Entry barriers, diminished, 128, 130–31
Environmental Protection Agency, 99,
  189–90, 205
Epson, 45
European investment in United States, 8
European Union, 160
Exchange rate, jobs and, 30–31
Exon-Florio Act, 186–87
Exports
  controls on technology, 84–86
  myths, 29–33
  shift to integration from, 204–206

F

Factories, 32–33
Farming, 65–68

Federal Aviation Act, 183
Federal Communications Commission,
  99, 112, 127, 185
Federal Deposit Insurance Corporation
  Improvement Act, 155
Federal Express, 10
Federal government. See United States
  Government
Federal Reserve, 157
Federal Technology Commercialization
  and Credit Enhancement Act, 105
Federal Trade Commission, 109, 112,
  113, 118, 119, 121, 132, 136
Federal Trade Commission Act, 112
Feltenstein, Andrew, 68
Fiber-optic technology, 146
Fibers, import controls, 55–58
Fields, Jack, 170
Financial institutions, global capital and,
  154–57
Firestone, 115
Fisher, Donald, 57
Fisherman's Marketing Association, 119
Flow International, 132
Food and Drug Administration, 97
Forbes, 152
Ford Motor Co., 59, 60, 96, 136, 190
Foreign Bank Supervision Enhancement
  Act, 157, 183
Foreign exchange transfers, 144–45, 150
Foreign trade. See International trade
Fox television network, 20
France, 92
Freuhan, Richard, 121–22
Freund, William C., 161, 169
Friedman, Milton, 53
Fuji, 16
Fujitani, Yoshitaka, 189

G

GAP, 57
Gates, Bill, 147
G.D. Searle, 89
GE, 17, 30
GE Capital, 156
Genentech, 132
General Ceramics, 186
General Electric, 17, 30
General Electric Information Services,
  126
Generally Accepted Accounting
  Principles, 158, 162
General Motors, 37, 58, 60

Allison Transmission Division, 132
Environmental Protection Agency and,
190
financial losses, 10
interactions with foreign companies,
58–59, 136
General Tire, 115, 116
Gerber, viii
Germany
multinational firms, 8
protectionism in, 174
small and midsized firms, 41
Getty, 120
Gilder, George, 65, 86
Gillette, 116
Glass-Steagall Act, 155
Global economy. See also International
trade
failure of America to adapt to, 1–25
shifting to, 201–11
Global Information Infrastructure, 195
GM. See General Motors
Goldman Sachs, 168
Goodrich, 115, 116
Goodwill, 162
Goodyear, 6, 96, 115, 116
Government. See also United States
Government
funding of innovation, 101–106
Grain farming, 67
Gramm, Phil, 58
Granfield, Michael E., 179
Great Britain
economic transition in 19th century, 74
foreign exchange trading in London,
150
telecommunications in, 20
Group of Seven, 13
Grove, Andrew, 96
Guiness Plc., 163

H

Haig, Robert, 151
Hamilton, Alexander, 55
Hanson Plc., 121, 218
Health care industry, 87, 92, 97–99, 217.
See also Pharmaceutical industry
Help Save America for Our Kids Future,
40
Herfindahl Hirschman Index, 124
Hertel, Thomas, 68
Hewlett-Packard, 30, 70, 88, 89, 91, 218
High-tech industries, 5, 48

High Technology Competitiveness, 78
Hitachi Corp., 91, 100, 138
Hollings, Fritz, 72
Holwill, Richard, 55
Honda, 18, 59, 173, 190, 194
Honda, Rimei, 34
Hoover, Herbert, 73, 75
Hormats, Robert, 34
Hufbauer, Gary, 18, 152, 180
Hurco, 62
Hutcheson, G. Dan, 117

I

IBM, 2, 103, 104, 128, 142, 193
DRAM production and, 145–46
laptop computers, 45, 83
overseas interactions, 18, 39, 138
ICL, 39
Immigration laws, 90–91
Import-relief laws, 207
Imports
controls on, 53, 54–58, 87–88. See also
Protectionism
value of, 30–31, 37
Industry. See Business
In-Focus Systems, 47
Information systems, 197–99
Infrared Research, 181
Ingersoll Rand, 132
Innovation
building infrastructure, 212–14
protectionism and, 76–107
revolution in, 82–88
shift from manufacturing to, 203–204
Institut Merieux, 120
Integration, shift from exports to,
204–206
Intel, 30, 83, 96, 104, 117, 131
Interdependence, shift from control to,
208–209
Interdependent competition, 16–17
Internal Revenue Code, 18, 188–89
Section 482, 177, 179
Internal Revenue Service, 97, 150–51,
177, 179, 190
International Accounting Standards
Committee, 162
International Monetary Fund, 13, 165
International trade. See also Global
economy
balance of trade statistics, 198
death of, 26–50
financial data, 12

managed, 51–75
myths, 28–33
Internet, 118, 132
Interoperability, 212–14, 216
Intuit, 118
Investment, foreign. See also Capital
  by American investors/firms, 8, 158
  national economy and, 42
  in United States, 20, 164, 172–94
IRS, 97, 150–51, 177, 179
Isolationism, 36, 40. See also
  Protectionism

J

Japan
  automotive industry and, 58–60
  computer industry and, 44–47, 62–65,
    87–88, 215
  funding of industries, 101
  government research, foreign firms
    particpating in, 105
  industry, 6, 40
  interdependent competition with,
    17–18, 29, 34, 44–47
  investment in United States, 173–74
  keiretsu system, 134–35
  protectionism in, 174
  steel industry and, 189
JESSI, 39
Jobs
  exports and, 30–31
  manufacturing, 175
  protectionism and, 71
  in textile industry, 57–58
Johnson and Johnson, 92
Joint ventures, 16–17
Jones Intercable, 127
J. P. Morgan, 156
Justice Department, 127

K

Kantor, Mickey, 51, 64
Kaplan, Seth, 69–70
Keiretsu system, 134–35, 137
Kellogg, 175
Keynes, John Maynard, 13, 23, 75, 148
Kidder Peabody, 169–70
Kimberly Clark, 121
Klingenberg, Martin F., 24, 112–13, 133,
  191
KLM, 194
Knowledge

capital and, 147
growth and transfer of, 199
interoperating, 214–15
as power, 80–82
Kodak, viii, 16, 136
Kohlberg Kravis Roberts, 9
Kubota Ltd., 137
Kyocera, 117, 193

L

Labor, low-skilled, 52
LaFalce, John J., 154
Laptop computers, 44–47, 83
Laws
  antidumping, 68–70, 87, 189
  antitrust, 109, 110, 155. (see also
    Antitrust policy)
  import-relief, 207
  regulation changes, 217
Leading Edge, 129
Lemaitre, Daniel, 98
Levitt, Arthur, Jr., 168
Lewis, William, 175
Licenses, technology, 81
The Limited, 96
Liquidity
  of capital, 152–53, 159
  of ideas, 15, 82, 95
  shift from competition to, 209–11
Litvack, Sanford, 120
Lochner, Philip R., Jr., 159
Lowe, Jeffrey, 199
Loyola University, 185
LSI Logic, 104

M

Machine-tool industry, 62, 77, 79
Mack, Connie, 152
Malkiel, Burton, 161
Manley, John, 211
Manufacturing
  facilities, 32–33
  jobs, 175
  shift to innovation from, 203–204
Marx, Karl, 23
Mathus, Roger, 100
Matsushita Electric, 92, 127
Mazda, 135
McAvoy, Clyde, 153
MCI, 20
McKinsey and Co., 174
McLaughlin, Brian, 62

McNealy, Scott, 86, 97
Medicine. See Health care industry; Pharmaceutical industry
Meiners, Roger, 99
Mercer, Robert, 6
Merck, 131, 134
Mergers and acquisitions, 6, 113–22. See also Antitrust policy
Microchip development, 1–2
Microcosm, 65
Micron Technology, 104
Microsoft, 83, 117, 118, 130
Milk, dry, 66
Mineral Leasing Act, 183
Ministry of International Trade and Industry, 101–102
Minolta, 16
Missile Technology Control Regime, 85
MITI, 101, 102
Mittelstand, 41
Mollica, Joseph, 134
Moore, James, 76
Moore, Robert, 182
Moore Corp., 186
Morita, Akio, 91
Morse, Ken, 41
Motorola, 15, 52, 104, 138
    in microprocessor market, 97
    overseas interactions, 15, 52, 104, 129
    Paging Products Group, 135
Mullins, David W., Jr., 156
Multi-Fiber Arrangement, 56
Multilateralism, shift from bilateralism to, 202–203
Mutual funds, 164–65

N
Nader, Ralph, 5
NAFTA, 35, 73–74, 167
Nalco Fuel Technology, 99
National Academy of Sciences, 85
National Association of Manufacturers, 85
National Competitiveness Act, 105
National Cooperative Research and Production Act, 138
National Flat Panel Display Initiative, 47
National Science Foundation, 5, 90, 93
National security, 182–86
National Steel, 119, 176
Navistar International, 136
NEC, 45, 104, 138
Nestlé, 11, 116, 159

Nike, 16, 96, 145, 199
Nissan Motor Corp., 135, 189
NKK America, 189
North American Free Trade Agreement, 35, 73–74, 167
Northwest Airlines, 194
Norton Co., 186
Notebaert, Richard, 126
Nucor Corp., 43
NUMMI, 136–37
N.V. Bakaert, 89

O
Oil/petroleum industry, 109, 120
Olson, James, 190
O'Neill, Tip, 200
Operation Bittersweet, 67
Outsourcing relationships, 199
Ownership, global, 199

P
Parker Pen, 116
Patents, 78, 99–101
Penzias, Arno, 110
Perot, Ross, 73
Peterson, Erik, 171
Petroleum/oil industry, 109, 120
Pharmaceutical industry
    cost of launching new drug, 92, 98
    federal regulations and, 19, 97–98, 107
    health and safety standards, 217
    overseas interaction, 92
    research collaboration, 134
Philip Morris, 175
Philips, 127, 135
Photocopier industry, 110, 119
Photography industry, 16
Polyconomics, 151
Prestowitz, Clyde, 63
Principles of Political Economy and Taxation, 27
Procter & Gamble, 98
Productivity
    protectionism and, 51–75
    wages and, 32
Profit, global definitions, 162
Protectionism, 17, 20, 21
    innovation and, 76–107
    productivity and, 50–75
    shift to diversity from, 206–207

Q
Quantum fund, 13
Quantum theory, 1, 2, 3

Quotas, 56, 61. See also Protectionism

R

Raytheon, 47
Razor and blade industry, 116
Reed, John, 156
Regulation K, 155
Relationships, 16–17
Republicans, 21–22
Research, global access and, 91–94
Ricardo, David, 27–28, 48
Rice industry, 67
RJR Nabisco, 9
Roberts, Paul Craig, 73
Robinson-Patman Act, 112
Roche Holdings, 132, 150
Rockefeller, John D., 109
Rodgers, T. J., 72
Rubin, Robert, 167
Russia, aluminum sales from, 70

S

Saatchi, Charles and Maurice, 48
Samsung, 33
Samuelson, Paul, 53
Sanders, W. J., III, 104
Sandoz, 150
Scale economies, 32
Schmidt, Helmut, 106
Schumpeter, Joseph, 76
Schwinn, 39
Scott Paper, 121
Seagrams, 194
Searle, 89
Securities and Exchange Commission, 158–65, 168–71
Securities markets, 143–44
Security, national, 182–86
Sematech, 39, 104, 117
Semiconductors, 36, 43, 146
    alliances with Japanese companies, 138
    development, 1–2
    pact with Japan, 63–65, 87–88
    Sematech and, 59, 104, 117
Servan-Schreiber, Jean Jacques, 193
Sharp Corp., 45, 46
Sherman Act, 112, 140
Siemens, 138, 191
Sikes, Alan, 104
Simons, H. C., 151
Singer, 44
Slater, Samuel, 80

Small firms, 41
Smith, Adam, 23, 27–28
Smith Corona, 218–19
Smokestack industries, 58–62
Smoot-Hawley tariffs, 36, 54, 73, 75
Software
    antitrust policy and, 118
    export controls on, 84–85
    patents and, 100–101
Sony Corp. of America, 91, 104, 127, 130
Soros, George, 13
Southwestern Bell, 126
Sovereignty, economic, eclipse of, 196–97
Soybean trade, 67
Spitzer, Alexander, 189
Sprint, 20, 126
Squibb, 91–92
SRI International, 105
Stalk, George, 96
Standard Oil, 108, 109
Steel industry, 42–43, 60–62, 121–22, 189
Stock exchanges, 144, 160
Stouffer Foods, 116
Strategic alliances, 137
Students, foreign, 78, 90
Sugar trade, 66–67
Summit Technology, 98
Sun Microsystems, 16, 88, 97, 100
Switzerland, 150

T

Tachonics, 186
Taxation
    capital and, 151–53
    of international business, 18, 93–94, 176–78, 187–88
    legislative changes, 218
Tax Reform Act, 153
TCI, 127
Technology
    American, 78–80
    export controls on, 84–86
    government obstruction, 77–78
    high-tech industries, 5, 48
    international transfer, 78–80
    speed of development, 95–97
Telecommunications Inc., 139
Telecommunications industry
    in Asia, 15
    AT&T breakup, 111, 125

Cable and Wireless, 16–17
copper wire depreciation, 146
export control laws, 84
federal laws and, 7, 19, 20
fiber optics, 146
offshore spending, 11
rapid change and government policy in,
124–28
Telecommunications standards, 214–15
Television, 20, 97
Tenneco, 137
Texaco, 120
Texas Instruments, 36, 97, 104
Textile industry, 55–58, 70–71, 80
Thailand, 65, 70
Thompson, Mark, 219
Thompson, Robert, 68
3M Co., 92, 96
Time Warner, 139
Tire industry, 115–16
Toshiba, 16, 45, 46, 104, 138
Toyota, 91, 135
Trade, international. See International
trade
Trade deficit, jobs and, 30–31
Trading Places, 63
Treasury Department, 165
Tsigas, Marinos, 68
Typewriters, 189, 218–19

U

Uenohara, Michiyuki, 138
Uniroyal, 115, 116
United States Government. See also
Antitrust policy; Protectionism
banking and, 154–57
capital and, 148–71

competitive policy, 108–41
computer industry and, 44–47
foreign investment and, 172–94
global innovation and, 76–107
managed trade and, 53–74
outdated policies, 17–18
regulatory overload, 217
response to global economy, 2–4, 6–7
Uruguay Round, 23–24, 100, 167
U.S. Taxation of International Income, 18
U.S. West, 84, 85, 139
USX, 61

W

Wages, productivity and, 32
Walker, Robert, 141
Wallman, Steven M. H., 168
Wang, 128, 130
Wealth of Nations, 27
Weidenbaum, Murray, 103
Westinghouse, 123
Wheat farming, 67
Whichard, Obie, 199
Whitman, Marina N., 106
Willens, Robert, 162
Wilson, Harold, 13
Windsor Declaration for International
Cooperation, 167
World Wide Web, 118

X

Xerox, 110, 119

Z

Zenith, 45
Zero-sum thinking, 33–35
ZF Friedrichshafen, 132